The Future of NATO

The Future of NATO

Regional Defense and Global Security

Andrew A. Michta
and
Paal Sigurd Hilde

University of Michigan Press
Ann Arbor

Published in the United States of America by
The University of Michigan Press
Printed and bound by CPI Group (UK) Ltd, Croydon, CR0 4YY

2017   2016   2015   2014   4   3   2   1

A CIP catalog record for this book is available from the British Library.

ISBN 978-0-472-07240-8 (cloth : alk. paper)
ISBN 978-0-472-05240-0 (paper : alk. paper)
ISBN 978-0-472-12072-7 (e-book)

Contents

Contents

Acknowledgments

The origin of this book was a seminar held as part of the research program NATO in a Changing World, a cooperation between the Norwegian Institute for Defense Studies and the Institute for Political Science at the University of Oslo. The program and seminar were made possible by a generous grant from the Norwegian Ministry of Defense.

We would like to thank Professor David Haglund and the anonymous reviewers for their helpful comments. The editors are grateful to Camilla Taufic, Magdalena Jackiewicz, and Ingrid Aune for their editorial assistance at various stages of this project.

Preface

As this book goes to press, European security is facing its most serious crisis since the end of the Cold War. The Russian annexation of Crimea in March 2014 in clear violation of international law has undercut the sovereignty and territorial integrity of Ukraine. Russian subsequent efforts to foment instability in Eastern Ukraine, combined with the presence of a sizeable Russian military force along the country's borders, have threatened to escalate the crisis further, with a real possibility that that region could also be severed from Ukraine. At a time when many have argued that Europe is moving beyond traditional hard power competition, geopolitics has returned to the continent with a vengeance.

NATO's response to the Ukraine crisis and the end of the ISAF operation seems likely to top the agenda at the September 2014 NATO summit in Newport, Wales. This combination makes the summit a turning point in the gradual shift of emphasis seen in the alliance from 2008. For twenty years, crisis management and stabilization operations outside NATO territory have dominated NATO's agenda both politically and militarily. Russia's intervention in Georgia in 2008 served as a catalyst for a gradual reemphasis on traditional tasks of deterrence and collective defense. For many reasons, ranging from Russian actions in Ukraine through the fiscal crisis to political and military fatigue from operations, NATO seems poised to go 'back to the basics' in coming years.

Russia's neo-imperial project—with Ukraine the immediate target though other countries like Moldova, Georgia, and possibly Kazakhstan are also in play—is now a geostrategic reality that will demand a NATO response. Calls for reassurance by allies in Central Europe and the Baltics, including the basing of U.S. military assets in the region, are clear indicators of how quickly and dramatically the security situation on NATO's northeastern periphery has changed. The crisis may further escalate if Russia decides to exert pressure on the Baltic members of NATO, especially Estonia and Latvia where the Russian ethnic community could be exploited by Moscow to foment instability.

Thus far the West has struggled to come up with a coherent and unified response to Russian aggression in East Europe. Competing national voices as different states have sought to balance their political and economic interest in relations with Russia with a larger collective security imperative have underscored how critical the NATO alliance has been in this crisis. The first symbolic, but important, reassurance to NATO members along the periphery came in the form of additional aircraft for air policing in the Baltics and for rotational training in Poland, including U.S. military personnel to support it. Ukraine has demonstrated that, notwithstanding long-term efforts to strengthen the EU's Common Security and Defense Policy (CSDP), NATO remains the sole effective security organization both in Europe and in the larger transatlantic sphere.

The crisis has already changed the dynamic of internal debates in NATO in anticipation of the next summit. It should be clear, however, that whatever strategy is ultimately adopted at Newport, NATO is not going to return to a Cold War outlook. Alliance members, particularly the United States but also the United Kingdom and others, will continue to expect NATO to engage in crisis management operations outside its territory—with Libya rather than Afghanistan serving as a model. Moreover, Russian actions will not stop the geopolitical rise of Asia-Pacific, though events in Ukraine may slow U.S. rebalancing towards that region. NATO's return to the basics will likely represent a "rebalancing back" towards the European region, not an abandonment of its globalized agenda.

Getting the balance right between in-area and out-of-area engagement will therefore remain a core challenge for the alliance in coming years. It is also the core theme of this book. The crisis in Ukraine thus serves to highlight the timeliness of this analysis and the debates it raises.

Andrew A. Michta
Paal Sigurd Hilde

Washington and Oslo, April 15, 2014

Introduction

*Regional versus Global Priorities—Can NATO
Get the Balance Right?*

Andrew A. Michta

Since the end of the Cold War the imminent demise of the venerable
North Atlantic Treaty Organization has been foretold more than once; yet
again and again, crisis after crisis, NATO has soldiered on, demonstrating
its institutional resilience. And today, despite the professed growing importance of the European Union (EU) as a security actor, the unpopularity
of current NATO missions, and clear disagreements among the members
about its purpose, NATO continues to be the key collective transatlantic security organization, which both the United States and Europe want
to keep. But staying alive is not the same thing as being effective. Today
the alliance is at an inflection point, faced with a set of challenges to its
resources, identity, and political will more serious than at any point since
the Berlin Wall was torn down.

Unlike previous bouts of post–Cold War self-doubt, in the last few years
NATO has been buffeted by economic and political forces strong enough
to undercut its residual strength. More than ever before it is struggling with
dwindling resources and declining public support, while defense budgets
in Europe implode. Ten years ago Europeans accounted for nearly half of
NATO's total expenditures on defense; today they total less than a third.
Even more ominous for the alliance are defense spending cuts in the United
States, while Washington looks to Asia as the high-risk area, and Europe's
security concerns seem to have become even more regional in scope.

NATO's strength has been tested by a decade of military operations in Afghanistan, the most immediate defining experience for NATO since the fall of the Wall. The much anticipated shutdown of its International Security Assistance Force (ISAF) in 2014 is not just symbolic but marks a change in how NATO is going to see itself going forward. ISAF has been the defining NATO mission since August 2003, when the alliance assumed the lead from the German-Dutch command rotation and by the end of the year decided to expand it to the entire territory of Afghanistan. After a decade of continued combat, security assistance programs, and state-building efforts, the impending end of the ISAF mission will be the end of an era in NATO's post–Cold War history and a landmark in transatlantic security relations. Amid the fiscal and political turmoil that has gripped the transatlantic community in the wake of the Great Recession, NATO has reached a point at which we need to discuss its core purpose going forward, lessons learned and yet to be learned, and the means necessary to keep this vital alliance relevant for another decade. As power shifts to Asia while the Middle East and North Africa sink deeper into crisis, this is not a theoretical proposition, but one with immediate and lasting policy implications. The transatlantic community of democratic states will need NATO even more in the coming years to serve as the linchpin of their security and defense, the preferred framework for collective action. To understand what needs to be done to keep NATO relevant, a practical, comprehensive, and structured analysis is needed of the strategic choices, structural adjustments, tasks, and resources going forward.

The guiding question of this book is NATO's future after Afghanistan. Here the debate focuses on two core questions—in-area missions versus out-of-area engagement—with the related and ever-more-intense argument over current and future tasks. These topics have been debated previously, but never has there been in the policy community such clear recognition that there must be a strong consensus on these issues, for in our resource-constrained environment, increasingly—and distressingly— NATO's mission risks becoming an either-or proposition. For the first time, as ISAF nears completion, the allies are no longer in a position to credibly argue that funding commitments can be deferred and that resources, especially U.S. power, will be there in abundance to compensate for shortfalls or mistakes. Priorities today are more urgent than at any time since the end of the Cold War, and consensus and sustainability are even more important than ever as the U.S. "pivot to Asia" has forced the alliance to adjust to the reorientation of American power. At the same time the need for mutuality is greater than before. The United States needs to rely on NATO when addressing global security threats, while the Europeans need to be certain that their regional security concerns, especially the resurgence of Russian power on Europe's periphery, will be addressed.

This book's immediate goal is to provide a comprehensive and structured analysis of NATO's adaptation to these new realities. It is the work of academics who in various ways have remained close to policy making throughout their careers. This practical, hands-on policy aspect is what sets this volume apart from most other comparable and recent publications. Several books on NATO have been published in the last few years, together representing somewhat of a surge in interest compared to the mid-2000s. Some of those have a narrow focus on specific issues, such as U.S. policy toward the alliance,[1] partnerships,[2] and operations,[3] notably the ISAF mission.[4] Others offer critical theoretical perspectives on NATO's persistence and evolution.[5] However, the majority of works currently on the market offer only a partial answer to the issue critical to the policy maker: not what is possible, but what is plausible. This book, in contrast, takes a broad perspective on NATO, informed by and aware of theoretical debates but not seeking to reargue theory, constructivist or otherwise. It aims to go beyond comparable volumes[6] to underscore the urgency of the fundamental in-area/out-of-area dilemma facing the alliance as the function of the balance between its regional and global priorities.

The Legacies

Since the fall of the Berlin Wall in 1990 NATO has undergone a profound transformation, even though for the general public it continues to evoke a somewhat Cold War era image of a regionally focused, collective defense organization built around Article 5 of the 1949 Washington Treaty, the "three musketeers' clause," whereby an attack on one member is treated as an attack on all. Indeed, although NATO's mission has expanded, Article 5 remains the bedrock of the alliance, paradoxically invoked for the first time in the wake of the terror attacks against the United States on September 11, 2001 (9/11). Whether one speaks of traditional territorial, transnational, or cyber threats, Article 5, with its expression of solidarity, is what gives NATO its continued vitality. The United States, with its power, resources, and commitment to the security and defense of Europe, has historically been the bedrock of allied security. In that sense NATO has never been an alliance of equals, and during the Cold War it often appeared more like a unilateral U.S. security guarantee to Europe against Soviet power, backed by nuclear weapons.

Since then NATO's mission has expanded as enlargement became an integral part of the postcommunist transformation of former Soviet clients in Eastern Europe. The first round of NATO enlargement took place in 1990 in tandem with the unification of Germany, when the five new Länder joined the Federal Republic. The Clinton administration's decision in the mid-1990s to make NATO enlargement into a vehicle for stabilizing and democratizing postcommunist Europe and making Europe "whole, free and at peace" widened the mission and changed the internal balance within the alliance.[7] It also brought with it additional tension in regional security perceptions between the "old" and "new" allies—a distinction that became the unfortunate reference for the U.S.-Europe divide in the run-up to the 2003 Iraq war. Enlargement was messy, but it kept NATO relevant. The consecutive enlargement cycles in 1999, 2004, and 2009 were accompanied by a concomitant change in the mission caused by NATO's decision in 1999 to war against Serbia during the Kosovo intervention. Enlargement also required adding new tasks. In the spring of 2004 NATO started air policing over the Baltic States, with fighter planes from different nations rotating to ensure control of the skies over Lithuania, Latvia, and Estonia.

But the critical operation that rewrote the book on how NATO performed out-of-area operations was the ISAF mission in Afghanistan. Its lessons and costs have factored into how NATO then approached the military intervention in Libya to protect civilians, an operation that ultimately led to the removal of Muammar Gaddafi from power. It was in part because of the experience of ISAF that in 2011 in Libya the United States took the back seat, in effect "leading from behind." And in the coming years these lessons will work themselves through NATO's political and military structures, reshaping how the alliance responds to future crises.

Adjustments to the structure of NATO have followed the new tasks, including the creation in 2003 of Allied Command Operations and Allied Command Transformation. The NATO Response Force (NRF) was launched at the 2002 Prague Summit; in 2006 at the Riga Summit, although NATO continued to work on its political transformation, it sought to focus on the mounting operational demands in Afghanistan.[8] Finally, the 2008 Bucharest Summit marked a watershed as both Ukraine and Georgia failed to obtain the much-coveted Membership Action Plan, the de facto precondition to the invitation to join the alliance. The 2008 Russo-Georgian war effectively ended the open-ended vision of NATO enlargement into the territory of the former Soviet Union.

Debates within the alliance continued to bubble up in the 2000s, moving from initial unity and solidarity with the United States after the 2001 terrorist attacks on the World Trade Center and the Pentagon through the growing tensions and disagreements in 2003 that preceded the U.S. invasion of Iraq. The alliance could agree to offer only a limited NATO Training Mission to the Iraqi government after the initial combat operations were concluded. By the end of the decade, although Europe stood by the United States as the Obama administration adopted the surge strategy in Afghanistan, skepticism about the operation was growing among the political and military leadership alike. NATO members continued to work together to implement the ISAF mandate, but individually they were looking for an exit timetable, proving the adage that though the West had all the watches, in the end the Taliban had all the time.

Three NATOs into One

Current debates in NATO over how best to define its mission reflect the axiom that ultimately nations live in neighborhoods, their size and threat environments shaping their individual and aggregate power requirements and reflecting their core security interests. Those geostrategic neighborhoods define the state's security optics. So today the alliance contains "three NATOs" of sorts, defined by the relative power, threat perceptions, and preferences of the member-states: (1) the U.S. vision of NATO as an expeditionary alliance capable of delivering security where needed, historically supported most strongly by the United Kingdom; (2) the Western European allies, who share a more regional focus, in which the idea of Europe is linked together into a liberal democratic club; and (3) what until 2012 could be described as the "quid pro quo alliance" in Central Europe and also endorsed by Norway, in which the willingness to buy into Washington's global expeditionary optics was viewed as a smart investment to ensure reciprocity in the event of a crisis. That third optic is increasingly up in the air, as the "new allies" see relatively limited benefits in exchange for their unequivocal support for America's global missions.

As NATO seeks to align its divergent identities, this book is ultimately about the meaning of allied solidarity going forward at a time when both the United States and Europe must grapple with persistent power deficits. This overarching question of NATO's identity can be broken down into smaller subsets. For example, how effective is the Comprehensive Approach really, what does burden sharing mean when priorities diverge, and what can we expect going forward? Finally, the most important question to consider is this: How is NATO to adapt institutionally and in terms of its command structure to respond to various expectations and remain credible? All these questions inexorably mark a return to the fundamentals of the competing strategic visions across the Atlantic, now even more so as the global power balance is in flux.

NATO must show political will to work toward a new consensus on priorities and burden sharing. The experience of Afghanistan and more recently that of Libya have demonstrated the need for greater participation from Europe, as well as the continued critical importance of U.S. engagement for NATO operations to succeed. In Libya, as elsewhere in the past, America had to play the pivotal role in reconnaissance, dynamic targeting, refueling, and command and control. The key challenge today, beyond the obvious and perennial capabilities debate—most recently addressed through the pooling-and-sharing "smart defense" formula touted at the NATO summit in Chicago in May 2012—lies in the alliance's ability to speak to the strategic requirements of both the United States and its increasingly disparate European allies. To put it differently, can NATO keep doing what it has been doing over the past two decades and avoid becoming hollowed out and dysfunctional in the process?

Today when one talks about the alliance that is seeking to adapt itself to divergent priorities, the geographic dimension still matters. To balance NATO's role in the traditional Euro-Atlantic space and keep it relevant to the growing challenges in South Asia, the Middle East, and North Africa, there must be give and take, and that requires political leadership. NATO continues to struggle with the challenge of rebuilding consensus, with some in Europe, such as the United Kingdom and Denmark, more open to this larger global role touted by Washington, while countries from the older Western core of the alliance, such as France and, increasingly, newer members from Central Europe like Poland, see NATO as a more regionally focused alliance. In 2012 the growing concern over the future role of Russian military installations in the Kaliningrad District returned the Central Europeans to the question of territorial defense more than at any point since the end of the Cold War. Increased Russian presence in the Kaliningrad District has also served as a wake-up call in Scandinavia, particularly for Norway, but also for non-NATO members like Finland and Sweden.

Shrinking resources and dwindling capabilities remain the key underlying drivers in that discussion. The current round of debate on NATO's future has also been reflected in the Libyan campaign. Here the Europeans seem to have learned some lessons from Kosovo, at least in part. In the Kosovo campaign the allies had to rely on the United States when it came to precision-guided munitions, the capacity for identifying targets, command and control, and managing the multiplicity of national assets in a rapidly changing combat environment. Unlike in Kosovo, the Libya campaign showed that while the depth of the available stores of specialized munitions in Europe was still insufficient, with key allies running out in short order, the capabilities of some European countries have improved somewhat, and the Europeans could serve the alliance as a whole in future conflicts. One could argue that it was a slow learning process, but it seems to offer hope for future NATO operations.

In addition to the capabilities issue, the other problem that undercuts allied solidarity is the frequent inability to prioritize. Since the Cold War NATO has been pursuing too many security errands. The alliance has been increasingly pushed into a veritable smorgasbord of defense- and security-related tasks: cyber defense, energy security, weapons of mass destruction (WMD) proliferation, Stability and Reconstruction (S&R) missions, out-of-area missions, territorial security, enlargement, partnership building, norm setting, and democratization. Recently there have been suggestions that NATO should also be ready to address the consequences of climate change—a point made on several occasions by the NATO Secretary General. But an alliance that purports to defend against all threats will be unable to defend well against the critical ones, especially as resource constraints force it to make choices. This book posits that instead of endlessly multiplying NATO's security tasks, after ISAF NATO needs to define its appropriate roles in different regions and go from there. How can it get the balance right between what is essentially a traditional territorial defense role of the alliance and the increasingly complex and evolving set of twenty-first-century challenges that are truly global, at a time when the Great Recession has imposed the most stringent resource constraints to date on defense budgets? This overarching question must drive the in-area/out-of-area debate going forward.

Toward a Regionally Grounded Global Alliance?

Throughout the ISAF mission NATO has sought to highlight the successes of the surge in Afghanistan, the reconstruction work, the increase in member and partner contributions, and the like. But two things are apparent today: for all the work done on the new Strategic Concept of 2010 and the marginally increased military contributions from Europe to ISAF, the transatlantic alliance has continued to struggle to establish a new identity, not just in word but also in deed. In addition, by Secretary General Anders Fogh Rasmussen's own admission, NATO is still not comfortable working the political and civilian security side of the street. As he put it, NATO has to better "institutionalize a broad and inclusive security dialogue and, where appropriate, partnership with relevant countries from around the world."[9] It appears NATO continues to struggle with the two tasks that since the 2006 Riga meeting it has declared to be the holy grail of security in the twenty-first century: working across sectors and partnering to lower the burden across the alliance. Combine this with the warning issued in 2011 by U.S. Secretary of Defense Robert Gates about the increasing disconnect between the United States and Europe, especially among the younger generation,[10] and the task of reforging the consensus and tying the divergent strands of security concerns into one remains daunting.

Ultimately NATO's effectiveness depends on the ability of the United States and Europe to forge a larger consensus about their stakes in preserving and protecting the current security regime beyond narrow interests. The most obvious answer to the question about NATO's future viability—and the organization is needed to secure the transatlantic space and beyond—is far-sighted leadership. Here a lot will depend on Germany as the leading European power, but an important role will also be played by France; the United Kingdom; and smaller states that have historically been closely aligned with the United States, such as Poland in Central Europe and Norway in Scandinavia. Without Germany taking the lead to reverse the dramatic decline in defense budgets across Europe, transatlanticists in the United States will be hard pressed to convince the public that continued commitment to Europe's defense in a time of crushing deficits and escalating debt is justified. To merge the three NATOs into one, the political leadership has to meet the challenge of resourcing the capabilities needed to put some meat on its new Strategic Concept of 2010 and meet critical capabilities requirements. How to do this in the midst of the longest and deepest economic crisis since the Great Depression is literally the multi-billion-dollar question.

These are the issues that must be addressed day to day by NATO's national authorities. They require vision at the highest level but also a great deal of practical bureaucratic skill in navigating the committee structures and building consensus. This practical approach in addressing the challenges facing NATO today is reflected in this book's choice of topics and contributors and in the conviction that whatever projections are made about strategy, tactics, and operations, they must cluster around the core debate about the "traditional versus global NATO." Apart from this introduction and a conclusion at the end, this book is organized into eight chapters: a background chapter followed by seven chapters in two parts. Chapters 2–4 focus on actors, and chapters 5–8 cover issues. The background chapter, by

Helge Danielsen and Helene F. Widerberg, sets out the overall theme of this volume, in-area and out-of-area, in a historical perspective. During the Cold War, the authors argue, NATO adopted a "nonpolicy" toward out-of-area engagements: not engaging directly, but rather quietly facilitating the engagement of allies in crises elsewhere. After the Cold War and some initial hesitation, NATO found a new mission in out-of-area operations in the Euro-Atlantic region in the 1990s, and from 2003 on a global scale. The authors argue that in the late 2000s the pendulum swung back from the nearly exclusive emphasis on out-of-area engagement toward a renewed balance between out-of-area and in-area engagement.

In chapter 2 Svein Melby analyzes how the United States has always seen, and will continue to see, NATO in the context of its global security interests. Although the United States has been the most vocal proponent of a wider global role for NATO, particularly in the 2000s, Melby argues that U.S. interests in NATO are not confined to using the alliance as a toolbox for operations. While the United States will likely continue to look to NATO in Europe for contributions to peace support operations, the author explores the fundamentals of the U.S. global approach to security and argues that "NATO remains of critical importance to the United States and will therefore continue to be a valuable instrument in the latter's global strategy."

Derek Averre's contribution (chapter 3) is a reminder of how important Russia remains for NATO. Russia is in many ways the outside actor that most strongly influences the in-area/out-of-area debate in NATO. The renewed self-confidence evidenced in Russian security and foreign policy in the mid-2000s served as a catalyst for the call in NATO to reemphasize Article 5 and collective defense. Averre analyzes how Russia's perception of the security situation in Europe differs markedly from that prevalent in NATO countries. He explores the challenges NATO will face in reconciling the need to reemphasize Article 5 while engaging Moscow in a more cooperative relationship.

In chapter 4 Janne Haaland Matlary analyzes how NATO's role as a "platform for coalitions of the willing and able"—a prominent feature of NATO's engagement in operations—will evolve after the end of ISAF. Military relevance and the willingness to take risks will continue to be important in the transatlantic burden-sharing perspective, Matlary argues, as European NATO allies not only face the challenge of continuing to show solidarity with the United States, but also take a leading role in addressing regional security challenges, notably on NATO's periphery. This risk willingness—or its lack in specific countries—Matlary traces to domestic political factors, notably to what she terms the "strategic culture."

In chapter 5 Helga Haftendorn examines the first of the specific issues covered in this volume: extended deterrence. With the end of the Cold War and the emergence of new priorities for the alliance, notably out-of-area operations, the issue of nuclear weapons slowly disappeared from NATO's political agenda. At the end of the 2000s, with the renewed emphasis on traditional security concerns, this debate reemerged ahead of the 2010 Lisbon NATO Summit. After a short review of the Cold War arguments, Haftendorn traces the development of the debate about extended deterrence in NATO from three perspectives: organizational, military, and political.

In chapter 6 Sten Rynning analyzes NATO's approach to comprehensive conflict resolution, termed the "Comprehensive Approach" by the alliance. Contrary to the debate about extended deterrence, the challenge of ensuring stable peace and security in the conflict zone through a comprehensive civilian-military effort gradually emerged in the 1990s with the widening engagement of NATO in out-of-area operations. Rynning explores the origins of NATO's approach to comprehensive conflict resolution, provides a critical analysis of its record in applying the Comprehensive Approach in Afghanistan, and suggests how NATO may seek to address the failures seen in Afghanistan.

Turning to the issue of the institutional adaptation of NATO in the post–Cold War period, in chapter 7 Paal Sigurd Hilde analyzes the development of NATO's command structure. Hilde identifies the need to enable NATO in its engagement in out-of-area operations as the most important overall driver for reform of the command structure in that period. Cost cutting has, however, become the most important factor shaping change in later years. Hilde argues that while the aim of a lean command structure is attractive, the reduction of NATO's institutional structure has the potential for adverse long-term consequences for the alliance.

In chapter 8 Jens Ringsmose analyzes the NATO Response Force (NRF), another key NATO structure, which he argues has "fallen victim to the strategic schizophrenia currently beleaguering NATO." After a brief history, Ringsmose assesses the utility of the force and concludes that so far it may be termed a qualified failure. While the NRF has served a purpose as a driver of military transformation, NATO's inability to reach consensus on employing the NRF in ongoing operations has severely weakened the allies' commitment. Ending on an optimistic note, Ringsmose sees a renewed utility for the NRF, despite its origins, in NATO's reemphasis on in-area assurance.

Andrew A. Michta provides the book's final chapter, tying together the various strands of the post-ISAF narrative to pose the larger question about NATO's continued viability and the in-area/out-of-area balance. He argues that to sustain the venerable alliance into the future, NATO needs to build on the experience of the ISAF mission as the most integrated operation in its history. It needs to embrace the premise that developments in various regions are increasingly interconnected, and that while it provides security for the member-states, it has to plan to address global threats. Though admittedly investment in defense is a hard sell at a time of economic hardship, Europe must stanch the bleeding in defense resources, and the United States needs to remain fully engaged in Europe and be prepared to lead in a crisis. The centerpiece of NATO's future is the strength of transatlantic relations going forward, with the recognition that despite post-Afghanistan fatigue, the United States and Europe remain essential to each other's security and prosperity, even more so today as power shifts to Asia, with Russia resurgent along NATO's northeastern periphery and the Middle East and North Africa (MENA) region imploding into chaos.

It should be clear from the selection of topics and the methodological approach that this book seeks to speak directly to the current policy debates, while offering the student of NATO and transatlantic security relations an insight into the larger questions confronting the alliance. It must be underscored that while the fiscal crisis is ultimately the greatest challenge to the transatlantic security system going forward, Afghanistan remains the most immediate "teaching moment" for NATO as its longest sustained deployment. If we cull the right lessons from it, they can be applied to future campaigns and in the process help NATO strengthen allied solidarity and refocus on the shared mission of providing for common security. The task of responsibly leaving Afghanistan as a truly common project for both Americans and Europeans is not simply an exercise in rhetoric or wishful thinking. It is in fact the test of statesmanship for the coming decade of accelerated global state-on-state competition, wherein the ability of the United States and Europe to work together and, yes, to sacrifice and take shared risks, will remain a pivotal element of global security.

Afghanistan will inevitably generate a lot of ink and many a bitter dispute after the dust has settled, with no shortage of finger-pointing and second-guessing. But as the authors of this book believe, the lessons that NATO draws from ISAF must also become lessons learned, with compelling comparisons to another era when an American war in a faraway land seemed to have poisoned transatlantic relations beyond repair, yet ultimately yielded a generation of leaders and strategic thinkers who by the 1980s brought the alliance together around shared priorities. With comparisons between Afghanistan and the Vietnam War cycling through academic and analytical circles, it is worth reminding ourselves that the Colin Powell/Norman Schwarzkopf generation served honorably as junior-grade officers in that earlier war, only to make that experience into truly one of "lessons learned." Similarly, in the coming decade the armed forces of all NATO member-states will be shaped and led by the very men and women for whom ISAF has been a formative experience.

And so, as NATO prepares to complete the ISAF mission in Afghanistan and readies itself for the summit in 2014, the allies have a chance to demonstrate foresight that goes beyond the post–Chicago Summit debates on the virtues of "smart defense" and recommit to the preservation of NATO as the premier security organization, which the transatlantic community and the West, broadly defined, continue to need. If we take the practical measure of NATO's experience in Afghanistan and—as this book argues—place it in the context of transatlantic security priorities going forward, we will get the balance right.

NOTES

All Web sites last accessed November 2013.

1. Stanley R. Sloan, *Permanent Alliance? NATO and the Transatlantic Bargain from Truman to Obama* (New York: Bloomsbury Academic, 2010); Ellen Hallams, *The United States and NATO since 9/11: The Transatlantic Alliance Renewed* (Abingdon and New York: Routledge, 2013).

2. Håkan Edström, Janne Haaland Matlary, and Magnus Petersson, eds., *NATO: The Power of Partnerships* (New York: Palgrave Macmillan, 2001).

3. Håkan Edström and Dennis Gyllensporre, *Pursuing Strategy: NATO Operations from the Gulf War to Gaddafi* (New York: Palgrave Macmillan, 2012).

4. Sten Rynning, *NATO in Afghanistan: The Liberal Disconnect* (Stanford, CA: Stanford University Press, 2012).

5. Michael J. Williams, *NATO, Security and Risk Management: From Kosovo to Kandahar* (Abingdon and New York: Routledge, 2009); Andreas Benhke, *NATO's Security Discourse after the Cold War: Representing the West* (Abingdon and New York: Routledge, 2012).

6. Gülnur Aybet and Rebecca R. Moore, eds., *NATO in Search of a Vision* (Washington, DC: Georgetown University Press, 2010); James Sperling and S. Victor Papacosma, eds., *NATO after Sixty Years: A Stable Crisis* (Kent, OH: Kent State University, 2012); Graeme P. Herd and John Kriendler, eds., *Understanding NATO in the 21st Century* (Abingdon and New York: Routledge, 2013).

7. James M. Goldgeier, *Not Whether But When: The U.S. Decision to Enlarge NATO* (Washington, DC: Brookings Institution, 1999).

8. Michael Ruehle, "NATO after Riga: A New Direction?" *World Security Network*, May 10, 2007, http://www.worldsecuritynetwork.com/NATO/Ruehle -Michael/NATO-after-Riga-%E2%80%93-A-New-Direction.

9. "Afghanistan and the Future of Peace Operations" (speech presented by NATO Secretary General Anders Fogh Rasmussen at the University of Chicago), http://www.nato.int/cps/en/natolive/opinions_62510.htm?selectedLocale=en (accessed September 8, 2010).

10. Greg Jaffe and Michael Birnbaum, "Gates Rebukes European Allies in Farewell Speech," *Washington Post*, June 10, 2011, http://www.washingtonpost.com /world/gates-rebukes-european-allies-in-farewell-speech/2011/06/10/AG9tKeOH _story.html.

Chapter 1

The Out-of-Area Question
in Historical Perspective

Helge Danielsen and Helene F. Widerberg

"Active Engagement, Modern Defense," NATO's new Strategic Concept, agreed upon at the 2010 Lisbon Summit, can be read as an attempt to strike a balance between NATO's engagement out-of-area and its commitment to challenges closer to home. Collective defense of the treaty area and global outreach are both seen as natural tasks for the alliance. NATO should be relied upon to "defend Allied Nations, to deploy robust military forces where and when required for [our] security, and to help promote common security with [our] partners around the globe."[1] The question of balancing collective defense and a global outreach was also central to the discussions leading up to the Lisbon Summit, within and beyond a group of experts led by Madeleine Albright. The 2010 concept should thus be seen as a compromise, reflecting differences in perceived security challenges and in expectations of NATO from different member-states. In practice this compromise may lead to a policy in which NATO continues to take on expeditionary challenges outside the Euro-Atlantic region and simultaneously tries to reassure—through a variety of political and military measures—member-states concerned with the future status of Article 5–based commitments. Does the apparent balancing of priorities reflect a development where the former division between in- and out-of-area challenges has been eroded? Or should the 2010 concept be seen as an expression of NATO's ambition to be an alliance with both regional and global orientation?[2]

The strategy revision gave the allies an opportunity to take an overall look at NATO's current and potential roles and missions, including its role in defending its core region versus expeditionary military engagements.

This issue has for obvious reasons been high on the agenda during the past decade, though discussions between (future) allies on NATO's role beyond the treaty area have been going on since before the alliance's birth.[3] There is, however, a new element to the recent and ongoing deliberations. The "out-of-area" discussions were previously caused by the desire of one or more allies to involve NATO in security issues outside the treaty area. Conversely, the debate preceding the Lisbon Summit was affected by concerns among some members that the focus on international operations had become too dominant and that it was time for NATO to put more emphasis on its traditional core tasks. Both these discussions, the concept itself, and subsequent developments show that different member countries have different ambitions for and different claims to the alliance.[4] One way of handling this situation would be for NATO to balance these aspects in a credible manner and to be both an expeditionary and a core area–oriented alliance.

NATO's policy on out-of-area questions during the Cold War has been described as a "nonpolicy," motivated by the need both to keep the Allies focused on the paramount task of collective defense and to keep NATO "out of trouble," that is, to avoid possible internal strife over such issues.[5] After the Cold War the alliance took steps out-of-area, mainly driven by events, but also based on a perceived need to redefine the purpose of NATO. The alliance gradually took on responsibilities beyond its borders during the 1990s. Since 2001 NATO has taken on a number of missions in areas such as Afghanistan, Iraq, and the Horn of Africa. In addition, the United States has turned more of its attention toward strategically important regions other than Europe. Some allies reacted to these developments with calls for measures to increase the credibility of collective defense as stated in Article 5.[6] Experts within NATO replied to such calls with a warning against spending too much time and effort on a dichotomy between Article 5 tasks and expeditionary operations. Jamie Shea, at the time director of policy planning in the Private Office of the Security General of NATO, argued in 2010 that "NATO must prepare for both types of operations—for its internal consensus as well as for its relevance as a multilateral security provider."[7] In its report the group of experts took a similar stand.[8] For the foreseeable future, assurance for the treaty-defined area *and* engagement beyond the treaty area should thus be seen as complementary, in the same way that defense and détente created a twin imperative from the late 1960s onward.[9] The report's clear recommendation that NATO strike a balance between its engagements in- and out-of-area was, as suggested above, taken seriously in the new concept.

How to balance a commitment to collective defense with perceived security challenges beyond the treaty area (either to the alliance as a whole or to one or more member-states) has been an issue of contention among the allies since the negotiations on the North Atlantic Treaty (NAT) before it was signed in 1949. The background for, meanings of, and conclusions to these discussions have varied over time, with the most obvious chronological break being the end of the Cold War. Throughout NATO's history, however, the decisions and policies on the balance between an out-of- or in-area orientation have been the result of the strategic situation of the alliance and of the need to balance collective interests with those of single members or groups of members. To a varying degree, this balancing act has been a challenge to alliance cohesion.

This chapter outlines NATO's handling of the out-of-area issue throughout the history of the alliance and addresses how different approaches to this question have affected it, mainly concerning questions of internal cooperation and alliance cohesion. Both in the past and today, the allies have had differing—and changing—points of view on NATO's role inside and outside of the treaty area. Discussing previous research on the subject, this chapter analyzes the attempt to balance core and expeditionary tasks in the 2010 Strategic Concept in historical perspective.

The Out-of-Area Issue during the Cold War

The description of NATO's Cold War approach to the out-of-area issue as a "nonpolicy" was coined by the Norwegian historian Frode Liland. His argument is that in addition to differences in interest, threat perceptions, and ideology, the choice by member-states to abstain from pushing for a common policy on out-of-area questions reflected a larger shared view. It was the realization that the common defense against the Soviet Union within the treaty area was of such importance that other challenges should not be allowed to create ruptures within the alliance.[10] The potential for such ruptures existed from the beginning, as the geographical and strategic orientations of the member-states were highly varied. The United States had global interests, whereas several European members had regional (and initially, colonial) ambitions, while other member-states, including the smaller European nations, had a more local orientation. Liland exemplifies how out-of-area problems were not handled as a matter of NATO as a whole. For example, NATO as an organization did not address the war in Korea. Parties directly engaged in Korea interacted either within the United Nations or bilaterally.[11]

The Korean War was of great importance for the development of NATO, however. The outbreak of war was in itself taken as proof that communist aggression could occur anywhere, and that preparations to resist an attack in Europe were due. It led to a consolidation of the alliance *within its core area* and to the development of an integrated military structure. In addition to the measures brought about by this interpretation of the war and its causes, the practical experience from taking part in a U.S.-led operation within a United Nations (UN) framework had an impact on norms of consultation and cooperation within NATO. It has also been suggested that U.S.-NATO relations indirectly put constraints on American military action in Korea, because an attack on China or the use of nuclear weapons most certainly would have caused a severe setback in the relationship between the United States and the rest of NATO.[12] To both the Truman and Eisenhower administrations, "preservation of the Alliance with Western Europe was more important than the war in Asia."[13]

The nonpolicy on out-of-area issues that was established during the Korean War remained the basis of NATO's approach to similar challenges throughout the Cold War. There were some exceptions to this rule. In the first half of the Cold War these were brought about by colonial (or postcolonial) crises; at a later stage they were caused by U.S. engagements outside the North Atlantic area.[14] The alternative to establishing an active out-of-area policy for NATO as a whole, followed by military engagements, was the use of political consultations and, in cases in which two or more NATO members had common interests in the use of force, the establishment of so-called coalitions of the willing. Liland's conclusion is that the combination of an official nonpolicy with these alternatives kept NATO "out of trouble," both in a general sense and concerning internal strife. The discussions on out-of-area questions and the resentment by member-states that pleaded for support from the alliance without getting it did, however, cause misgivings within NATO. Liland's argument is that the level of conflict would have been higher if it were not for the nonpolicy, combined with the previously mentioned alternatives.[15]

Other scholars have provided interpretations similar to Liland's. In a study from 1990 Douglas Stuart and William Tow show how the out-of-area issue during the Cold War can be thought of in terms of balancing general and particular interests. They provide a comprehensive analysis of how NATO before 1989 dealt with "the difficulty of maintaining a regionally demarcated multilateral alliance comprising nations that recognize important security interests beyond the Alliance's perimeters."[16] Their point of departure is an interpretation of how alliance cohesion is affected by the nature of the international system. They argue that in a bipolar system characterized by opposing blocs, a common threat perception, and a hegemonic leader within each alliance, common interests will prevail. The pursuit of particular interests will not be given a priority that would threaten to seriously disrupt alliance cohesion.[17] When the discussions on different out-of-area problems nevertheless caused disagreements within NATO, this was in part due to false (and exaggerated) expectations. Both large and small members overestimated the degree to which other allies would perceive a particular security interest of one state as the general interest of the alliance. The presence of such discussions, and of expectations for that matter, is all the more understandable because both the establishment of NATO itself, and later the establishment of the "nonpolicy" on out-of-area issues, were the result of deliberations on the shape and purpose of the alliance. According to Stuart and Tow, the possibility for disagreement, as well as the basis for false expectations, had its origin in potentially conflicting paragraphs in the North Atlantic Treaty. On the one hand, Article 4 on consultations allows allies to bring security interests and challenges to the attention of NATO, regardless of geography. Article 4 thus throughout NATO's history has provided an opportunity for members to try to engage the alliance (or single members) in activities outside the treaty area. The geographic limitations of Article 6, on the other hand, in both a formal and a practical sense provided the foundation on which to build the "nonpolicy." This was so not least because these limitations contributed to highlighting the dominant, common security threat to the North Atlantic area represented by the Soviet Union and the Warsaw Pact.[18]

This does not mean that Article 6 *prevented* disputes and misgivings linked to the out-of-area security challenges of one or more member-states, but rather that it provided a means to keep the internal level of conflict fairly low. As a part of the NAT, Article 6 not only regulated the geographic extension of the mutual security guarantees set forth in Article 5 but also set limits to the subjects and the kinds of security issues the members could bring to each other's attention in a formal NATO setting. The article has been described as a "circuit breaker" because, notably during the Cold War, it provided an instrument to prevent the escalation of out-of-area discussions to an unpleasant level. Despite the presence of such a legalistic argument, out-of-area issues also led to a series of situations in which the use of different forms of diplomacy within the alliance was warranted. These took the shape of mutual information and consultations, the coordination of policies, and in some cases (notably the Suez crisis) conflict resolution.[19] Veronica M. Kitchen has argued that NATO members handled the out-of-area issue, both during and after the Cold War, based not only on the norms and agreements laid down in the Atlantic Treaty but also on a *social norm*. This social norm is rooted mainly in the experiences from the Suez crisis, defining mutual duties and responsibilities. According to Kitchen, during the Cold War period the treaty norm of mutual defense was accompanied by a social norm holding that military operations by member-states outside of the treaty area were secondary. They should not be brought before the Atlantic Council, even if this technically was an option provided in Article 4.[20] In those cases in which one member-state wanted to mobilize other allies for support in operations outside the treaty area, they dealt with the issue bilaterally. Kitchen sees this as an example of how "norms of security within the Atlantic Community depended on more than what was written in the NATO treaty."[21] Such a statement is fairly uncontroversial, but concerning the out-of-area policy of NATO during the Cold War, the established practice can be said to have been based on a relatively straightforward interpretation of the relevant treaty articles. In other words, the "social norm" and the "treaty norm" were fairly similar.

One could thus simply argue that a situation, the Suez crisis, in which the out-of-area engagement of two allies created a crisis of confidence within the alliance, invoked the treaty norm. Alternatively, one can see NATO's handling of the Suez affair after the crisis as a *clarification* of the alliance's in- versus out-of-area orientation in this period. Sten Rynning sees this case as "illustrative of the limits of the Atlantic agreement in these early alliance years," particularly regarding alliance policies toward the broader Middle East.[22] The outcome of the crisis, or rather NATO's way of leaving the controversies behind, was an agreement to focus on the treaty area and to put more weight on political consultations. Simultaneously, the allies left it up to the UN to deal with the Suez crisis, and the United States pursued a strategy toward the Middle East that was more or less independent of NATO. Rynning argues that this approach "helped sustain the Atlantic community as such," an argument that fits well with Liland's idea of a nonpolicy.[23]

Veronica Kitchen argues that the primacy of mutual defense was not provided in the North Atlantic Treaty, but rather "institutionalized in the discursive structure and identity of the Alliance."[24] This implies a reading of Article 5 compared to the other articles of the treaty that, in our opinion, underplays the significance of the mutual commitment expressed by the allies in that article. Furthermore, the claim appears to be ahistorical, as it does not take into account the prehistory and the context of the NAT. It also overlooks the significance of the Korean War in NATO policies regarding the out-of-area issue. This is not to say that we refute the belief that NATO's policy on this and other issues is the result also of social norms for allied interaction that have been developed over time. However, we suggest that "treaty norms" and "social norms" should not be seen as dichotomies, but rather stress the interplay between them in situations— particularly during the Cold War—in which allies differed on challenges outside the treaty area.

Nevertheless, both the primacy of mutual defense and the social norm that security issues beyond the treaty area should not be dealt with in formal NATO channels were stronger after the Suez crisis than before it.[25] This was the case in part because already existing norms were challenged by some allies and defended by others. Attempts by France and the United Kingdom to involve NATO were rejected by the United States and Canada, among others, on the basis of Article 6, and to some extent Article 4. Thomas Risse-Kappen has described the Suez crisis as the "most significant incident of transatlantic non-cooperation during the 1950s."[26] The U.S. decision to coerce its allies was based on the view that the United Kingdom and France had violated alliance norms to such a degree that a kind of retaliation was warranted that would otherwise be unheard of. His analysis shows that a set of norms was already established before the crisis but also points out that the Suez experience led to a revision of NATO rules and procedures for consultation.[27]

Notwithstanding the establishment of a nonpolicy and the presence of a "circuit breaker," out-of-area questions did play an important role within NATO throughout the Cold War and highly influenced the development of the alliance. The driving force behind the out-of-area discussions within NATO changed around 1960. In the first half of the Cold War the European colonial powers brought political and military challenges in their colonies or former colonies to the attention of the alliance. They did so either by soliciting support from NATO or by handling challenges linked to decolonization and interests outside of Europe in ways that affected the alliance. From the early 1960s onward the out-of-area issues on NATO's agenda were a result of the increased global engagement of the United States. In addition to this chronological division, attempts have been made to classify out-of-area disputes on the basis of their characteristics.

A typology developed by Stuart and Tow, based on thirty-one cases from the Cold War period, identifies five types of situations related to out-of-area challenges that have had implications for NATO: (1) situations in which the policies of one ally created concerns of *guilt by association* among other members, (2) situations in which one member has seen the actions of another ally as an intrusion into its *domaine reservé*, (3) situations in which members have tried to solicit the support of others either by appealing to alliance solidarity or by using alliance mechanisms, (4) out-of-area situations in which the activities of one member have raised the issue of internal burden sharing, and (5) situations that have illustrated differences either in the understanding of what constitutes a common interest or in threat perceptions within the alliance.[28] In addition, out-of-area-problems can include a combination of one or more of these five types. According to Stuart and Tow, both the Suez crisis in 1956 and the French involvement in Indochina combined all five characteristics. European reactions to decolonization throughout the 1950s raised American concerns of guilt by association on several occasions, but also brought about European reactions to U.S. involvement in what the colonial powers saw as internal matters. Situations arose in which European members sought allied support but did not receive it to the desired degree.

From the late 1960s to the end of the Cold War the issue of burden sharing was raised, especially in the form of American criticism of other member-states concerning contributions (economic, moral, or military) to what the United States perceived as common security threats outside the treaty area.[29] The issues of contention sparking an out-of-area dispute could also differ from one period to another. While *domaine reservé* discussions mainly took place during the 1950s and 1960s, disagreements over threat perception and discussions over burden sharing dominated in the second half of the Cold War.[30]

It should be added that even if NATO did not engage directly in out-of-area issues during the Cold War, the member-states had a more flexible approach to the geographic limitations of the treaty area in the 1980s than in earlier decades. This reorientation was in part brought about by the Soviet invasion of Afghanistan, one of several developments that altered the threat perception of a number of NATO countries. It strengthened the belief that the security situation in, for example, Southwest Asia and the Persian Gulf area, could have repercussions for the security and stability of the North Atlantic area. The practical expression of this was that the traditional means of dealing with out-of-area challenges—consultations and coordination of activities—were supplemented by measures. These included the deployment of personnel in Europe "to maintain the necessary force levels for deterrence in the event that individual allies felt compelled to utilize NATO designated assets to respond to a crisis outside the Treaty area."[31] The political basis for such measures had been established in the Strategic Concept of May 1957, commonly referred to as MC 14/2 (and best known for establishing "massive retaliation" as NATO's nuclear doctrine). It stated that allied military planning should take into consideration that some of the member-states had security commitments outside of the core area, and that it would be in the interests of the whole alliance if such issues were attended to. An example is the acceptance by other NATO members that they would compensate for the reduced American presence in Europe caused by the increased U.S. engagement in Southwest Asia after the Iranian revolution and the Soviet invasion of Afghanistan.[32] NATO's reactions to these events represented a strong modification of the established nonpolicy on out-of-area questions, yet was not a disposal of the approach altogether.

The allied reactions to the changing security situation in the Gulf area and beyond are an example of both continuity and change in NATO's manner of addressing the out-of-area question. On the one hand, the main aspects of the nonpolicy were maintained. Initial responses were *not* a display of unity, and a common response developed slowly. On the other hand, the reactions represented a development, a modification, pointing toward a new approach to out-of-area-engagements after the Cold War. At the time the Afghanistan crisis was seen as a display of a lack in alliance cohesion, raising American concerns regarding burden sharing within NATO. In retrospect, the increased focus on allied cooperation on an out-of-area issue that the Americans pushed for from this incident and throughout the 1980s was more successful than was acknowledged at the time, as the European allies—however reluctantly—both supported and compensated for U.S. efforts in the region.[33] Liland has argued that the deployment of seventy-five warships by six NATO countries to the Persian Gulf in 1987, facilitated by Germany and Norway taking over duties in European waters, was in *reality* (though not formally) an out-of-area operation.[34] Even if the alliance was not engaged directly in the 1980s, a development and change in policies had occurred. NATO played a different role in the 1980s than it had done earlier, because it functioned as "a mechanism for generating informal coalitions composed of allies and intended to interfere in Middle Eastern politics."[35] Both the Carter and Reagan administrations, after having considered other alternatives, addressed situations outside the treaty area in cooperation with several allies, without formally engaging NATO in their efforts.[36]

This approach helped to maintain NATO's nonpolicy, at least in theory. There were other cases, such as Korea and the Falklands, in which more than one NATO member opted for the use of military power outside the treaty area. The involvement of the alliance itself—and thus the disruption of the nonpolicy—was avoided by establishing coalitions of the willing, or by what has been described as the ad hoc establishment of "shadow alliances."[37]

Finally, crises like the Suez and the Soviet Union's invasion of Afghanistan are examples of how international situations with serious implications for NATO (as they raised issues concerning cohesion, solidarity, and burden sharing) were not allowed to develop beyond a certain level, to prevent interallied strife. According to Wallace Thies, the internal "healing process" in both these examples started even before the crises themselves were resolved.[38] We argue that the "nonpolicy," in combination with allied consultations, contributed to this.

Our initial goal was to understand the changing approaches to the out-of-area issue in light of changes in the wider strategic and political context that NATO policies were a part of. As already suggested, the main factor affecting how NATO dealt with this issue during the Cold War was the perceived political and military threat from the Soviet bloc in the Euro-Atlantic area. This common worldview not only led to the establishment of NATO, but also contributed to maintaining common defense based on Article 5 as the main task of the alliance throughout the period in question. Even the slight modification of the nonpolicy in the early 1980s should be interpreted in light of bipolarity and thus differs in more than one way from the post–Cold War approaches to the out-of-area issue.

The Out-of-Area Issue after the Cold War

After the end of the Cold War and the dissolution of the Soviet Union, NATO's death was predicted by a string of international relations (IR) scholars. Realists like John Mearsheimer argued that "it is the Soviet threat that provides the glue that holds NATO together," and that without this threat the United States was likely to abandon its allies, eventually resulting in the disintegration of NATO. Similarly, Stephen Walt claimed that without a common and unifying foe, the alliance would gradually dissolve.[39] Others argued that in order to survive, NATO should seek new tasks and challenges.

The slogan that NATO should go "out-of-area" to avoid going "out of business," coined by U.S. Senator Richard Lugar,[40] characterized the ensuing debate on NATO's role and area of action. Lugar's phrase had a double meaning: the alliance should both expand its membership and take on responsibility for security tasks *outside* the treaty area.[41] This somewhat strict either/or assertion has been nuanced by Ronald Asmus, Richard Kugler, and Stephen Larrabee. Their contention was that to avoid following the Soviet Union and the Warsaw Pact into the history books, NATO had to demonstrate continued relevance not only at home but also beyond its borders. They argued that NATO should adjust to the new security environment and remain relevant by *combining* its traditional task of territorial defense with out-of-area engagements, rather than maintain the two as separate phenomena:

> It is no longer possible for NATO to concentrate on the strategic luxury of territorial defense. The dividing line between "in-area" and "out-of-area" crisis, so clearly drawn under the Cold War, has become ambiguous and artificial. Redefining alliance commitments in both areas, and finding the proper balance between the two, is the fundamental issue facing the Alliance.[42]

The end of the Cold War thus represented a break with the established (non)policy on the out-of-area issue, and the hierarchy of tasks, in which territorial defense was previously paramount, became less clear. NATO redefined its purpose and engagement outside the treaty area in the 1990s, initially regarding its periphery, and then, after 2001, the area beyond the Euro-Atlantic region. Throughout the post–Cold War years the allies have confronted the task of dealing with the challenging debates on NATO's balance between out-of-area engagements and territorial defense; in other words, the alliance's cohesion and solidarity, purpose, role, and relevance.

From the 1990s onward NATO adjusted its involvement beyond the treaty-defined area through a dual-track approach. First, it engaged in cooperation with former adversaries and opened up for widening of the treaty area. Second, it took on a more active crisis management role and developed a new policy for operations beyond the allied region. While the alliance on one side prepared to expand the core area of territorial defense by including new members, on the other side it prepared to shift emphasis from that area to territories beyond its borders. In an analysis in 1999 Torunn Laugen Haaland argued that NATO's shift toward a new out-of-area policy had been driven by events, mainly the dissolution of the Soviet Union and the Yugoslav Civil War, rather than by allied strategic thinking.[43] According to Sten Rynning, during these events important allies first got caught up in a game of influence and later failed to take the lead in different, though crucial, situations.[44] Haaland describes the changes in NATO's out-of-area role in the 1990s as a development in three main phases. In the first phase, from 1990 to 1992, the established policies stayed largely unchanged. In the second phase, from 1992 to 1995, the alliance became gradually involved in the Balkan wars by engaging in Bosnia-Hercegovina.

In the third phase, from 1995 to 1999, NATO fully embraced an independent out-of-area role.

The alliance took some time to adjust to the new strategic situation after the Cold War. During the 1990 Gulf War, NATO did not take on a formal role and was only marginally involved. This was mainly due to strong reluctance to adopt an increased out-of-area role among several members, who worried about alliance cohesion and weakened commitment to Article 5. The Strategic Concept of 1991 affirmed that territorial defense was still the core task of NATO. NATO as such should not take on operations outside treaty borders.[45] However, there was some change in rhetoric about the nature of the alliance, in line with the ambition to create a "Europe whole and free." In spite of the confirmation of territorial defense as a priority, the 1991 concept, specifically in its chapter on crisis management and conflict prevention, took NATO one step further toward a new out-of-area role: it could take on a broader approach to security, possibly even begin to operate outside its old borders.[46]

This first phase after the Cold War was followed by two periods in which NATO became gradually involved in crises and conflicts outside its core area. In the Balkans the alliance initially supported peacekeeping activities on a case-by-case basis under the Conference on Security and Cooperation in Europe (CSCE) and UN Security Council (UNSC) authority. Later NATO's role became increasingly active and independent. The 1990s saw it move from reluctance to involvement in the area beyond the Article 6 boundaries and from peacekeeping to peace enforcement.[47] In the Bosnian War, from April 1993 NATO imposed a no-fly zone in Operation Deny Flight, and in 1995 it conducted air strikes on Serbian targets during Operation Deliberate Force. The first deployment of ground troops took place when the IFOR (Implementation Force) replaced UNPROFOR (United Nations Protection Force) in 1995. NATO's independent role was illustrated when the alliance intervened in the Kosovo conflict in Operation Allied Force in 1999, without a UNSC mandate. This shift in policy was reflected in the Strategic Concept of 1999. Here, conflict prevention and crisis management were defined as fundamental security tasks for the alliance.[48]

External events also continued to be a driving force behind NATO's out-of-area engagements in the new millennium. Between 2001 and 2007 NATO increased its out-of-area role, and missions expanded in scope, nature, and geographic range. The 2001 terrorist attacks against the United States were a watershed in the interpretation of the international security environment. They shifted the debate within NATO from how the alliance should meet threats in the Euro-Atlantic region to how it could meet threats independent of their origin. This opened the way for operations at strategic distance and portended not only a regional but also a global role for the alliance. NATO countries agreed that the alliance "must be able to field forces that can move quickly to *wherever* they are needed."[49] With an increasing number of out-of-area missions, of which ISAF was the most important, NATO's agenda was dominated by its global engagement.[50] Partly as a backlash against this, but also due to the Russo-Georgian war in August 2008, some allies called for increased emphasis on collective defense and Article 5 capabilities. Both new and old members reacted to what they saw as neglect of territorial defense. Had new tasks been prioritized at the expense of the core task? This was expressed, for example, in nonpapers (initiatives not dealt with by the Council) such as the Norwegian "core area initiative."[51] The 2009 Declaration on Alliance Security can be seen as an early attempt to address these worries. Article 5 and collective defense were confirmed as NATO's cornerstone, but the declaration also stated that NATO should improve its ability to meet security challenges that had an impact on allied territory. This was to be irrespective of whether threats "emerge[d] *at strategic distance or closer to home*" and was to strengthen NATO's role in crisis management and conflict resolution "*where our interests are involved.*"[52]

NATO's increased out-of-area engagements have spurred debates and exposed intra-alliance differences, challenging cohesion and cooperation, as experienced during the Cold War. The new approach to out-of-area issues after 1990 has not necessarily made them easier to handle or resolve. In his study on NATO's engagement in the broader Middle East, Sten Rynning shows how difficulties in coordinating policy goals, interests, and diverging views on the use of force among allies have caused internal dispute. These factors are relevant to NATO's handling of out-of-area issues in general: Is it of common interest to involve the alliance in missions outside the treaty area? If so, for what reasons, to what extent, and on what legal basis? How shall military and political burdens be shared? Against this background, Rynning argues, it would be for the benefit of alliance cohesion if NATO qua alliance did *not* engage in the Middle East or elsewhere, but rather took on a function mainly as a coalition-making framework.[53]

Coalitions of the willing have remained an option for member-states to manage crises outside the core area when consensus on collective action has been absent. Operation Enduring Freedom in Afghanistan, the main military response of the United States after 9/11, is one example of this. The Bush administration chose to align with the United Kingdom, bypassing NATO's offer of assistance and solidarity after the alliance had invoked Article 5 for the first time. NATO's contributions were therefore initially limited to the patrolling of U.S. airspace, followed by joint actions like Operation Active Endeavour in the Mediterranean. The 2003 Iraq intervention, which caused severe ruptures between NATO allies, was carried out by a U.S.-led coalition. The air strikes on Libya in 2011, based on UNSC Resolution 1973, were initially led by a smaller group of NATO members (including the United States, France, and the United Kingdom). All of these coalition-based operations have later been supplemented or replaced by joint allied operations: NATO took responsibility for the ISAF operation in Afghanistan in 2003, established a training mission in Iraq, and took over the leadership of Operation Unified Protector in Libya.

A new chapter of allied engagement started with NATO's involvement in the Balkans. In the following years, especially after the turn of the millennium, the balance between in-area and out-of-area emphasis shifted as NATO took on new roles in distant areas in an increasing number of non–Article 5 operations. NATO has thus become more of an international security organization rather than a strictly regional defense alliance. As Jennifer Medcalf has pointed out, NATO has taken on a number of global roles:

> NATO as a global defender, demonstrated by its naval patrols in the Mediterranean following 9/11; global enabler, for example, the logistical support given to [African Union] operations in Darfur and Somalia; NATO as a global stabilizer, most obviously seen in its role in Afghanistan; NATO as a global trainer, as demonstrated by its role building capacity in the Afghan and Iraqi security forces; and finally NATO as a global relief provider through the assistance it gave to Pakistan and the United States following natural disasters.[54]

NATO's global dimension has been much debated. Ivo Daalder and James Goldgeier have argued that the alliance should expand and include members from outside the Euro-Atlantic region in order to be better able to handle international security challenges more broadly and over a strategic distance.[55] Rynning, however, argues that NATO's joint operation in Afghanistan reflects "an important degree of political maturity that not even the troubled diplomacy surrounding the Iraq War could break."[56] Mads Berdal and David Ucko have argued that "NATO (had) read too much into the consensus on peacekeeping in the 1990s and failed to consider future more serious challenges."[57] According to Andrew Bacevich, Afghanistan "is the decisive test of whether the Alliance can handle large-scale, out-of-area missions."[58] His conclusion that the result has been a disappointing and dysfunctional alliance is based on the cultural differences among "Europeans (who) had long since lost their stomach for battle" and the Americans, who try to "nurture a muscle-flexing new NATO."[59]

Despite the many disputes and challenges out-of-area missions in general and ISAF in particular have raised, former Secretary General Jaap de Hoop Scheffer repeatedly pointed to the mission in Afghanistan as "priority number one."[60] This demonstrated how clearly the balance had shifted toward out-of-area operations residing at NATO's core. In the words of former U.S. NATO permanent representative Nicholas Burns, relations between the United States and Europe were "increasingly a function of events in the Middle East, Asia and Africa."[61] The shift triggered an intra-alliance, as well as academic debate on NATO's role and engagements in a larger geographical theater. Timo Noetzel and Benjamin Schreer have pointed out that "collective defense and the principles of solidarity are no longer at the forefront of many allies' considerations," and that "there no longer exists a solid consensus within the Alliance about the hierarchy of roles the organization is to perform."[62] In their view, a process of disintegration has accelerated in recent years because of diverging opinions on the role of military power in international politics and the role of military alliances in general. Veronica Kitchen has also made the point that the hierarchy of tasks and roles has eroded since NATO went out-of-area. She goes further than Noetzel and Schreer, claiming that as "NATO's definition of its area of primary responsibility meant that the old distinction between in- and out-of-area no longer applied, and the rules on how to agree or disagree on such matters, defined during the Cold War by the strict hierarchy established by the out-of-area norm, did not either."[63] She also argues that the distinction between Article 5 on collective defense and Article 4 on consultation has become "meaningless."

The new Strategic Concept of 2010 and the process leading up to its adoption can be seen as an effort to reconcile highly differing positions within NATO. Both before and during this process there was talk of distinctive intra-alliance groups with conflicting views on NATO's international and regional engagement.[64] Noetzel and Schreer claimed that NATO had "developed from a fixed 'two-tier' into a rather fluid 'multi-tier' alliance where a 'reformist' tier advocated a global NATO, a 'status quo'-oriented tier was reluctant to question existing strategic and doctrinal foundations, and a 'neo-traditionalist' tier advocated a return to the classical task of collective defense."[65]

However, the task of collective defense and the primacy of Article 5 have gained increased support in the alliance as such, as seen in the 2010

Strategic Concept and the renewed emphasis on contingency planning and collective defense–based exercises. As mentioned previously, the 2010 concept declares that the alliance can be relied upon to defend member nations, deploy forces where needed, and promote security globally, in cooperation with allies and partner nations.[66] In our view, this is in line with the view of the Declaration on Alliance Security and the report of the expert group. Other scholars, like Ringsmose and Rynning, see the new Strategic Concept as a shift toward a more global NATO and argue that behind the affirmation of Article 5's continued relevance, the new concept suggests fewer geographical limitations and a globalized way of thinking. In their view, it is an expression of NATO's development toward becoming a political and global organization, rather than a regional and military one. This is outlined as "subtle" but not "trivial" in the hierarchy of NATO's responsibilities.[67] We argue, however, that this can be seen as more than just a verbal affirmation of the significance of Article 5. It can also be seen as an attempt to accommodate those predominantly newer and flank members who have argued that the alliance needs to raise its profile and increase visible assurance at home in order to avoid a decrease in public support.

Given that the new concept can be interpreted in many different ways, there is reason to believe that NATO's role in international security policy will be driven by external, and unforeseen, events also in the future.[68]

It can be argued that NATO in its new concept has made an effort to strike a balance between in- and out-of-area engagements, such as by keeping an eye on emerging dangers evolving outside the treaty area while also putting more weight on collective defense of the core area. This approach has gained support from so-called reformist allies, including the United States and United Kingdom, who have realized the strategic self-interest of having an alliance in which the members both have confidence in its security guarantee and support engagements outside the treaty area. In addition, the experiences from former and ongoing operations out-of-area have demonstrated the danger of NATO's credibility being too closely linked to these operations. Karl-Heinz Kamp is one of several scholars who have argued that NATO, after Afghanistan, should return to its core principles and "its roots as a classic security alliance." A balance of tasks will still be necessary, however. Kamp argues that even if NATO should return to its core tasks, it would "have to look beyond its territorial boundaries, because globalization is also relevant for security."[69]

In our reading, the 2010 Strategic Concept gives increased priority to Article 5, while it also states that according to Article 4, NATO remains the "forum for consultations on all matters that affect the territorial integrity, political independence and security of its members," and that "any security issue of interest to any ally can be brought to the NATO table."[70] This gives Article 4 an important role in today's complex security environment, though it upholds a meaningful rather than meaningless distinction between the two articles. NATO has adjusted its strategy and purpose to fit a world with new threats and a permanently altered meaning of geography. Simultaneously, the alliance has acknowledged that to remain relevant, NATO must be able to guarantee the mutual security of its members.

Conclusions: 2010 in Historical Perspective

The background for NATO's 2010 Strategic Concept was the significant set of changes in both regional and global security challenges since 1999. The Strategic Concept, to a high degree, was retrospective and based on historical experience, as it highlighted practices and policies that were already part of NATO's repertoire without being mentioned in the previous concept.[71] At the same time, "Active Engagement, Modern Defense," also addresses possible future developments and older issues (such as nuclear proliferation) with a renewed urgency. Concerning the policy on out-of-area operations in NATO, the concept even includes recommendations that may shape the alliance for years to come and not just formalize established practices. The concept does not represent a complete break from the out-of-area policies developed during the post–Cold War period but still seeks to show the proponents of a greater NATO engagement and visibility in-area that their concerns are taken seriously. As mentioned in the introduction, whereas some member-states have wanted more of a balance between these two types of engagements, based on the view that they are contradictory, the group of experts recommends an increased balance, on the grounds that these are complementary tasks. From a historical perspective this line of argument is highly interesting, as it is fairly similar to arguments from the Cold War era, which suggest that security concerns outside of the treaty area, affecting one or more of the allies, should be regarded as a concern of all. The difference is that today there is a higher degree of consensus on such a position and on the presence of potential global threats.

Claims have been made that the boundaries between mutual defense of the treaty area and an orientation out-of-area have been blurred or even "eroded" in the post–Cold War period.[72] It has also been argued that the allies have not adapted to this new reality, in the sense that they have not clarified what their responsibilities to each other are. More specifically, Veronica Kitchen has argued that the subordination of consultations as mandated in Article 4 to Article 5 responsibilities characteristic of the

Cold War period was challenged as NATO reoriented toward the defense of common values rather than of a geographic area. She also suggests that this development, along with the Balkan experience, has brought about the beginning of change in the social norm giving preference to Article 5 challenges.[73] Another approach to the relationship between in-area and expeditionary operations after the Cold War is presented by Sten Rynning, who sees the Cold War approach, in particular the practice established in the 1980s, as a possible example for the future of NATO. By continuing to use NATO as a basis for coalition making, rather than involving the alliance outside the treaty area, it can continue to function as a tool for those members who have an increasingly global security approach, without putting the alliance itself at risk. Rynning argues that by using the alliance to generate political and military support, without engaging NATO in a military sense, one avoids weakening transatlantic cooperation.[74] This analysis is sensitive to an element of continuity in NATO's history and also allows for viewing NATO as a more multifaceted organization, in which the members have some common, and many differing, security objectives.

The concerns expressed by some members over the expeditionary character of NATO, and the ensuing initiative to reengage NATO in-area, to a certain degree echo the debate on the out-of-area issue during the Cold War. The potential conflict between the general interest of NATO and security interests of one or more member-states is one such similarity. Current efforts to integrate an out-of-area perspective with closer attention to the core area can thus be seen as a balancing act in which the real issue at stake is weighing general and particular interests. Or perhaps it should be seen as an attempt at bridge building between the very different interests found among the allies, be they "particular" for certain members or "general" for groups of members. One way or another, the real test of the efforts to integrate core area and out-of-area commitments will be how they are followed up in practice in decades to come, not just in the final text of the Strategic Concept, but in political and military terms.

NOTES

All Web sites accessed in November 2013 if not otherwise specified.

1. From the preface of "Strategic Concept for the Defence and Security of the Members of the North Atlantic Treaty Organisation" (adopted by heads of state and government in Lisbon), http://www.nato.int/nato_static/assets/pdf/pdf _publications/20120214_strategic-concept-2010-eng.pdf.

2. See, e.g., Veronica M. Kitchen, "NATO's Out-of-Area Norm from Suez to Afghanistan," *Journal of Transatlantic Studies* 8, no. 2 (June 2010): 105–17; and Jens Ringsmose and Sten Rynning, "Introduction: Taking Stock of NATO's New Strategic Concept," in *NATO's New Strategic Concept: A Comprehensive Assessment*, DIIS Report 2011:02, ed. Jens Ringsmose and Sten Rynning (Copenhagen: Danish Institute for International Studies, 2011), 7–22.

3. The "out-of-area" issue has historically spanned more than one dimension. The geographical scope of NATO—the area covered by the mutual commitment to common defense in line with Article 5—is one such dimension. Another is of a more political and ideological nature, for example, the debate over a "global NATO." Finally, there is an operational dimension, concerning whether and on what grounds NATO should engage militarily beyond its own borders. It is this final aspect that is the main subject of this chapter.

4. See, e.g., Timo Noetzel and Benjamin Schreer, "Does a Multi-tier NATO Matter? The Atlantic Alliance and the Process of Strategic Change," *International Affairs* 85, no. 2 (2009): 211–26.

5. See Frode Liland, *Keeping NATO Out of Trouble: NATO's Non-policy on Out-of-Area Issues during the Cold War*, Forsvarsstudier 4/99 (Oslo: Institutt for Forsvarsstudier, 1999).

6. Jens Ringsmose and Sten Rynning, *Come Home, NATO? The Atlantic Alliance's New Strategic Concept*, DIIS Report 2009:04 (Copenhagen: Danish Institute for International Studies, 2009).

7. Jamie Shea, "NATO at Sixty—and Beyond," in *NATO: In Search of a Vision*, ed. Gülnur Aybet and Rebecca Moore (Washington, DC: Georgetown University Press, 2010), 22.

8. North Atlantic Treaty Organization, *NATO 2020: Assured Security, Dynamic Engagement; Analysis and Recommendations of the Group of Experts on a New Strategic Concept for NATO* (Brussels: NATO Public Diplomacy Division, May 17, 2010), http://www.nato.int/cps/en/natolive/official_texts_63654.htm.

9. North Atlantic Treaty Organization, *NATO 2020*, 12.

10. Frode Liland, "Explaining NATO's Non-policy on Out-of-Area Issues during the Cold War," in *A History of NATO: The First Fifty Years, 1949–1999, Volume 1*, ed. Gustav Schmidt (Basingstoke/New York: Palgrave, 2001), 173f.

11. Liland, *Keeping NATO Out of Trouble*, 176; Lawrence Kaplan, *NATO Divided, NATO United: The Evolution of an Alliance* (Westport, CT/London: Praeger Publishers, 2004), 9ff.

12. See Thomas Risse-Kappen, *Cooperation among Democracies: The European Influence on U.S. Foreign Policy* (Princeton, NJ: Princeton University Press, 1995), 46ff. and 63.

13. Risse-Kappen, *Cooperation among Democracies*, 77.

14. Among the exceptions are the inclusion of (French) Algeria in the treaty area; the Indochina Resolution of 1952; the membership of Greece and Turkey—and hence the orientation toward the Mediterranean and the Middle East as (possible) areas of interest; limited common policies on Cuba in the early 1960s; and limited policies subsequent to the Soviet invasion of Afghanistan (Liland, *Keeping NATO Out of Trouble*, 113ff.).

15. Liland, "Explaining," 188f.; see also Liland, *Keeping NATO Out of Trouble*.

16. Douglas Stuart and William Tow, *The Limits of Alliance: NATO Out-of-Area Problems since 1949* (Baltimore, MD: Johns Hopkins University Press, 1990), 3.

17. They also point out that a bipolar situation in which the allies have "nowhere else to go" provides an opportunity to push particular interests within the alliance, at least in rhetoric, to a much higher degree than in a multipolar situation, in which an *exit* option is (somewhat) more likely, and thus requires a more cautious approach; see Stuart and Tow, *Limits of Alliance*, 4f.

18. Stuart and Tow, *Limits of Alliance*, 314.

19. Douglas Stuart, "NATO's Future as a Pan-European Security institution," *NATO Review* 41, no. 4 (August 1993): 15–19, http://www.nato.int/docu/review/1993/9304-4.htm.

20. See Veronica M. Kitchen, *The Globalization of NATO: Intervention, Security and Identity* (London and New York: Routledge, 2010); and Kitchen, "NATO's Out-of-Area Norm," 105f.

21. Kitchen, "NATO's Out-of-Area Norm," 107f.

22. See Sten Rynning, "NATO and the Broader Middle East, 1949–2007: The History and Lessons of Controversial Encounters," *Journal of Strategic Studies* 30, no. 6 (2007): 905–27.

23. Rynning, "NATO and the Broader Middle East."

24. See Kitchen, *Globalization*, 7

25. See Kitchen, *Globalization*, 39.

26. See Risse-Kappen, *Cooperation among Democracies*, 83.

27. Risse-Kappen, *Cooperation among Democracies*, 92–96.

28. Douglas T. Stuart, "The United States and NATO Out-of-Area-Disputes: Does the Cold War Provide Precedents, or Merely Prologue?," in *A History of NATO*, ed. Gustav Schmidt (Basingstoke/New York: Palgrave, 2001), vol. 1, 129; Stuart and Tow, *Limits of Alliance*, 9.

29. Stuart, "United States and NATO," 130ff.

30. Stuart and Tow, *Limits of Alliance*, 12ff.

31. Stuart, "NATO's Future."

32. It should be noted that this policy was the result of a NATO communiqué, not based on informal agreements or "coalition-of-the-willing"-like measures (Liland, *Keeping NATO Out of Trouble*, 116). Both MC 14/2 and subsequent measures in line with it were brought about by increased Soviet activities toward countries in the so-called third world. Military responses were not, however, considered to be the most appropriate reaction to such Soviet activities, which were mainly perceived of as a political and/or social challenge. See Frode Liland and Helge Pharo, "Norge og striden om NATOs geografiske virkeområde," in *NATO 50 år: Norsk sikkerhetspolitikk med NATO gjennom 50 år*, ed. Chris Prebensen and Nils Skarland (Oslo: Den Norske Atlanterhavskomité, 1999), 186.

33. Wallace J. Thies, *Why NATO Endures* (Cambridge, UK: Cambridge University Press, 2009), 226, 239.

34. Liland, *Keeping NATO Out of Trouble*, 123.

35. Rynning, "Broader Middle East," 914.

36. Rynning, "Broader Middle East," 917.

37. Stuart, "United States and NATO," 124.

38. Thies, *Why NATO Endures*, 241.

39. See, e.g., John Mearsheimer, "Back to the Future: Instability in Europe after the Cold War," *International Security* 15, no. 1 (1990): 52. Stephen Walt, "The Ties That Fray: Why Europe and America Are Drifting Apart," *The National Interest*, no. 54 (Winter 1998/1999), http://www.comw.org/pda/swalt.pdf.

40. Richard G. Lugar, "NATO: Out of Area or Out of Business" (speech presented to the Overseas Writers Club, June 24, 1993), cited in Jennifer Medcalf, *Going Global or Going Nowhere: NATO's Role in Contemporary International Security* (Bern: Peter Lang, 2008).

41. See, e.g., Rebecca Moore, *NATO's New Missions: Projecting Stability in a Post-Cold War World* (Westport, CT: Praeger Security International, 2007), 24. The expression was later also used in the debate on NATO's purpose and role outside of the treaty area.

42. Ronald Asmus, Richard L. Kugler, and Stephen F. Larrabee, "Building a New NATO," *Foreign Affairs* 72, no. 4 (1993): 38.

43. Torunn Laugen Haaland, *Stumbling into a New Role: NATO's Out-of-Area Policy after the Cold War* (Oslo: Institutt for Forsvarsstudier, Forsvarsstudier 5/1999), 10.

44. Sten Rynning, *Nato Renewed: The Power and Purpose of Transatlantic Cooperation* (New York: Palgrave Macmillan, 2005), 23.

45. Laugen Haaland, *Stumbling into a New Role*, 12 and 23ff.

46. North Atlantic Treaty Organization, "The Alliance's New Strategic Concept," 1991, paragraphs 31–33. http://www.nato.int/cps/en/natolive/official_texts_23847.htm.

47. Laugen Haaland, *Stumbling into a New Role*, 33.

48. North Atlantic Treaty Organization, "The Alliance's Strategic Concept," 1999, paragraphs 6 and 10, http://www.nato.int/cps/en/natolive/official_texts_27433.htm.

49. North Atlantic Treaty Organization, "Final Communiqué of the Ministerial Meeting in Reykjavik," May 14, 2002, paragraph 5, http://www.nato.int/cps/en/SID-3672FD28-4108CD25/natolive/official_texts_19577.htm.

50. Examples of NATO out-of-area operations since 2001 include the NATO Training Mission in Iraq from June 2004, the humanitarian relief operation in Pakistan (October 2005–February 2006), support to the African Union peacekeeping mission in Sudan (June 2005–December 2007), and airlift support in Somalia (assisting an African Union mission since June 2007). "NATO's Operations and Missions," http://www.nato.int/cps/en/natolive/topics_52060.htm.

51. "Strengthening NATO—Raising Its Profile and Ensuring Its Relevance" (unpublished manuscript, 2008). The Norwegian paper later received support in a Baltic and an Italian nonpaper.

52. North Atlantic Treaty Organization, "Declaration on Allied Security," 2009, http://www.nato.int/cps/en/natolive/news_52838.htm.

53. Rynning, "Broader Middle East."

54. Medcalf, *Going Global*, 26–27.

55. Ivo Daalder and James Goldgeier, "Global NATO," *Foreign Affairs* (September/October 2006), http://www.foreignaffairs.com/articles/61922/ivo-daalder-and-james-goldgeier/global-nato.

56. Rynning, "Broader Middle East," 919.

57. Mads Berdal and David Ucko, "NATO at 60," *Survival* 51, no. 2 (April 2009): 63.

58. Andrew Bacevich, "Let Europe Be Europe: Why the United States Must Withdraw from NATO," *Foreign Policy* (March/April 2010), http://www.foreign policy.com/articles/2010/02/22/let_europe_be_europe.

59. Bacevich, "Let Europe Be Europe."

60. See, e.g., Jaap de Hoop Scheffer, "Press Briefing at Riga Summit," Brussels, November 26, 2006, http://www.nato.int/docu/speech/2006/s061124a.htm.

61. R. Nicholas Burns, "A Renewed Partnership for Global Engagement" (remarks at the European Institute Annual Gala Dinner, Washington DC, December 28, 2005), *DISAM Journal* 28, no. 2 (Winter 2006): 78–82.

62. Noetzel and Schreer, "Does a Multi-tier NATO Matter?," 215–19.

63. Kitchen, "NATO's Out-of-Area Norm," 111.

64. See also Gareth Chappel, "What Future for 'Out-of-Area' Operations after Afghanistan," *PISM Policy Paper*, no. 4 (March 2011).

65. Timo Noetzel and Benjamin Schreer, "Does a Multi-tier NATO Matter? The Atlantic Alliance and the Process of Strategic Change," *International Affairs* 85, no. 2 (2009): 212.

66. See North Atlantic Treaty Organization, "Strategic Concept," 2010.

67. Ringsmose and Rynning, "Introduction," 2.

68. As shown previously, Ringsmose and Rynning interpret the main character of the new Strategic Concept somewhat differently than we do. Interestingly, the contributions to the DIIS report the two have edited are not consistent on this issue. Some contributors tend to agree with the editors, others tend to see the concept as a "balancing act," and some point out that the concept can be read as a reflection of a lack of allied agreement on the issues discussed here. See DIIS Report 2011:02.

69. Karl-Heinz Kamp, "NATO after Afghanistan," *US Naval Institute Proceedings* 136, no. 36 (June 2010): 55.

70. North Atlantic Treaty Organization, "Strategic Concept," 2010, paragraph 5.

71. Both in the ongoing discussions on the new Strategic Concept and in NATO's policies on the out-of-area issue after 2001, there are elements of continuity from the Cold War era, for example, concerning the possible use of consultations and in the use of coalitions of the willing as an alternative to mobilizing the alliance as such. Nevertheless, it would be simplistic and inaccurate to see the current attempts at balancing the in- and out-of-area commitments of NATO as a mere synthesis of the Cold War policies with the post–Cold War ones.

72. Kitchen, *Globalization*; Ringsmose and Rynning, "Introduction."

73. Kitchen, *Globalization*, 109f.

74. Rynning, "Broader Middle East."

Chapter 2

NATO and U.S. Global Security Interests

Svein Melby

The efficiency with which NATO carried out its expeditionary military operation in Afghanistan was long viewed as the critical test of the future role of the alliance in U.S. global strategy. If NATO failed that test, it was argued, the organization would lose its strategic value to the United States and could even cease to be a key international institution. But as NATO and the United States are winding down their at best partially successful military operations in Afghanistan, there is much less discussion about the negative long-term implications for NATO's role in U.S. security policy. And while the Obama administration in its latest strategy document—*Sustaining U.S. Global Leadership*—announced an increased focus on Asia and troop drawdown in Europe, it has also stated, in unequivocal terms, the continued importance of Europe and NATO to U.S. interests.[1]

As proof of this, the Obama administration came out strongly in support of NATO's new Strategic Concept with its emphasis on collective defense, and among other things, has promised to participate more in alliance military exercises. The U.S. "leading from behind" use of NATO in the 2011 Libya operation may also indicate a new role for the alliance in U.S. global strategy. The continued U.S. emphasis on the alliance may come as a surprise, given the earlier debate about NATO and Afghanistan, but it should not. While NATO's operation in Afghanistan is an important factor in Washington's evaluation of the organization, it is far from the most decisive. To fully understand U.S. interests in NATO and to put the Afghanistan question in its proper context, Washington's evaluation needs to be viewed in a wider U.S. geopolitical context. It is through this kind of analysis that one can explain the logic of the Obama administration's NATO policy.

A geopolitical analysis of U.S. interests in NATO can be divided into three components, all of which are discussed in the following sections. First is *NATO's role in handling direct threats to U.S. national security*. Second is *NATO's role in securing the great power balance in Eurasia*. Third is *NATO's role in securing and deepening the transatlantic institutional community*.

NATO and Direct Threats to U.S. National Security

Historically, NATO has not been an important instrument for the United States in handling direct threats to its national security. Generally the country has based this part of its strategy on national instruments, mainly its military defense and deterrence capability. However, in its role in the great power context, NATO has done its part to reduce the level of threat to U.S. national security.

The direct threat from other great powers has diminished since the Cold War. Russia is far from representing the same threat as the Soviet Union, and the direct threat from China is still relatively modest. However, a military confrontation with China appears to be the most likely future major war scenario from a U.S. perspective.[2] While the threat from China will probably continue to increase in the years to come, NATO is not expected to play a role in U.S. efforts to meet that threat. As in the Cold War days, any direct threat from a great power against U.S. national security will still probably consist of an attack, or threat of an attack, with nuclear weapons, and needs to be handled with U.S. national instruments. Nor is there any indication that the United States will seek to involve NATO in any direct military role in the event of a conventional military confrontation with China in Asia.

Although there are some indications that the great power dimension in U.S. security policy is acquiring renewed importance, it will probably never regain the same dominant role it had during the Cold War. September 11, 2001, marked a watershed in American security policy, and the "new challenges" on the political agenda must be expected to remain a permanent part of U.S. threat perception. The new threats consist of a combination of terrorism, rogue states, failed states, and the spread of WMD. In other words, threats from nonstate and state actors are less amenable to national means than those from other great powers. Therefore, an ability to meet these new threats requires the integrated use of the whole arsenal of national and international instruments. The emergence of these threats has therefore made U.S. national security more dependent,

generally speaking, on international collective institutions and cooperation with other states. This represents an important structural change in
the parameters of U.S. policy, and one should expect the United States to
elevate the role of instruments like NATO, even in the handling of direct
threats to its national security.

As early as the 1990s the United States tried to make new challenges
an important matter for NATO, but it was only after the terror attacks of
September 11, 2001, that these questions were made a top issue on the
organization's agenda. While NATO has taken several initiatives in this
field, the Afghanistan operation is by far the most important.[3] And because
the terror attacks on the United States were carried out by an organization based in Afghanistan, there was, and still is, a direct link between the
security situation in this area and U.S. national security. To prevent the area
from once again being used for launching an attack on the United States is
therefore a vital security concern for Washington. And it is in this context
that NATO's efforts in Afghanistan make the organization more directly
involved in U.S. national security than was previously the case.

Both during the 2008 presidential election campaign and his first years
in office, President Barack Obama gave even greater priority to Afghanistan in U.S. national security. According to the U.S. president, the goal of
the operation was to defeat Al Qaeda in Afghanistan and force the Taliban
and other insurgent groups on the defensive. Obama's strategy was based
on the principles of counterinsurgency: that responsibility for security in
Afghanistan could successfully be transferred to the Karzai government,
and that the Taliban could be forced to see a diplomatic, political solution as preferable to continued military resistance. To reach these goals,
President Obama more than doubled the number of American troops in
Afghanistan.[4] This military escalation was combined with the setting of a
fixed date—July 2011—for the start of the military drawdown and transfer
of responsibilities to the Afghans. At the November 2010 Lisbon Summit,
NATO announced its intention to complete the transfer of responsibilities by the end of 2014.[5] The deadline and process were reaffirmed in a
U.S.-Afghan agreement signed by presidents Obama and Karzai on May 1,
2012, and by the NATO Summit in Chicago, May 20–21, 2012.[6]

Military escalation and fixed dates for the military drawdown and transfer of security signal both the importance of this operation to the Obama
administration and its determination not to let the Afghanistan engagement be a driving premise for U.S. foreign policy indefinitely. In his speech
at West Point in December 2009, the president emphasized that he would

never let the military operation in Afghanistan undermine the economic and domestic political basis of a forceful U.S. foreign policy. "Nation building" at home, he said, was his foremost goal.[7] The combination of escalation and drawdown illustrates the fine balance Obama thinks he needs to succeed in Afghanistan and secure long-term American global interests.

Enabling NATO to carry out expeditionary operations, including warfare, S&R, and nation building, was one of the key reasons behind U.S. efforts to change the organization after the Cold War.[8] Although the Balkan operations in 1995 and 1999 were the first steps in this process, Afghanistan has been far more important in this regard. As the more than ten years of military operations in Afghanistan now approach their end, it is possible to summarize some of their main lessons.[9] Even though NATO in 2003 took on the responsibility to lead the ISAF operation, this collective responsibility was not reflected in the share of the military burden accepted by the member-states. On the contrary, in many member-states domestic political factors led governments to impose limitations on their forces, particularly in terms of participation in the toughest war fighting part of the operation. In practice, responsibility for the most demanding parts of the operation fell to a small number of countries, notably the United States, the United Kingdom, Canada, the Netherlands, Australia, and Denmark.

It was widely expected that the inauguration of a new U.S. president in January 2009 would lead to some correction of this imbalance. That did not happen.[10] Instead, the increase in the number of U.S. troops led to a clear Americanization of the war and a relative reduction of NATO's military role. Further, the United States continued to receive most assistance in war fighting from the same small group of countries. The lack of symmetry required those with the heaviest war fighting responsibilities to organize their own sequence of meetings, even at the ministerial level, to coordinate their war efforts. To some extent, the NATO system did accept a kind of formalized alliance within the group, which seemed to confirm the existence of a "coalition of the willing" as a part of NATO.

From an American perspective, and for both political and military reasons, NATO has proved to be ill-suited for carrying out military operations based on the principle of counterinsurgency.[11] This is not surprising, insofar as NATO, throughout most of its existence, has been dominated both politically and militarily by defensive strategies and plans for securing the territorial integrity of the member states. Most NATO members also lack training in such use of military force, not to mention the absence of an offensive strategic culture and unwillingness to tolerate casualties, which expeditionary counterinsurgency-type operations require.[12] NATO's territorial and defensive orientation started to change during the 1990s, but most states that joined the Afghanistan operation were not prepared for the use of force implicit in the tactics of counterinsurgency. The reluctance to participate in the fighting may be seen as a clear illustration of this.[13] As a general conclusion, the readiness and ability of NATO member-states to take part in stability operations and peacekeeping are certainly superior to their willingness and ability to perform expeditionary-type war fighting. When it comes to the use of military force, NATO has often not functioned as a collective organization, but rather as a resource pool for the forming of an ad hoc coalition.

Two fundamental factors appear to have impeded NATO's capacity to carry out military operations in Afghanistan. First, there are obviously differences between American and European views of the threat from terrorism and failed states in general, and of an Al Qaeda and Taliban-ruled Afghanistan in particular. Washington seems to consider the threat from terrorism something qualitatively new and imminent, whereas Europeans believe it to be neither new nor imminent. This in turn leads to different conclusions about the importance of fighting terrorism compared to taking care of other security challenges and consequently to different assessments of the urgency of the Afghanistan operation to Western security. Second, there is a fundamental disagreement on how best to handle these "new threats." There is widespread consensus, in theory at least, that any strategy designed to meet challenges like those in Afghanistan must be a mixture of soft and hard power instruments. But while military means are considered of critical importance in Washington, most European governments put a similar emphasis on political and economic efforts.

These differences in the emphasis put on soft and hard power instruments are likely to limit the possibility of a consensus that can unite NATO members on when and how to act in Afghanistan-like conflicts. The critical question is, however, whether these differences are structural and timeless or a result of political attitudes that can be changed over time. Robert Cooper argues that Europe and the United States have indeed reached different phases of historical development, of which different understandings of national interests and different approaches to conflict resolution are two of the most prominent attributes.[14] Robert Kagan argues that the differences between the United States and Europe in handling security challenges are mostly due to their differences in capabilities. In other words, two different authors see the described security policy differences as structural in character.[15] If Cooper and Kagan are right, then the Afghanistan engagement is the most obvious illustration of the difficulties involved in using an organization like NATO to execute such operations, and at best it can be expected to function as a platform for the formation of ad hoc coalitions.

In his 2009 Nobel Peace Prize acceptance speech, however, President Obama seemed to question the existence of structurally based transatlantic differences in threat assessments and approaches to conflict resolution. According to Obama, all security policy and all handling of conflicts must be based on certain simple, universal, and timeless principles about human nature and international politics. Evil exists in the world, said Obama, and it is impossible to base security policy on the premise that human nature can be fundamentally changed. Animosities and conflicts cannot be eliminated; the best one can do is to build mechanisms that reduce the number of conflicts and contain the negative effects of them. War will, as a consequence of this, from time to time be necessary as an instrument to obtain peace and stability.[16] The use of military power, according to Obama, is a necessary precondition for both national security and conflict resolution. This was especially the case when faced with opponents like those in Afghanistan. Thus in two different speeches at the end of 2009, at West Point and in Oslo, Obama tried to reestablish a security policy orientation similar to what was previously defined as Cold War liberalism—a flexible combination of hard and soft power.[17]

If Obama's thinking, with its prominent role for military force, were to be accepted in Europe as the main approach to peace and stability forces, it might be possible to bridge the transatlantic differences. This could become a watershed in transatlantic relations and facilitate a common understanding of why and how NATO can be used as a global instrument for conflict resolution. The rationale behind the NATO-led Libya operation seems to fit nicely with this way of thinking and may be seen as a signal of European acceptance of Obama's approach to conflict resolution. However, the support in NATO for this military operation was far from unanimous, and it does not seem to have established a broad transatlantic consensus on how to approach future conflict situations. Syria is one example. So while NATO operations like those in Afghanistan should not be completely written off, they would seem to be highly unlikely, in fact, so unlikely that the United States cannot base its contingency planning on the use of the alliance for such purposes.

While the experience in Afghanistan has demonstrated that the United States cannot trust NATO to be a major instrument in its handling of new threats to national security, it is unlikely to seriously impact Washington's conception of NATO's role in dealing with direct threats to U.S. national security.

The emergence of new threats to the United States does not mean the end of traditional security challenges. Indeed, they are an ever-present structural element of the international system. Therefore, it was highly relevant early on to question the strategic wisdom of the enormous focus on new threats in U.S. security policy. History also tells us that it is rather unlikely that the United States would ever manage the military transformation required to successfully handle these new challenges through expeditionary counterinsurgency operations.[18] As the Afghanistan experience showed, not only European NATO members, but also the United States, struggled to succeed with counterinsurgency-type operations. Their effectiveness is also open to question. There is good reason to ask whether the terrorist threat and the problems of failed states will continue to dominate the U.S. security agenda the way they did in the aftermath of 9/11. Instead, one could argue, it would have been sensible for Washington at an early stage in the post-9/11 period to formulate its global strategy on the basis of a complex and nuanced threat evaluation. In addition, there was even better reason to doubt whether Iraq and Afghanistan would be the determining factor in how the United States would use military force in the future.

The negative experiences from Afghanistan and Iraq, the prevailing trend in global security affairs, and a stalling U.S. economy have justified skepticism about future American involvement in counterinsurgency and stabilization operations. Better intelligence; surgical precision drone attacks; and tailored, small-scale deployments of ground forces are far more cost-effective in fighting terrorists than the use of large, traditional military forces. Further, military-based nation building in Afghanistan has had limited success. All this, combined with the need to cut defense spending and handle an economically and militarily stronger China, has prompted the United States to make a new strategic reassessment.[19] Not surprisingly, this process has already moved U.S. global strategy back to its classical emphasis on geopolitics, with military priorities favoring naval- and air-based power projection in the Pacific Ocean, Indian Ocean, and the Persian Gulf regions. In other words, U.S. strategy and military priorities have changed fundamentally from the initial post-9/11 years.

The geopolitical approach provides the platform for making an analysis of NATO's continued strategic value to the United States.[20] As a consequence, not only is any new Afghanistan-type operation an unlikely option for NATO, it also has only a very modest chance of becoming part of U.S.

contingency planning. It is not clear whether the Afghanistan experience has changed NATO's already minor role when it comes to direct threats to U.S. national security. But collective instruments generally have greater priority in the Obama administration than efforts to contain these new threats.

NATO and Eurasian Stability

The United States has long sought to influence the balance of power in Eurasia. It has been particularly important to forestall the emergence of an ideologically hostile hegemonic power on this continent. Stability and balance of power are key elements. What happens on the Eurasian continent in this regard impacts the relative balance of power internationally, and with it the character of the international system. In other words, this is a discussion of the basic premises for sustaining U.S. global leadership.[21]

Successful influence on the balance of power in Eurasia will decisively affect not only the fight against terrorism, but also U.S. ability to handle a number of its other major security challenges. Insufficient American influence and regional instability would increase the risk of conflict in several areas of Eurasia, making the spread of WMD more likely and the flow of energy less secure and more costly.

NATO helped the United States reach these goals in Eurasia during the Cold War in several ways. The organization was important both to contain the power of the Soviet Union and to create stability and predictability. NATO's enlargement has served a similar purpose in preventing the emergence of a destabilizing power vacuum in Eastern Europe in the aftermath of the collapse of the Soviet Union and in creating efficient institutional barriers against potential Russian attempts at revanchism. NATO's enlargement has also contributed to widening the zone of democratic stability. This is in itself important to U.S. interests, but it also makes it much easier for the United States to focus on, and use, its resources in other areas in Eurasia where security concerns are a lot more pressing. Hence, NATO has continued to help the United States tackle the great power challenges in Eurasia even after the end of the Cold War. In sum, NATO is still important to U.S. ability to shape the security landscape on this continent.

There is much to indicate that NATO, by its very existence, will continue to be the main pillar of the institutionalized European security order. In this role, the organization will continue to contribute to stability and predictability regarding the balance of power in the Eurasian region. As long as NATO exists, potential Russian expansionism will be contained, and there will be less renewed anxiety about Germany's role. In addition, the United States will have sufficient influence on the security policy ambitions of the EU. All of this is important for the United States to reach its geostrategic goals in Eurasia.

In the foreseeable future there is no realistic alternative to NATO for upholding Eurasian stability. Consequently, if NATO were to be dissolved, the United States would lose a valuable asset. However, it should be noted that Russia represents a fundamentally smaller challenge to the global power position of the United States than did the Soviet Union, making this aspect less important to the former. This is so because Russian capabilities today are incomparably smaller than the Soviet Union's, and because major trends suggest a weaker rather than a resurgent Russia.[22] This being said, Putin's Russia continues to think in terms of spheres of interest in its foreign policy and approaches its relations to the United States through competition rather than cooperation. Russia's reaction to the recent crisis in Ukraine should be a clear reminder of this.

Seen from an American perspective, the question of how to handle Russia must therefore be based on elements of both change and continuity: change because the challenge has diminished and the center of gravity of great power politics has moved from Europe to Asia, and continuity because Russia can be seen as a weakened and somewhat more nationalistic version of the Soviet Union. The continued use of NATO to secure U.S. interests in Eurasian great power politics will require the United States to manage a delicate balance between understanding Russian security interests and the concerns and anxieties of the new NATO members about Russia. If America cannot do this, it could provoke Russian overreaction and/or erode East European trust in NATO and the United States. Both factors could cause instability and internal problems in NATO, undermine its stabilizing and balancing functions, and reduce its role in U.S. global strategy.

The changes to the U.S. missile defense plans for Europe made by the Obama administration in 2009, and especially the way the decision was communicated, serve as an illustration of what is at stake. Poland and the Czech Republic joined the original American plan mainly because American defense installations there were considered important, adding credibility to American guarantees in the case of Russian attempts at political-military intimidation. They perceived this to be of special importance after Russia's military operations against Georgia in 2008.

While the United States argued that the missile plans were solely a defensive measure against a potential missile threat from Iran, Russia viewed the project from the start as yet another U.S. ploy to gain power and influence in an area that had been part of the former Soviet empire and was still considered a Russian sphere of interest. According to official American statements, Obama's missile defense decision was motivated by new intelligence about Iranian missile programs and by technological factors.[23] Nevertheless, Russia, Poland, and the Czech Republic (and probably other NATO members as well) perceived this decision primarily through the historically European way of security policy thinking.

Given the positive reactions from Moscow on the revised American plans, the U.S. decision may have been seen by Russia as a tacit acceptance of Russia's right to operate in spheres of interest in Europe, even including countries that are members of NATO. Worries that the Russians could be right, combined with weakened trust in both NATO and U.S. security guarantees, explained the reactions of Poland and the Czech Republic. The governments of both countries also felt the American decision demonstrated ignorance of the security needs of these countries and of the historical context in which these interests had to be considered. All this made it necessary for the Obama administration to send Vice President Joseph Biden to the region, where he went out of his way to underscore the continued viability of the U.S. security guarantees.[24] The NATO Summit's renewed emphasis on collective defense and NATO-Russian cooperation on missile defense can be seen as an important effort by NATO and the United States to strike the right balance between security reassurances for the new members and openness to Russian concerns. This 2009 missile defense incident illustrates the fact that NATO still has an important stabilizing role to play in European security policy, even if that function is not as critical to U.S. interests as it was during the Cold War.

The role of the United States in European security—formalized by the North Atlantic Treaty—has been key to European political and economic integration for decades.[25] NATO's existence, in other words, has been a necessary precondition for the emergence of the EU as a major building block in the institutionalized European political order. A division of labor between NATO and the EU, in which the former is responsible for security policy and defense matters and the latter for political and economic questions, has been seen as logical and positive from an American perspective. This way, the two organizations strengthen each other and promote stability and predictability in Europe. The strategy has been of great importance in securing U.S. interests. However, the crux of the issue is whether NATO still is the best way to secure U.S. interests or if an alternative institutional division of responsibility could serve them better.

One development that the United States will try to prevent is an autonomous EU that would try to compete with NATO on important security issues. This could lead to a situation in which NATO is no longer needed, with the EU becoming a real competitor to the United States, not only in Europe but in world politics in general. Such a development could have a major impact on the relative international balance of power and on the character of the international system, moving it toward multipolarity. The U.S. government will certainly do its best to maintain a unipolar international system, or at least a system with an institutional structure that allows the United States to dominate the international agenda and the approaches chosen in international problem solving. An EU that could replace NATO as the central European institution, even in security policy, is incompatible with U.S. interests and must therefore be opposed. While the financial crisis, weak economic outlook, and internal political problems in the EU reduce the likelihood of such a scenario, the United States has to seriously consider it in long-term planning.

To avoid this possibility, it is important that the United States do what it can to enable NATO to continue to deliver in the security and military fields. The questions are then what this requires of NATO, and to what extent the United States is politically able and willing to give NATO the priority necessary to make this possible. In discussing these questions, it is reasonable to divide the NATO members into two categories with different outlooks on what is expected of the United States. For most of the Cold War allies, the handling of the residual Russian threat is primarily viewed as a "fire insurance policy" for a remote scenario. These countries view NATO mostly as a forum to influence American foreign and security policy and as an important mechanism to keep the superpower on the collective track in the implementation of this policy. Many new members approach the question quite differently. For them, NATO is almost entirely a means of getting American security guarantees against Russian attempts at political and military intimidation. For the United States to satisfy the first group it must be willing to integrate the transatlantic dialogue in its security policy making. The United States must give these states at least the impression that it is listening to their arguments and takes their views seriously. In other words, what is required is a minimum level of American multilateralism.

For the new members, the continued, long-term credibility of U.S. guarantees is the critical factor. Serious doubts about this could have a devastating effect on their opinions of NATO. In sum, all this indicates that the United States must demonstrate politically, and through its military dispositions, that it still gives priority to the Article 5 aspect of NATO alliance. This implies that there is a limit to how far the United States can push NATO to undertake expeditionary military operations and focus on out-of-area conflicts. Reduced American emphasis on expeditionary anti-terrorist operations should make it easier for the United States to support efforts to maintain NATO's collective capability to defend member states' territories and to avoid an eventual competition with the EU. Keeping military bases in Europe, participation in military exercises in Europe, and the building of a ballistic missile defense system could all be important measures here. American support of NATO's new Strategic Concept, with its emphasis on collective defense, illustrates that the Obama administration understands what is at stake here. Also, in *Sustaining U.S. Global Leadership* the Pentagon not only makes plans for reducing the U.S. force levels in Europe, it also signals greater participation in exercises and rotational military presence in the region. In addition, anchoring the missile defense program in NATO can be seen as part of the same policy.[26]

There is no doubt traditional ambivalence in the United States when it comes to the role of the EU. America must strive to balance measures that prevent a powerful and independent EU and measures that make the EU an important contributor to European stability and balance of power. As already argued, the United States will therefore be greatly interested in a formalized division of labor between NATO and the EU, supplemented by bilateral arrangements between the United States and the EU. The established arrangement, which gives NATO primary responsibility for military warfare while the EU will mainly carry out humanitarian and police operations, seems to be exactly the right recipe for the United States. It would likely be of little concern to America if EU operations included more regular warfare, as long as the troops and the other military resources were subject to NATO authorization. If, on the contrary, the EU started to act independently of NATO and established its own military organization for such purposes, the United States would try to block it.

Many U.S. politicians and defense experts have complained, throughout most of NATO's existence, about the lack of European defense efforts. From time to time they have also warned that the United States will soon be unwilling and unable to live with the existing imbalance in burden sharing.[27] For NATO, it would of course be beneficial if the Europeans strengthened their defense efforts. But seen from a geopolitical perspective, the United States has good reason to be satisfied with a militarily relatively weak Europe, which mainly uses other instruments of power to secure its interests. It is this situation that gives the United States its enormous influence and creates important stability. With a militarily strong Europe, the conflict potential would probably increase, and the European great powers would be likely to operate in a much more assertive and independent way relative to the United States. In other words, a much tougher political and military environment would exist that could easily become a major challenge to U.S. interests. NATO's continued existence and the current distribution of roles within the alliance effectively prevent such a scenario.

The rise of China (and India) and increasing economic and strategic interest in Asia have clearly made the Pacific Ocean, Indian Ocean, and Persian Gulf region the center of gravity in U.S. foreign and security policy.[28] This was also the main conclusion of the Pentagon's latest strategy review. It is therefore only reasonable to ask whether this will diminish U.S. strategic interest in Europe and NATO's role in U.S. global strategy. At first glance, that would appear to be the case. The United States will have to adapt its security priorities and reallocate military resources, which among other things will require force transfers from Europe to Asia. Yet a closer examination of the question reveals that the answer is not that simple. A good case can even be made that European stability and the continued viability of NATO are as critical to the United States as before.

In securing its interests, the United States must always look at Eurasia as one entity, and the main objective is to prevent or contain the emergence of a Eurasian hegemon. It is through this perspective that U.S. policy toward China must be analyzed. To succeed with its main goal, the United States needs a policy based on a combination of military containment and political-economic dialogue. Realistically, the United States will be unable to handle China unilaterally. It can only succeed if it manages subtly to leverage other regional powers and through burden sharing. To put it simply, the United States needs to position itself as the key stabilizing power in the very delicate Asian system of balance of power and win over regional actors, even China, in support of this role. To fulfill this role, the U.S. Navy and traditional power projection are key instruments. But to fully concentrate on this extremely difficult task, it will also be of critical importance to maintain a stable European order and use it as a platform for the expansion of the existing democratic zone of stability. This will prevent any challenges to U.S. relative power from this part of the Eurasian continent, and it will also prevent the reappearance of the potential for major conflicts in Europe. In other words, it will secure a major U.S. interest in the

European region and free resources that would be decisive in U.S. efforts to handle the situation in Asia. And as previously described, the United States can secure an institutionalized European order with small resources. It requires only minor maintenance and awareness.

Keeping NATO in good shape is therefore both a cost-effective and strategically smart way for the United States to achieve its main goal in Eurasia and secure continued U.S. global leadership. As Robert Kagan has argued in *The World America Made*, the international order and norm system are mostly a function of the global distribution of power.[29] This means that the existing institutionalized order in Europe is greatly dependent on U.S. ability to secure its international leadership. It is therefore in the interests of both Europe and America that the United States be given the possibility to focus its resources and awareness on Asia. That may be what it takes to prevent Chinese domination of Eurasia, which would have far-reaching implications for the international institutional architecture and norm system.

NATO and the Institutionalized Transatlantic Community

When discussing why NATO remained the leading security policy institution after the end of the Cold War, several experts have referred to the importance of what can best be defined as the transatlantic institutional community.[30] Still, there is no agreement on the origin of this community. Was it an already existing community with deep historical roots that formed a critical political basis for establishing NATO in the first place? Or is this community primarily a by-product of NATO, something that has started to live its own life regardless of changing threats to the member-states?[31] Whatever the outcome of this important debate, this dimension of NATO cooperation is of great interest to the United States.

The transatlantic institutional community has several aspects. First, NATO is an institutionalized security policy alliance of democracies with similar value and norm systems. The participation of states with non-democratic governments has been a rare exception. For those exceptions, membership in NATO has almost always strengthened the democratic forces in those countries. Second, NATO cooperation has established a deeply anchored institutional culture in the member-states. In most of the member-states, national defense and security policy is often discussed with a certain concern for how domestic decisions will fit into NATO's wider policy. There exist strong structural mechanisms that give the NATO system some influence in the defense planning of each member-state. This institutional element is therefore integrated as a logical feature of national planning processes. Finally, NATO members (perhaps also most nonmember European states) have something that may best be described as a common approach to problems of European security, based on a collective way of thinking. In other words, there is a basic interest in the continuation of a collective, institutionalized European security order and a willingness to see national security interests in a broader European context.[32] This was clearly demonstrated in the Clinton administration's use of concern about the future of the European collective security order to argue for the necessity of a NATO engagement in the Balkan conflict during the 1990s. All this indicates that the institutionalized transatlantic community is a successful forum for coordinating the policy of the member-states.

It should also be noted that over time NATO has acquired a considerable political and military bureaucracy. It not only has close relations with member-states' own national political and military organizations, but also has close relations with many other international organizations and institutions working on related security policy issues. While such institutional-bureaucratic factors cannot secure the continued existence of NATO, they will certainly reduce the organizational impacts of changes in the international security environment.[33]

The very existence of this transatlantic institutional community has provided a means by which the United States can rally support and legitimacy for its policy that otherwise would have been hard to come by. And as the international influence of the United States is expected to become increasingly dependent on its role as a hub in a networked world, NATO represents a uniquely tailored instrument for America to fill that role.[34] At the same time, this community has also given the other members a channel to influence American policy, which few if any of them could achieve on their own. The existence of the community has of course not guaranteed a unified policy. In some cases that is not possible. In general, however, the existence of the community has greatly increased the likelihood of some form of consensus and mutual influence.

In a situation where the main focus of U.S. foreign policy is moving away from Europe, it is reasonable to ask whether the community can continue as a mechanism to unify Western policy. It could be argued that it will be more difficult to reach consensus as common interests may be harder to find than before. Some even argue that with its new global priorities, the United States will be more likely to lose patience with its allies and may even start to look for other partners to help it cope with the new types of security challenges.[35] But that idea works best in theory. In the real world it would be difficult for the United States to find states easier to work with than its current allies in NATO. As I have argued, those allies still have a genuine interest in working with the United States and helping it reach its global strategic goals. The transatlantic institutional community has another important function. Through the norms and rules that the community helps establish for its members, the likelihood of conflict among those very same states is reduced. And not least, the community has created a culture in its approach to conflicts that makes it highly unlikely internal conflicts will result in military confrontation. Being part of the community is considered of intrinsic value and creates a social pressure to adhere to its norms and rules. As a consequence, it is extremely difficult for a democratic state to pursue a policy over time that is not supported by other democratic states.[36] This institutional community is therefore an important barrier against the return to a nationalist type of security order in Europe. The zone of stability is largely the result of exactly this: the extension of the community and the values it represents.

It should be obvious that it is in American interests to maintain, and even strengthen, this community. And without a doubt, during its sixty-four years NATO has been vital to the creation and maintenance of the transatlantic institutional community. The NATO option is therefore the safest way to maintain this important pillar in American foreign and security policy. Even a NATO with a smaller military component is probably sufficient to keep the community alive and well. Keeping NATO as a functioning organization is probably the best, safest, and especially the most cost-effective option for the United States.

Concluding Remarks

The Afghanistan experience shows that NATO as a collective organization is not suited for this kind of conflict engagement. In the pursuit of counterinsurgency operations, the United States can at best only expect to use NATO as a pool from which to form ad hoc coalitions. But as discussed, several military and security policy factors and certain domestic, political, and economic issues render such engagements much less important in U.S. global strategy than was the case in the early aftermath of the terrorist attacks on September 11, 2001. An evaluation of NATO's Afghanistan engagement is unlikely to have any significant effect on the role of the alliance in U.S. global strategy.

Yet as I have argued, NATO's role in U.S. global strategy is far from simply a question of the success of the organization in Afghanistan-type military operations. It is a lot more complex and has to be approached from a U.S. global geopolitical perspective. This analysis explains that

NATO remains of critical importance to the United States and will therefore continue to be a valuable instrument in the latter's global strategy. It is through the maintenance of the NATO-dominated European institutional order that America can best handle traditional challenges to its power and also make necessary realignments to remain the stabilizing force in both Asia and the Middle East. Further, it is through this role that the United States can contain a rising China and reach its goal of preventing a Eurasian hegemon. Without NATO, it is far more difficult to see how a less powerful United States would manage to keep its dominant role in the international system. In other words, NATO's existence is still crucial to U.S. national interests.

NOTES

1. U.S. Department of Defense, *Sustaining U.S. Global Leadership: Priorities for 21st Century Defense* (Washington, DC: DOD, January 2012).

2. This threat assessment is described in the last edition of the National Security Strategy published by the Bush administration in 2006. See George W. Bush, *The National Security Strategy of the United States* (Washington, DC: The White House, 2006). For an expert dialogue about the threat from China, see Aaron L. Friedberg and Robert S. Ross, "Is China a Military Threat?," *National Interest* (September/October 2009): 19–34.

3. For more on NATO's role in the fight against international terrorism, see Renée de Nevers, "NATO's International Security Role in the Terrorist Era," *International Security* 31, no. 4 (Spring 2007): 34–66. See also Anton Bebler, "NATO and Transnational Terrorism," *Perceptions* (Winter 2004/2005): 159–75, http://sam .gov.tr/wp-content/uploads/2012/01/Anton-Bebler.pdf; and Bjørn Olav Knutsen, "NATOs rolle i kampen mot internasjonalterrorisme," *Internasjonal Politikk* 66, no. 1 (2008): 35–64.

4. The White House, Office of the Press Secretary, "Remarks by the President in Address to the Nation on the Way Forward in Afghanistan and Pakistan," Eisenhower Hall Theatre, United States Military Academy at West Point, West Point, New York, December 1, 2009, http://www.whitehouse.gov/the-press-office /remarks-president-address-nation-way-forward-afghanistan-and-pakistan.

5. See North Atlantic Treaty Organization, "Declaration by the Head of State and Government of the Nations Contributing to the UN-mandated, NATO-led International Security Assistance Force (ISAF) in Afghanistan," Lisbon, November 20, 2010, http://www.nato.int/cps/en/natolive/news_68722.htm.

6. The White House, Office of the Press Secretary, "Fact Sheet: The U.S.-Afghanistan Strategic Partnership Agreement," May 1, 2012, http://www.whitehouse .gov/the-press-office/2012/05/01/fact-sheet-us-afghanistan-strategic-partnership -agreement.

7. White House, Office of the Press Secretary, "Remarks by the President."

8. It was not only a question of refocusing the political and military organization, it was also necessary to promote a new expeditionary strategic culture in

NATO. For more on this American way of thinking, see *Hearing Before the Foreign Relations Committee, US House of Representatives*, May 3, 2006 (statement of Dan Fata, Deputy Assistant Secretary of Defense for European and NATO Policy), http://www.dod.mil/dodgc/olc/docs/TestFata060503.pdf.

9. For an extensive evaluation of NATO's ability to carry out counterinsurgency operations, see Christopher M. Schnaubelt, ed., *Counterinsurgency: The Challenge for NATO Strategy and Operations*, NDC Forum Paper, no. 11 (Rome: NATO Defense College, November 2009), http://www.ndc.nato.int/download/downloads.php?icode=139.

10. For a broader debate on these forces, see "Europe and Afghanistan" (editorial), *New York Times*, December 14, 2009.

11. For more analysis of NATO and its counterinsurgency capacity in Afghanistan, see Benjamin Schreer, "NATO and Counterinsurgency: Lessons from Afghanistan," in Schnaubelt, *Counterinsurgency*.

12. For more on this way of using military force, see Sverre Diesen, "Afghanistan-krigens utfordringer," November 5, 2009, http://www.minerva.as/?p=7853. See also Timo Noetzel and Martin Zapfe, "NATO and Counterinsurgency: The Case of Germany," in Schnaubelt, *Counterinsurgency*.

13. Diesen, "Afghanistan-krigens utfordringer."

14. See Robert Cooper, *The Breaking of Nations* (New York: Atlantic Monthly Press, 2003).

15. See Robert Kagan, *Of Power and Paradise* (New York: Alfred A. Knopf, 2003).

16. See The White House, Office of the Press Secretary, "Remarks by the President at the Acceptance of the Nobel Peace Prize," Oslo, December 10, 2009, http://www.whitehouse.gov/the-press-office/remarks-president-acceptance-nobel-peace-prize.

17. For an excellent evaluation of Obama's general political way of thinking, see David Brooks, "Obama's Christian Realism," *New York Times*, December 15, 2009, http://www.nytimes.com/2009/12/15/opinion/15brooks.html.

18. For some important arguments against emphasizing Afghanistan-type engagements and "counterinsurgency" operations, see Leslie Gelb, *Power Rules: How Common Sense Can Rescue American Foreign Policy* (New York: HarperCollins, 2009). See also Andrew Bacevich, "The Petraeus Doctrine," *Atlantic Monthly* (October 2008), http://www.theatlantic.com/magazine/archive/2008/10/the-petraeus-doctrine/306964/; and Michael Horowitz and Dan A. Shalmon, "The Future of War and American Military Strategy," *Orbis* 53, no. 2 (2009): 300–318.

19. See U.S. Department of Defense, *Sustaining U.S. Global Leadership*.

20. See *The QDR in Perspective: Meeting America's National Security Needs in the 21st Century* (Final Report of the Quadrennial Defense Review Independent Panel) (Washington, DC: United States Institute for Peace, 2010).

21. For an introduction to this approach to geopolitics, see Zbigniew Brzezinski, *The Grand Chessboard: American Primacy and Its Geostrategic Imperatives* (New York: Basic Books, 1997).

22. Demographic projections indicate that the Russian population will fall from 140 million in 2014 to about 110 million in 2050. For more about Russian demographics, see Matt Rosenberg, "Population Decline in Russia," *About.com*, May 31, 2006, http://geography.about.com/od/obtainpopulationdata/a/russiapop.htm.

23. For more of the official American arguments, see Robert Gates, "A Better Missile Defense for a Safer Europe," *New York Times*, September 20, 2009.

24. For more about Vice President Biden's visit to Eastern Europe, see Peter Baker, "Mending Fences, Biden Assures Poland That U.S. Is Watching Over It," *New York Times*, October 22, 2009.

25. See Josef Joffe, "Europe's American Pacifier," *Foreign Policy* 54 (Spring 1984): 64–82.

26. U.S. Department of Defense, *Sustaining U.S. Global Leadership*.

27. A relatively new and good illustration of this American frustration can be found in Secretary of Defense Robert Gates's farewell speech to the NATO Council in 2011. U.S. Department of Defense, "Secretary of Defense Speech: The Security and Defense Agenda (Future of NATO)," as delivered by Secretary of Defense Robert M. Gates, Brussels, Belgium, Friday, June 10, 2011, http://www.defense.gov/speeches/speech.aspx?speechid=1581.

28. For more about this geopolitical shift, see Christopher Layne, "The Global Power Shift from West to East," *National Interest* (May/June 2012): 21–31.

29. See Robert Kagan, *The World America Made* (New York: Alfred A. Knopf, 2012).

30. Karl W. Deutsch had the original idea about the existence of this security policy community in 1957. See Karl W. Deutsch, Sidney B. Burrell, and Robert A. Kann, *Political Community and the North Atlantic Organization in the Light of Historical Experience* (Princeton, NJ: Princeton University Press, 1957).

31. For more on recent research into the causes of NATO's continued relevance after the Cold War, see Wallace J. Thies, *Why NATO Endures* (Cambridge: Cambridge University Press, 2009). See also Günther Hellmann, "Inevitable Decline versus Predestined Stability. Disciplinary Explanations of the Evolving Transatlantic Order," in *The End of the West? Crisis and Change in the Atlantic Order*, ed. Jeffrey J. Anderson, G. John Ikenberry, and Thomas Risse (Ithaca, NY: Cornell University Press, 2008), 28–52.

32. We are here discussing things with certain similarities to what Robert Cooper terms "the postmodern world." But it is important to remember that Cooper does not think the United States can be placed in that group. For more on his three levels of development, see Cooper, *Breaking of Nations*.

33. A realist like Stephen Walt argues that the more institutionalized an organization is, the greater is the possibility for its survival when the basis for the organization changes. See Stephen Walt, "Why Alliances Endure or Collapse," *Survival* 39, no. 1 (1997): 156–79.

34. For an analysis of the role of networks in U.S. foreign policy, see Ann Marie Slaughter, "America's Edge: Power in a Networked Century," *Foreign Affairs* 88, no. 6 (2009), http://www.foreignaffairs.com/print/63722.

35. For this way of reasoning, see Jeremy Shapiro and Nick Witney, "Towards a Post-American Europe: A Power Audit of EU-US Relations," *European Council on Foreign Relations*, November 2, 2009, http://ecfr.3cdn.net/05b80f1a80154dfc64_xlm6bgxc2.pdf.

36. For more on this argument, see Robert Kagan, "A Decent Regard," *Washington Post*, March 2, 2004.

Chapter 3

Dealing with Russia

A New 2020 Vision?

Derek Averre

The conflict with Georgia in August 2008—the first time post-Soviet Russia waged war beyond its borders—was a sobering event for the West. The United States, seen by President Mikhel Saakashvili of Georgia as his country's foremost ally, could do nothing to prevent the conflict or the ultimate de facto independence of South Ossetia and Abkhazia. The EU was limited to a postconflict peacekeeping and reconstruction role and was excluded from the separatist territories. The Organization for Security and Cooperation in Europe (OSCE), the only pan-European security organization, was effectively nowhere to be seen. Of more direct relevance to this analysis, the conflict was not dealt with by the NATO-Russia Council (NRC), the principal forum for relations between the alliance and Russia. The lack of effective security mechanisms for dealing with conflicts in wider Europe was thus exposed, and any hopes of a strategic partnership between Russia and NATO appeared to have been laid to rest.

Since the 2008 conflict, the Obama-inspired "reset," followed by the U.S.-Russia strategic arms control agreement, the resumption of full relations in the NRC, the positive mood of the Lisbon summit, and the revitalization of NATO-Russia cooperation on shared challenges—not least Russia's assistance to ISAF—have signaled a more constructive, albeit pragmatic and cautious, approach by the West to dealing with Russia. Numerous problems remain, however. Amid differing threat perceptions and conflicting priorities among NATO member states, former Warsaw Pact countries, uncertain over the extent of future U.S. commitment to Europe and strategies for extended deterrence, are seeking the reaffirmation of

Article 5 guarantees against aggression by Russia. Operation Unified Protector, the alliance's out-of-area operation in Libya, ostensibly to protect the civilian population, was seen by Moscow as no more than a cover for plans to force the Gaddafi regime from power.

NATO's 2010 Strategic Concept, while conveying a rhetorical commitment to partnership, disguises a lack of trust in Russia's leadership and its strategic ambitions; an informed source reports on the widespread "Russia fatigue" among NATO member-states and the "sombre" mood that characterizes the relationship.[1] Kamp concludes that "disappointment about mutual misperceptions and unfulfilled expectations is about to transform the entire partnership. NATO has come to the painful recognition that there is hardly anything in common for effective cooperation."[2] Despite the alliance's other functions—as a political "toolbox" for crisis management and postconflict reconstruction and a focal point for cooperative security partnerships—Moscow remains convinced that defense and deterrence remain NATO's pivotal tasks, and that its actions are motivated by a desire to contain and marginalize Russia. The looming problems of ballistic missile defense (BMD) in Europe and security arrangements in Eurasia following the withdrawal of NATO forces from Afghanistan after 2014—a pivotal moment for the alliance, as Andrew Michta makes clear in the introduction to this volume—complicate the picture even further.

Meanwhile, as demonstrated by its involvement in the Syrian conflict, Russia continues to bid for a more influential global role. In Moscow's eyes the failure of the West's political leadership demands not only a thoroughgoing overhaul of the architecture of European security governance, but also the "democratization" of the new "polycentric" international order on the basis of equality and collective security.[3] The question thus arises: What are the prospects for NATO and Russia finding enough common ground to consolidate the post–Cold War gains of cooperative security? Russian foreign minister Sergei Lavrov has voiced a blunt summary of Moscow's position: "There should be no exclusivity in our common area as regards the most sensitive sphere—the military-political dimension of security. To remove the problem of the false choice between the EU/NATO and Russia, faced by many countries, we need something inclusive, reaching beyond NATO and the NRC."[4] The NATO-Russia marriage of convenience appears badly in need of a counselor.

This chapter first focuses on NATO's new Strategic Concept (NSC) and assesses the alliance's attempts to engage Russia in a more cooperative relationship to manage common security challenges. It then highlights the key issues on the NATO-Russia agenda that are likely to shape that relationship in the near future. The penultimate section examines in more detail the out-of-area issue and Moscow's response to the evolution of NATO's strategic identity. Finally, the chapter explores the prospects for a radical shift toward a deeper partnership that would allay Moscow's traditional mistrust of a potentially hostile military alliance and establish a coherent strategy for shared management of international security.

I argue that, while NATO member-states recognize Moscow's growing international influence and will seek to mitigate differences, the NSC at best places limitations on the partnership and at worst threatens to perpetuate the security dilemma in Europe. Farther afield, unless NATO reins in its ambitions and seeks a more collective approach to security management, Moscow will continue to assert its global clout to contest its out-of-area missions where they are not sanctioned by the UN Security Council. As Lavrov has argued, NATO must not act as a "global surgeon" prescribing "radical intervention" in complex internal conflicts.[5]

The 2010 NATO Strategic Concept

The period from the Georgian crisis to the Lisbon summit was marked by blunt pronouncements by Russia's foreign policy establishment, which were firmly rooted in the accumulated disappointments of the previous decade. The 1997 NATO-Russia Founding Act had miscarried over the alliance's intervention in the former Republic of Yugoslavia over Kosovo and the first of a fresh wave of enlargements. Both coincided with the adoption of the 1999 NATO Strategic Concept, with its claim to the right to conduct out-of-area operations beyond the allies' territory.[6] The NRC— which succeeded the Permanent Joint Council instituted by the Founding Act—has produced a limited number of cooperative security measures but has not developed into a forum for real deliberation over strategic issues. In Moscow's eyes, Russia remains effectively sidelined from European security decision making on key issues. The enlargement of what it considers a largely unreconstructed NATO is seen as the main danger, if not an immediate threat, to European security[7]; the West still pursues "a course of inertia, nourished by a spirit of triumphalism and an attempt to secure assimilation of the geopolitical space abandoned by the Soviet Union. . . . This messianic ardor is the best recipe for a repetition of the mistakes made at the beginning of the 1990s."[8]

The alliance's attempts to preserve its political-military supremacy in wider Europe, as well as conflicting interpretations of international law as it relates to the right of intervention in sovereign states, continue to bedevil what is otherwise an increasingly interdependent relationship. Lavrov has attacked the "cold war prejudices . . . aimed at globalizing the policy of NATO-centrism, spreading it far beyond Europe's borders, including projecting military force essentially to any region of the world without the sanction of the UN Security Council."[9] Russia's former envoy to NATO, Dmitrii Rogozin, attacked the alliance for avoiding substantive discussions on military matters and trying to divert Moscow's attention to "soft" security issues, and for its intention to acquire exclusive functions in energy security and cyber defense: "transforming NATO into the world's policeman, something like Orwell's Big Brother, can not suit Russia."[10] An authoritative Russian commentator argues that if "the alliance is not transformed into a peacekeeping organization with Russian participation but remains a closed military bloc, and its military infrastructure moves right up to our borders . . . the growing alienation between [Russia and the West] will represent one of the main threats to national and international security."[11]

Moscow's demand for inclusion in European security governance was crystallized in its proposals for a European Security Treaty[12] that would "make the principle of indivisibility of security juridically binding and universally applicable in the Euro Atlantic region"[13] in line with the provisions of the UN Charter and in accordance with the 1999 Charter for European Security. Presented by Moscow as a return to the Helsinki process, the European Security Treaty is effectively designed to prevent any repeat of intervention by NATO in sovereign states and the further enlargement of the alliance and to ensure an equal voice for Russia in decision-making on key issues affecting European security. The treaty focuses much less on the humanitarian principles that reflect evolving conceptions of security in Europe, in particular the "values agenda" espoused by NATO and the EU. Unsurprisingly, this vision of a pluralist greater Europe has met with a cool reception; it remains on the NRC agenda, but there is little appetite in Washington and Brussels to change security arrangements that have served NATO-EU Europe well.[14] Even given the interdependence between Russia and the major actors and institutions in the European security space, the challenge of translating the principle of cooperative security into juridically binding arrangements requires sustained political commitment and trust, which are currently lacking.

The debates in the run-up to the publication of the NSC in November 2010 reflected this lack of trust on the part of NATO member-states. The NSC is at first glance a very constructive document. Its leitmotifs are the contemporary security challenges faced by the alliance and its readiness for engagement with its principal partners, among which Russia rates a special mention. Disputes with Russia are highlighted, notably short-range nuclear weapons in Europe and conventional arms control, but there is an undertaking to seek cooperation with Russia on BMD. NATO-Russia cooperation "is of strategic importance as it contributes to creating a common space of peace, stability and security. NATO poses no threat to Russia. On the contrary we want to see a true strategic partnership between NATO and Russia ... with the expectation of reciprocity from Russia."[15] Despite these rhetorical flourishes, however, the NSC glosses over the preparatory report by the group of experts, appointed by Secretary General Rasmussen and led by Madeleine Albright, which concentrated much more on the security dilemmas that still bedevil relations with Russia.[16]

The alliance's core tasks and principles remain largely unchanged in the 2012 Chicago Summit Declaration. It reaffirms the NSC's commitment to Article 5 collective defense and nuclear deterrence, as well as to developing robust, mobile, and deployable conventional forces to carry out both Article 5 responsibilities and the alliance's expeditionary operations for conflict management. NATO's commitment "to the purposes and principles of the Charter of the United Nations" is restated, but there is no indication that NATO military action will require a UN Security Council resolution. The alliance will also take on new tasks, including protection of energy infrastructure and transit routes, cyber defense, and planning for the security impact of emerging technologies. The Chicago Summit Declaration reaffirms the commitment, made at the 2008 Bucharest Summit, to Georgia's membership of NATO and to enhanced cooperation with Ukraine. Russia is promised political consultations and practical cooperation, but commitment to joint action within the NRC remains vague.[17]

Following the 2010 Lisbon Summit the reform of the NRC was put on the agenda, and Rasmussen initiated a more constructive approach to dealing with Moscow. The experienced foreign ministry diplomat Aleksandr Grushko, who succeeded the more combative Rogozin, has emphasized a positive trend in relations.[18] The register of practical cooperative activities to deal with new threats and challenges has been boosted. The NSC in general received a qualified welcome from Russia's leadership; Lavrov spoke of a qualitative breakthrough toward a strategic partnership in which "we are overcoming the logic of negative interdependence based on the confrontation of military capacities, on the threats and counter-threats: we start our ascension towards the logic of positive interdependence."[19]

Yet the main contentious issues, which are preventing the two sides overcoming the post–Cold War legacy, are no nearer to resolution.[20] In

Russian eyes the enlargement of NATO perpetuates dividing lines and raises the risk of containment, or in the worst case, confrontation. Moscow remains wary of the location of NATO infrastructure in the territory of new member states and of support for Georgia in its bid for membership in the alliance through the latter's "open door" policy. NATO's Operation Unified Protector in Libya—enforcing an arms embargo and a no-fly zone—was seen by Moscow as exceeding the mandate of the UN Security Council resolution (Russia had abstained from voting) and designed through "humanitarian intervention" to effect regime change.[21] The operation provoked a heated response from Russia's foreign policy establishment in defense of what it considers the fundamental norm of sovereignty in international law.[22]

The lessons of NATO intervention in the former Republic of Yugoslavia—in Moscow's eyes the question of Kosovo's independent status "remains open"—and the U.S.-led invasion of Iraq remain central to Russia's thinking. Conservative and nationalist politicians and commentators—who still form a substantial section of Russia's domestic political spectrum—have scarcely changed in their antipathy to NATO and remain skeptical about its proclaimed transformation and its intentions toward Russia.[23] The ambivalence toward Russia in Western political establishments and the lack of strategic clarity in the NSC beyond vague commitments to partnership with Russia hinder any genuine breakthrough in relations.[24] Enhanced relations in the NRC do not hold out the promise of a genuine strategic partnership in which Moscow's core security concerns are taken into account: NATO's claim to be a value-based security community, not exclusively a threat-based military bloc,[25] cuts no ice in Moscow in the absence of a clear set of juridically binding and predictable rules aimed at constructing a single European security space, as Lavrov wastes no opportunity to reemphasize.[26] The notion that the security of NATO-Europe is the security of everyone is flatly rejected by Moscow.

The Emerging NATO-Russia Agenda

Since the establishment of the NRC engagement has tended to focus on making incremental gains in cooperation over common security threats and challenges. There has been progress on military-to-military cooperation and enhancing defense transparency, crisis response, and Russian logistical support to ISAF, including support for the Afghan air force. The updated NRC Action Plan on Terrorism, drawing on a Joint Review of Common Security Challenges endorsed at the Lisbon Summit, is expanding the scope of the fight against terrorism, including via the Cooperative Airspace Initiative, and managing its consequences.[27] Moscow has welcomed agreement on aspects of WMD counterproliferation; protecting navigation routes and dealing with piracy; countering the narcotics threat emanating from Afghanistan; rescue at sea; and civil emergency planning, including protecting infrastructures against terrorist and technogenic disasters.[28]

Important though these activities may be, any coherent future NATO strategy in forging a closer relationship with Russia must focus on the main issues that form the basis for strategic stability. Foremost among these are NATO's BMD plans, which in Moscow's eyes have now become a litmus test of the alliance's readiness to effect a qualitative shift toward meaningful strategic cooperation and respect for Russia's core security interests.[29] The November 2010 Lisbon NRC meeting agreed to institute joint BMD threat assessment,[30] and intensive talks have been going on between Moscow and both NATO and the United States. Ongoing efforts in the NRC to review how independent NATO and Russian BMD systems might work together are aiming at establishing a joint Missile Data Fusion center and joint Planning Operations Centre.[31] Expert assessment has also underlined the need for cooperation.[32]

There are substantive hurdles to overcome, however. Moscow has roundly criticized the U.S. "phased adaptive approach," which will form the basis of NATO's European BMD to counter the threat posed by third parties' (particularly Iran's) missiles, stating that it risks unbalancing strategic stability. An authoritative Western assessment has emphasized that regardless of the likelihood that Russia can use asymmetric measures to neutralize the threat from the NATO system, Russia's military planners will be forced to put in place far-reaching countermeasures; NATO's plans may provoke "opportunistic or hawkish elements within the Russian ... political and military establishment. . . . [T]he bottom line is not intentions, but capabilities."[33] Moscow has, indeed, warned of "a phased adaptive response": putting missile early warning stations on combat alert, reinforcing protection of Russia's strategic arsenal, equipping new strategic ballistic missiles with advanced missile defense penetration warheads, and deploying offensive weapons in the west (including Kaliningrad) and south of the country. Furthermore, Russia's participation in the strategic arms treaty with the United States may be reviewed once BMD reaches a certain stage.[34] The modernization of air-space defense capabilities has already been made a priority for the Russian military.[35]

The decision by the Obama administration in March 2013 to cancel the SM-3 block IIB program, the fourth phase of BMD, which could have intercepted strategic missiles, would appear to allay Moscow's main concerns. The creation of centers for operational exchange of intelligence and early warning data and for joint planning and cooperation of missile defense operations should go some way toward reassuring Moscow and engage its support for a policy to deal with potential proliferators.[36] In fact, independent Russian experts have cast doubt on the strategic threat posed to Russia by NATO's BMD plans.[37] Moreover, both U.S. and Russian commentators have underlined that missile defense can only reduce, not eliminate, the threat of ballistic missiles, and that a political solution needs to be found as part of a broader political-military partnership.[38] Despite the alteration in U.S. plans, however, Moscow is still claiming that transparency in BMD planning is insufficient and is seeking juridical guarantees, as well as clear "objective" criteria regarding the geographical scope and technical capabilities of the later stages of the BMD system beyond 2022, to ensure that it does not undermine Russia's strategic capability.[39]

The problems facing NATO and Russia are, arguably, less technical than political. The demand for "objective" criteria—presumably meaning access to operationally significant information—may well be hostage to the lack of trust that vitiates the relationship. Authoritative experts have argued that neither the U.S. nor the Russian military and defense complex is interested in cooperation that might tip their hands and upset narrow political and bureaucratic agendas.[40] The ultimate stumbling block is that Washington will not countenance any missile defense strategy that allows for a measure of joint political control with Russia. The United States may well yet again be seen by Russians as driving European security arrangements to the detriment of strategic and regional stability.

Russia is also insisting that BMD be linked with other outstanding arms control issues and take into account its broader concerns over strategic stability. Moscow is uneasy about U.S. strategic high-precision non-nuclear and space-based weapons, which are not limited by arms control agreements, and indeed over the "breakout potential" of U.S. strategic offensive nuclear weapons.[41] The Obama administration, under some pressure from disarmament lobbies and the U.S. Senate, is seeking talks on increasing transparency over and reducing Russia's tactical nuclear weapons (TNW) in the European theater—again, never dealt with by any arms control treaty. But Moscow insists on addressing the imbalance in conventional forces via the Adapted Central Forces in Europe (CFE) Treaty—which is currently in cold storage, with no immediate sign of resolution—since Russia's TNW in Europe compensate for its conventional force weakness (and may potentially be used to counter NATO's BMD system).[42] The presence of large numbers of Russian TNW makes it difficult in turn for the United States and NATO to make a case for withdrawing theirs, not least due to concerns about a diminishing U.S. commitment to Europe. Experts have argued that withdrawal would enhance the credibility of disarmament and nonproliferation policies of alliance members, with no real loss of security; NATO could make it clear that they are only one element of its force posture and try to link the issue with missile defense and other arms control initiatives.[43] While the current consensus view in the alliance is to promote transparency and confidence-building measures with Russia on the issue of TNW, there are splits within NATO. Some countries, such as Germany and Norway, might support withdrawal of U.S. TNW as part of improving relations with Moscow. Several Central European states would be strongly opposed to such a unilateral move.[44]

In many ways this issue goes to the heart of the "traditional" NATO-Russia debate over European security: Does Moscow still represent a threat to its smaller neighbors, and to what extent does NATO really threaten Russia and its key interests? The deployment of NATO's infrastructure closer to Russia's borders, alliance military exercises in northern Europe, and the promise of accession to Georgia—fraught with the potential for confrontation, given Russia's support for South Ossetia and Abkhazia—perpetuate the problems of the 1990s, despite substantial changes in the political map of Europe. Whether the political will exists to unravel the complicated knot of political-military issues and build on a relatively benign post-Lisbon relationship is open to doubt.

Out of Area—Out of the Business of Cooperation?

Beyond "traditional" questions of strategic stability, the out-of-area issue is the other key point of contention in NATO-Russia relations, in spite of shared interests in managing potential conflicts and combating emerging security threats. Russia is directly affected by the risk of long-term instability presented by failing states, Islamist jihadism, and corruption-fueled drug trafficking. As suggested earlier in this chapter, functional cooperation over Afghanistan—NATO's primary operation in recent years, and high on the NRC agenda—has been largely positive. Moscow has granted transit to and return transit from that country through Russian territory and airspace of ISAF goods and personnel, notably via its facility in Ulyanovsk, as well as contributing to training and equipping Afghan security forces. Moscow has also declared itself ready to consider a more active role in national reconciliation, economic reconstruction, and humanitarian assistance in

Afghanistan.[45] Although a more comprehensive joint strategy with NATO to stem the flow of drugs from Afghanistan has made limited progress, with Moscow deploring the alliance's reluctance to establish closer relations with the regional military alliance (the Cooperative Security Treaty Organization [CSTO]),[46] counter-narcotics training via the NRC has produced good results. Improved governance in a turbulent Central Asia—indeed, in Eurasia more widely—to ward off further terrorist and trafficking inroads into the region will scarcely be possible without cooperation with Moscow and other states in the region.

Citing Russia's strategic interests in Central Asia, President Vladimir Putin has, however, voiced suspicions about Washington's plans to retain military bases in Afghanistan "without a clear mandate, aims and periods of function" following the withdrawal of NATO combat forces after 2014, as part of its wider plans to station military facilities in the region.[47] These suspicions stem from concerns over the loss of Russian influence in a fragmenting region; despite the threats posed by longer-term instability, Moscow is still more fearful of allowing external influence to take root in the Central Asian region and prefers to support "friendly" governments there.[48] Russia's cooperation with NATO's "Resolute Support" training and advisory mission in post-2014 Afghanistan must therefore be underpinned by a new UN Security Council resolution, which would provide clarity about the alliance's strategic tasks and ensure a collective approach to security management in the region.

Afghanistan is only one aspect of a larger problem in which the evolution of the alliance—not only in terms of force projection capabilities but also of political aspects of developing partnerships to legitimize missions with a global reach—comes at a time when Russia is more prepared, and has greater capacity, to take on a more global role. It is beyond the scope of this chapter to speculate on likely future theaters for NATO missions, what the prospects are for mobilizing partners to participate, and indeed, whether missions on the scale of Operation Unified Protector will prove possible. In any case, Moscow's traditional insistence on UN Security Council sanction for military intervention in sovereign states—as suggested above, reinforced by the lessons of Kosovo in 1999, Iraq in 2003, and Libya in 2011—has become a core tenet of its foreign policy. It is Russia's response to the apparently insoluble collision among the principles of respect for sovereignty, intervention, and the humanitarian imperative inherent in "responsibility to protect." This bottom line has been only too visible in Syria, where Moscow's key demand is clear: no regime change in the case of complex internal conflicts. A Russian contribution to joint peace enforcement or peacekeeping missions is possible, given agreement with NATO on military and not just political aspects of a joint approach to peacekeeping, but only on a legal basis that excludes a repeat of Kosovo or the Libya scenario.[49]

A New 2020 Vision?

How might the alliance and its member-states use the more constructive positions in Russia's foreign policy to coax Moscow into enhanced cooperation? In the run-up to the Lisbon Summit, Rasmussen emphasized the need for a "virtuous circle" of trust and confidence, concentrating less on values and more on shared principles as the basis of a genuine partnership[50] in which "NATO-Russian security cooperation [is] an established feature on the international security landscape."[51] This was publicly reciprocated by Moscow; following the NRC meeting in November 2010, then president Dmitrii Medvedev acknowledged that "everyone spoke of the need to develop partnership relations, develop an alliance, and we even heard the term 'union'."[52]

A growing consensus that the evolving threat environment in Eurasia necessitates a greater role for Russia in security governance appears to have influenced this trend. Former senior German policy figures have revived the debate over Russia's admittance to NATO, proposing "a strategic framework for the three centers of power: North America, Europe and Russia."[53] Influential U.S. voices have called "for NATO to make a serious effort to bring Russia into the post-war settlement" and "pick up on Moscow's call for fresh thinking about a 'new European security architecture'."[54] Zbigniew Brzezinski has suggested that NATO should rethink its reservations about a formal link with the CSTO, proposing "a joint agreement for security cooperation in Eurasia and beyond," as well as an arrangement with the Shanghai Cooperation Organization (SCO)—thereby engaging China—in the form of a NATO-SCO council.[55] Sam Nunn argues that shared challenges, particularly nuclear arms control and nonproliferation, demand Russia's cooperation and asks:

> Does the expansion of membership to new states obligate us to incur enormous increases in defense budgets or be forever committed to Cold War concepts of deterrence ... has expansion primarily become a political exercise? ... Finally, are Russia and the West destined to continue the assumption that Russia will always be outside the Euro-Atlantic security arc?[56]

In Moscow, experts at the Institute of Contemporary Development, in a joint study with the International Institute of Strategic Studies, advocate a NATO-Russia strategic concept to underpin a Euro-Atlantic security community.[57] The concept of a security community is central to the Euro-Atlantic Security Initiative, which has brought together former senior policy makers and recommended a long-term vision for Russia's inclusion.[58]

These proposals present a new conceptual framework within which a genuine vision beyond 2020 may be constructed. As suggested, however, they run counter to strategic and political differences that promise to last well into the next decade. Differing perceptions of the strategic environment between NATO and Russia (indeed, to an extent among NATO member-states) and approaches to managing security crises—BMD, Operation Unified Protector over Libya, the Syrian conflict—seem to rule out a paradigm shift in relations. Divergent views on key security and defense planning issues are deep rooted; joint decision making with Russia would risk diluting the "unique and essential role" (to cite the NSC) that the alliance plays in global security. Ultimately, Moscow will not compromise on its core national security interests, nor will it reconcile its traditional commitment to the UN Charter with membership in an alliance that assumes the function of an "enabler" for military action out-of-area without a Security Council resolution.

The Asia-Pacific and Eurasian "vectors" in Moscow's world outlook gain importance in terms of Russia's global strategy. As Thomas Gomart argues, Russia's traditional dilemma of how to move closer to Europe "is changing with the rapid shift of global influence towards the Asia-Pacific region. . . . [I]t is now a question of how to position itself in relation to Europe in creating its global identity."[59] Debates among senior Russian officials and experts have drawn similar conclusions:

> The United States has long been shifting the focus of its global strategy to Asia . . . while viewing Europe as an important, yet secondary ally. Russia now also has a much wider choice of opportunities and partners. . . . Moscow no longer views the European vector of cooperation as an absolute priority over the development of all-round ties and interaction in the Asia-Pacific region.[60]

The globalization of NATO, without a closer and more constructive relationship with Russia and greater clarity in alliance strategy, is thus likely to complicate relations further. Russia's relations with China would also come under scrutiny in the event of integration with NATO.

The political hurdles stem from ambivalence in Russian foreign policy thinking, deriving from a tension between two conflicting aspects. One was summed up by Rogozin while still ambassador to NATO and reflects the antipathy toward the alliance among nationalist political elites: "As long as Russia has the means to guarantee its sovereignty, as long as we have the means to repel any aggression, we are self-sufficient."[61] This claim to strategic independence reinforces the deep reservations within the establishments of NATO member-states over Russia's political development. Strategic independence and "great power" status is without doubt a crucial element in Russia's global identity. However, it coexists with the second key aspect in official thinking: the need to play a more influential global role. A growing awareness of the complex dependencies and constraints faced by Russia generates a call for partnership with the leading Western countries; as Lavrov argues, "Russia's foreign policy is determined by long-term aims for the complex modernization of the country, the diversification of its economy and its transition to an innovative model of development. . . . Russia does not need confrontation."[62] Moderate elements within Russia's political elite recognize that the "hardware" of European security—its architecture, institutions, and regimes—cannot operate without adequate "software"—a common "ideational platform" or shared values.[63] But problems of historical identity, together with mistrust stemming from security concerns in a still-divided Europe, produce a fundamental, unresolved ambivalence in Russia between a desire for rapprochement with NATO-EU Europe and an emphasis on strategic self-sufficiency.

Conclusions: Common Interests and Unfinished Business

In many respects writing on Russian foreign policy contains a striking resemblance to Western assessments of the changed post–Cold War international environment.[64] Both stress the need for (1) cooperative management of regional instability and emerging security challenges, (2) the importance of recalibrating and building on global institutions and recognizing the danger of "deglobalization" and consequent defection of states from international agreements, and (3) the imperative of "network diplomacy" in an interdependent international order. As suggested above, the emphasis on collective approaches and on the potentially huge contribution Europe can make to Russia's development is a constant in current Russian foreign policy thinking. Putin is pragmatic enough to understand that he must work within the existing institutional framework in Europe. Lavrov has underlined Russia's commitment to working with NATO and voiced his belief in dependable expectations of peaceful change that form the basis of a security community: "I think we have not been enemies for a long time. Nobody can imagine even in their worst nightmares that we will go to war with each other."[65]

Yet there is much unfinished business, in terms both of revitalizing arms control regimes and reaching strategic accommodation in Europe and of developing a genuine partnership that may deal cooperatively with challenges farther afield. It is clear that the underlying assumptions of the West's policy for much of the post–Cold War period—how to integrate Russia into a Western liberal democratic security order—must now be reconsidered. The risk remains, not only of failing to move from a "non-war community" to a "mature" security community, but also of reproducing security dilemmas between a defense alliance and a nuclear great power, mitigated only by limited cooperative activities—a variation on détente, based on containment together with pragmatic transactions.[66] In a definitive article over a decade ago, a former U.S. ambassador to NATO spoke of the post–Cold War need for

> a set of attitudes, practices, policies, and institutions that can find common value in a different means of ordering relations among states. . . . [T]here would have to be developed profound, common understandings about the nature of power and security in Europe and about the respective roles of Russia, NATO, other institutions, and individual allies. These understandings are still far in the offing, if they can be achieved at all.[67]

Working toward these common understandings is a tall order and will require scrupulous and painstaking negotiation on a complex and resource-sapping agenda in a fast-changing international environment; as the Arab Spring, and indeed the current crisis in Ukraine, have proved, it is nigh on impossible to predict where the next flashpoint will arise.

A dual agenda—regional and global—has emerged in NATO-Russia relations, highlighted by Lavrov: "We may say that two main factors are of key importance in strengthening security in the Euro Atlantic region: the degree of readiness in Russia and NATO to jointly solve problems inherited from the past . . . and their ability collectively to counteract risks arising beyond the region."[68] Put simply, Russia is back as a global power. If NATO is to succeed in mitigating security dilemmas with Russia, it will need to exercise the kind of political will that has only occasionally been evident since the end of the Cold War, paying greater heed to Moscow's views in its decision making in order to change mutual perceptions. As a leading European commentator argues, "Western alliances . . . will have to learn to accommodate and manage disagreements: on threat assessments, on priorities, and on appropriate policy options."[69] The ultimate aim should be NATO and Russia, together with the EU, acting as the linch-pin of a community of interests, if not values, based on deeper engage-ment and underpinned by cooperative agreements on a number of specific issues.[70] Engaging Russia in facing global challenges on a broader security and political front—using the kind of flexible approach that will be crucial in NATO's future partnerships strategy[71]—may ultimately contribute to mitigating Russia's sense of exclusion from the European security com-munity.[72] But there is a long road ahead.

NOTES

The author gratefully acknowledges comments on a draft of this chapter by Paal Sigurd Hilde, Norwegian Institute for Defense Studies, and Mark Webber, University of Birmingham.

1. Karl-Heinz Kamp and Heidi Reisinger, "Political and Military Coopera-tion or NATO-Russian Roulette?" (Conference Report, Research Division, NATO Defense College, June 2013).

2. Karl Heinz Kamp, *NATO's 2014 Summit Agenda*, NATO Defense College Research Paper No. 97 (Rome: NATO Defense College, September 2013), 3.

3. See Sergei Lavrov, "International Relations in a Turbulence Zone: Where Are the Points of Support?," *Diplomaticheskii ezhegodnik*, December 29, 2012, http://www.mid.ru/bdomp/brp_4.nsf/0/D126FA2FC8FF917B4425798200209721 (accessed May 9, 2012).

4. Sergei Lavrov, "The Euro-Atlantic Region: Equal Security for All," *Rus-sia in Global Affairs*, July 7, 2010, http://eng.globalaffairs.ru/number/The_Euro -Atlantic_Region:_Equal_Security_for_All-14888 (reproduced from an article in *Revue Défense Nationale* [May 2010]).

5. Sergei Lavrov, "International Relations in a Turbulence Zone," 2011, http://www.mid.ru/brp_4.nsf/newsline/263A1015041B1BBA4425797500416F7A.

6. For an overview see Derek Averre, "From Pristina to Tskhinvali: The Leg-acy of Operation Allied Force in Russia's Relations with the West," *International Affairs* 85, no. 3 (2009): 576.

7. See the 2010 Russian Federation Military Doctrine (text in Russian), http://www.mid.ru/bdomp/ns-osndoc.nsf/e2f289bea62097f9c325787a0034c255/2a959a 74cd7ed01f432569fb004872a3!OpenDocument (accessed September 10, 2010).

8. G. B. Karasin, "The Cold War and Its Policy" (speech presented at Cam-bridge University, November 18, 2009), http://www.mid.ru/bdomp/brp_4.nsf/0 /B45D0A6284AF1305C325767400474BE0 (accessed May 9, 2012).

9. Sergei Lavrov, "Russian Diplomacy in a Changing World," *Federal Yearbook* 23 (April 30, 2010), http://www.mid.ru/bdomp/brp_4.nsf/0/4E37152B4A140C1EC 325771C004C7DBB (accessed May 9, 2012).

10. "The Choice Facing NATO," *Nezavisimaya gazeta*, May 17, 2010, 9; Dmitrii Rogozin [Russian representative to NATO], "The West Is Avoiding Our Initiatives," *Izvestiya*, December 2, 2009, 5.

11. Sergei Kortunov, "The World Military-Political Situation in 2025," *Mezhdunarodnaya zhizn'*, no. 4 (2010): 107.

12. The European Security Treaty focuses on four areas: the fundamental principles of relations between states; arms control regimes and confidence and security building measures (CSBMs); the principles of conflict settlement; and new threats and challenges. See *The European Security Treaty after Corfu*, SEC.DEL/242/09, September 14, 2009 (Russian version produced by PIR-Center, Moscow). Follow-up proposals on arms control, modernization of the 1999 Vienna Document on CSBMs, and the CFE Treaty have been drafted by Moscow. Vladimir Voronkov [Director of the Department of Pan-European Co-operation of the Ministry of Foreign Affairs of Russia], "Statement at the Joint Meeting of the OSCE Forum for Security Co-operation and the OSCE Permanent Council," September 15, 2009, FSC-PC.DEL/28/09.

13. Sergei Lavrov, "Press Conference Following OSCE Annual Review Conference on Security," Vienna, June 23, 2009, http://www.mid.ru/brp_4.nsf/0/F3332 10311BA05EBC32575DF00304D03 (accessed November 9, 2009).

14. "No Need for New European Security Treaty—NATO Chief," *RIA Novosti*, October 8, 2010, http://en.rian.ru/world/20101008/160881510.html (accessed July 1, 2013). See also Nicolas Sarkozy and Angela Merkel, "Security, Our Joint Mission," *Le Monde*, February 4, 2009; Hillary Clinton, "Speech at L'Ecole Militaire, Paris," January 29, 2010, www.state.gov/secretary/rm/2010/01/136273.htm (accessed July 1, 2013).

15. North Atlantic Treaty Organization, "Active Engagement, Modern Defense," 2010, http://www.nato.int/lisbon2010/strategic-concept-2010-eng.pdf (accessed November 29, 2010).

16. North Atlantic Treaty Organization, *NATO 2020: Assured Security, Dynamic Engagement; Analysis and Recommendations of the Group of Experts on a New Strategic Concept for NATO* (Brussels: NATO Public Diplomacy Division, May 17, 2010), http://www.nato.int/cps/en/natolive/official_texts_63654.htm. The report warns that "old rivalries could resurface . . . efforts at political intimidation could undermine security along its borders" (p. 6) and states that "*Provided NATO stays vigilant, the prospects of direct military attack across the borders of the Alliance is slight*" (p. 8; emphasis added). NATO should try to engage Russia but "[b]ecause Russia's future policies toward NATO remain difficult to predict, the Allies must pursue the goal of cooperation while also guarding against the possibility that Russia could decide to move in a more adversarial direction" (p. 16). NATO needs to be ready for both a stabilization operation out of area and "a major combat operation in Europe *against a serious adversary*" (p. 40; emphasis added). It warns of the "conflicting signals about [Russia's] openness to further cooperation with NATO . . . no one should doubt NATO's resolve if the security of any of its member states were to be threatened" (pp. 26–27). During a visit to Moscow for consultations, Albright was blunt: "We believe that every country should have the right to exercise its legitimate and sovereign rights—including the right to join or not to join an alliance. . . . We do not accept the idea that large countries have spheres of interest

that give them license to dominate their neighbors" (speech presented at Moscow State Institute for International Relations, February 11, 2010, www.nato.intcps /en/natolive/opinions_61448.htm [accessed September 10, 2010]). This echoes the 1999 Strategic Concept, which included a similar "hedge against the risk of backsliding in Moscow" (David S. Yost, "Assurance and US extended deterrence in NATO," *International Affairs* 85, no. 4 [2009]: 759).

17. North Atlantic Treaty Organization, "Chicago Summit Declaration," 2012, http://www.nato.int/cps/en/natolive/official_texts_87593.htm (accessed July 11, 2013).

18. Ambassador Grushko, interview with author, Brussels, July 1, 2013; "Bloc Thinking Has Not Completely Outlived Itself in the Political-Military Sphere," interview with Aleksandr Grushko, envoy to NATO, by Elena Studneva, *Mezhdunarodnaya zhizn'*, no. 11 (2012).

19. Sergei Lavrov, "Speech at the 47th Munich Security Conference," February 2011, http://www.securityconference.de/Lavrov-Sergey-V.696.0.html?&L=1 (accessed February 9, 2011).

20. For a definitive analysis, see Dmitrii Danilov, "Russia and NATO: Dilemmas of Strategic Partnership," *Russian International Affairs Council* (June 2013), http://russiancouncil.ru/inner/?id_4=2032#top (accessed July 9, 2013).

21. Vladimir Putin, "Russia and the Changing World," *Moskovskie novosti*, February 27, 2012, http://premier.gov.ru/eng/events/news/18252 (accessed April 23, 2012); "Bloc Thinking."

22. See, for example, Evgenii Voronin, "The Problem of Legitimacy of Armed Intervention: The Libyan *casus belli*," *Mezhdunarodnaya zhizn'*, no. 8 (2012).

23. See, for example, "Russia-NATO after Lisbon," *Mezhdunarodnaya zhizn'*, no. 1 (January 2011): 32–44.

24. See Hans-Joachim Spanger, "The Future for NATO," *Mezhdunarodnaya zhizn'*, no. 3 (March 2011): 94–106; Aleksandr Orlov, "Russia-NATO Relations in the Context of the North Atlantic Alliance's 2010 Strategic Concept," *Mezhdunarodnaya zhizn'* (January 1, 2011): 85–93. David Yost notes the agreement among NATO allies—which subsequently emerged in the WikiLeaks dossier—to prepare contingency plans for the defense of the Baltic states: "NATO's Evolving Purposes and the Next Strategic Concept," *International Affairs* 86, no. 2 (2010): 501.

25. Karl-Heinz Kamp summarizes this argument—"[NATO's] interests are primarily 'Western' interests. The West, not as a geographical but a political category, describing the community of democratic, pluralist, market oriented countries, is a reality . . . a lasting European security architecture will be dominated by NATO and will be in its general orientation a 'Western' one"—in *The Indivisibility of Security: Russia and Euro-Atlantic Security*, ed. Andrew Monaghan, NATO Defense College nonpaper (Rome: NATO Defense College, December 2009), 49.

26. Sergei Lavrov, speech presented at international conference "Military and Political Aspects of European Security," Moscow, May 23, 2013, www.mid.ru/brp _4.nsf/newsline/A92136C46841A2A044257B74002DBEF2 (accessed June 20, 2013).

27. See "NATO-Russia Action Plan on Terrorism," April 15, 2011, www.nato -russia-council.info/en/official-documents/official-document-07; and "Meeting of the NATO-Russia Council at the level of Foreign Ministers held in Brussels,"

April 19, 2012, http://www.nato-russia-council.info/en/official-documents/official
-document-19-04-2012/ (accessed May 9, 2012).

28. "NATO-Russia Council Practical Cooperation Fact Sheet, April 2013,"
http://www.nato-russia-council.info/media/96614/final_2013_04_17_nrc_fact-
sheet_en_and_fre.pdf; Grushko, interview with author.

29. "Bloc Thinking."

30. North Atlantic Treaty Organization, "NATO-Russia Council Joint Statement," November 20, 2010, http://www.nato.int/cps/en/natolive/news_68871.htm
(accessed December 6, 2010).

31. North Atlantic Treaty Organization, "Chicago Summit Declaration," 2012,
http://www.nato.int/cps/en/natolive/official_texts_87593.htm?mode=pressrelease
(accessed June 7, 2012).

32. See Richard Weitz, "Illusive Visions and Practical Realities: Russia, NATO
and Missile Defense," *Survival* 52, no. 4 (2010): 99–120; and Nikolai Sokov, "Missile Defense: Towards Practical Cooperation with Russia," *Survival* 52, no. 4 (2010):
121–30.

33. Yousaf Butt and Theodore Postol, *Upsetting the Reset: The Technical Basis of
Russian Concern over NATO Missile Defense*, Special Report No. 1 (Washington, DC:
Federation of American Scientists, September 2011), 10, 30.

34. Dmitry Medvedev, "Statement in Connection with the Situation Concerning the NATO Countries' Missile Defense System in Europe," November 23, 2011,
http://eng.news.kremlin.ru/transcripts/3115 (accessed March 30, 2012).

35. Dimitrij Medvedev, "Address at Expanded Meeting of the Defense Ministry Board," March 20, 2012, http://eng.news.kremlin.ru/transcripts/3562 (accessed
March 30, 2012).

36. "NATO Deputy Secretary-General's Enthusiasm for Missile Defence Is
Undiminished, Despite Russian Opposition," *NATO Watch*, June 17, 2013, http://
www.natowatch.org/node/979 (accessed July 11, 2013).

37. V. Esin and S. Rogov, "US Zaporozhets Cannot Catch Our Mercedes,"
Nezavisimaya gazeta, March 28, 2013, 3; A. Arbatov and V. Dvorkin, *The Great Strategic Triangle*, Carnegie Papers (Moscow: Carnegie Moscow Center, April 1, 2013),
23–24.

38. See Weitz, "Illusive Visions and Practical Realities"; Aleksei Arbatov,
"Nuclear Disarmament: Dead-end or Pause?," *Mirovaya ekonomika i mezhdunarod-
nye otnosheniya*, no. 2 (2012): 3–18.

39. S. A. Ryabkov, deputy foreign minister, interview in *Golos Rossii*, June 1,
2013, http://www.mid.ru/brp_4.nsf/newsline/051BDC1D8B9E952844257B7C003
A0F9D (accessed June 20, 2013).

40. Arbatov, "Nuclear Disarmament"; see also Butt and Postol, *Upsetting the
Reset*, 12.

41. Alexey Fenenko, "Russian and U.S. Nuclear Policies after the Cold War,"
Russia in Global Affairs, no. 3 (2011), http://eng.globalaffairs.ru/number/After-the
-Reset-15928.

42. Malcolm Chalmers and Simon Lunn, *NATO's Tactical Nuclear Dilemma*,
RUSI Occasional Paper (London: Royal United Services Institute, March 2010);
Alexei Arbatov, "A Russian Perspective on the Challenge of U.S., NATO, and
Russian Non-Strategic Nuclear Weapons," in *Reducing Nuclear Risks in Europe:*

A Framework for Action, Nuclear Threat Initiative, November 17, 2011, http:// www.nti.org/media/pdfs/NTI_Framework_Chpt8b.pdf?_=1322702907 (accessed May 9, 2012).

43. Riccardo Alcaro, *Combining Realism with Vision: Options for NATO's New Strategic Concept* (Rome: Istituto Affari Internazionali, May 2010), 10–11; Arbatov, "A Russian Perspective."

44. David S. Yost, "Adapting NATO's Deterrence Posture: Report on a Workshop in Tallinn 4-6 May 2011," June 2011, http://www.ndc.nato.int/download /downloads.php?icode=294. For NATO's consensus position on Russia's TNW, see North Atlantic Treaty Organization, "Deterrence and Defence Posture Review," May 2012, http://www.nato.int/cps/en/natolive/official_texts_87597.htm ?mode=pressrelease (accessed November 26, 2013).

45. See speech by Lavrov at the International Conference on Afghanistan, Kabul, July 20, 2010, http://www.mid.ru/brp_4.nsf/0/E6BEB2613842F7 FEC3257766004B3739 (accessed September 10, 2010).

46. The CSTO is a military alliance comprising Russia, Belarus, Armenia, Kazakhstan, Kyrgyzstan, and Tajikistan.

47. Putin, "Russia and the Changing World."

48. See Marlène Laruelle, *Russia's Strategies in Afghanistan and Their Consequences for NATO*, NATO Defense College Research Paper no. 69 (Rome: NATO Defense College, November 2011). As a leading Russian commentator argues, Moscow needs to rethink its rejection of "good governance" as a key strategy for the stabilization of weak or authoritarian regimes; Andrei Zagorski, "The Limits of a Global Consensus on Security: The Case of Russia," in *Global Security in a Multipolar World*, ed. Luis Peral, Chaillot Paper no. 118 (Paris: EU Institute for Security Studies), 69.

49. Grushko, interview with author. See also "Bloc Thinking."

50. Anders Fogh Rasmussen, "Success Generates Success: The Next Steps with Russia" (speech presented at Istituto Affari Internazionale, September 17, 2010), http://www.nato.int/cps/en/natolive/opinions_66265.htm (accessed September 23, 2010).

51. Carnegie Endowment, "NATO-Russia: Partners for the Future" (Carnegie Moscow Center event transcript, Moscow, December 17, 2009), http://www .carnegieendowment.org/events/?fa=eventDetail&id=1508 (accessed May 4, 2010). Fogh Rasmussen is cool in this speech on further enlargement to the East, stating that new members would have to contribute to overall security in the Euro-Atlantic area: "We do not import problems into the NATO alliance."

52. "News Conference Following NATO-Russia Council Meeting," Lisbon, November 20, 2010, http://eng.news.kremlin.ru/transcripts/1345/print (accessed January 20, 2011).

53. Volker Rühe, Klaus Naumann, Frank Elbe, and Ulrich Weisser, "It's Time to Invite Russia to Join NATO," *Spiegel Online*, August 3, 2010, http://www.spiegel.de /international/world/0,1518,druck-682287,00.html. See also Charles A. Kupchan, "NATO's Final Frontier," *Foreign Affairs* 89, no. 3 (2010), http://www.foreign affairs.com/articles/66217/charles-a-kupchan/natos-final-frontier. There is a history of eminent U.S. statesmen advocating Russia's accession to NATO; see James A. Baker III, "Russia in NATO?," *Washington Quarterly* 25, no. 1 (2002): 95–103.

54. See, for example, Charles Kupchan, "Decision Time: NATO's Hard Choices," *NATO Review* (2009), http://www.nato.int/docu/review/2009/0902/0902_NATO FUTURE/EN/index.htm (accessed November 26, 2013).

55. Zbigniew Brzezinski, "An Agenda for NATO," *Foreign Affairs* 88, no. 5 (2009), http://www.foreignaffairs.com/articles/65240/zbigniew-brzezinski/an-agenda -for-nato (accessed November 26, 2013). Dmitri Trenin argues that Moscow's preferred form of engagement would be "a NATO-CSTO committee flanked by permanently neutral states, such as Ukraine"; he points out that the lack of CSTO support for Russia's recognition of independence for South Ossetia and Abkhazia demonstrated that these countries are no longer "Russia's clients, but sovereign states" ("Russia's Sphere of *Interest*, Not *Influence*," *Washington Quarterly* [October 2009]: 14).

56. Sam Nunn, "NATO Nuclear Policy and Euro-Atlantic Security," *Survival* 52, no. 2 (2010): 14–15.

57. *Towards a NATO-Russia Strategic Concept: Ending Cold War Legacies; Facing New Threats Together* (London/Moscow: IISS/INSOR, November 2010), 5, 6.

58. Carnegie Endowment, *Toward a Euro-Atlantic Security Community*, Carnegie Endowment for International Peace, final report, February 2012, http://carnegie endowment.org/files/EASI_FinalReport.pdf (accessed May 9, 2012).

59. Thomas Gomart, "Europe in Russian Foreign Policy: Important but No Longer Pivotal," *Russie.Nei.Visions* 50 (May 2010), http://www.ifri.org/?page =contribution-detail&id=6050&id_provenance=97 (accessed November 26, 2013).

60. Sergei Karganov and Timofei Bordachev, "Towards a New Euro-Atlantic Security Architecture" (Report of the Russian Experts for the Valdai Discussion Club Conference (London, December 8–10, 2009), http://vid-1.rian.ru/ig/valdai /European_security_eng.pdf (accessed November 26, 2013).

61. Aleksandr Grishin, "Three Scenarios for Russia Joining NATO," *Komsomol'skaya Pravda*, September 6, 2010, 1.

62. Lavrov, "Russian Diplomacy in a Changing World."

63. Konstantin Kosachev [Chairman of the State Duma International Affairs Committee], "Values for the Sake of Unification," *Vremya novostei*, March 22, 2010, 6. Kosachev paints a sobering picture of the alternative: "If we don't achieve real agreement over values and a common understanding of the fact that there are no grounds for conflict here . . . we will build at best a 'peaceful coexistence of two systems' model, along the lines of the peaceful times of 1970s '*détente*.' And at worst we will all the time reproduce the 'cold war' in one form or another"; "Russian and NATO: Coincidence of Values," *Izvestiya*, February 3, 2010, 6.

64. See North Atlantic Treaty Organization, *NATO 2020*, 14.

65. Sergei Lavrov, interview by *Rossiiskaya gazeta*, October 1, 2010, http://www .mid.ru/brp_4.nsf/0/39E55A022F510F9AC32577AF002203BD (accessed January 20, 2011).

66. A former head of NATO's liaison office in Ukraine puts it more starkly: "Within the Western alliance, political energy that was once focused on achieving a 'Europe whole, free, and at peace' has shifted to other theatres—first Afghanistan and now Libya—leaving a perception of *de facto* strategic accommodation to . . . a Russian sphere of influence dominated by a Eurasian value system" (James Greene,

"Russian Responses to NATO and EU Enlargement and Outreach," Chatham House Briefing Paper, June 2012, 18).

67. Robert E. Hunter, "Solving Russia: Final Piece in NATO's Puzzle," *Washington Quarterly* 23, no. 1 (2000): 120, 133.

68. Article in special issue of *Rossiya v global'noi politike*, May 23, 2013, http://www.mid.ru/brp_4.nsf/newsline/3580E088EFF44F0E44257B74002EF301 (accessed June 20, 2013).

69. Constanze Stelzenmüller, "The West Runs Out of Power," *Policy Review*, no. 172 (April–May 2012): 91. A recent research paper asks similar questions but goes no further than recommending the preservation of the NRC, given "the relatively limited current and foreseeable level of partnership/cooperation [with Russia]."

70. "We need to 'think about broadening the community of responsible stakeholders, specifically to include Russia,' basing engagement conceptually on the (albeit elastic) notion of 'an inclusive security community'" (Dmitry Trenin, "Transatlantic Security in the 21st Century: Do New Threats Require New Approaches?" [Hearing before the Committee on Foreign Affairs, U.S. House of Representatives, March 17, 2010]); *Euro-Atlantic Security: One Vision, Three Paths* (Brussels/Moscow/New York: East-West Institute, June 23, 2009).

71. See Karl-Heinz Kamp and Heidi Reisinger, *NATO's Partnerships after 2014: Go West!*, NATO Defense College Research Paper no. 92 (Rome: NATO Defense College, May 2013); and Ioanna-Nikoletta Zyga, *Emerging Security Challenges: A Glue for NATO and Partners?*, NATO Defense College Research Paper no. 85 (Rome: NATO Defense College, November 2012).

72. See Brent Scowcroft, Joseph Nye, Nicholas Burns, and Strobe Talbott, "U.S., Russia Must Lead on Arms Control," *Politico* (October 13, 2009), http://www.politico.com/news/stories/1009/28201.html; Nunn, "NATO Nuclear Policy and Euro-Atlantic Security"; "The Right Direction for U.S. Policy toward Russia" (report from the Commission on U.S. Policy toward Russia, Washington, DC, March 2009). This commission, composed of leading policy practitioners and commentators, recognizes that Washington cannot expect "to create its own sphere of influence on Russia's borders while simultaneously seeking a constructive relationship with Russia."

Chapter 4

Burden Sharing after Afghanistan

Janne Haaland Matlary

[NATO is divided] between members who specialize in "soft"
humanitarian, development, peacekeeping, and talking tasks, and
those conducting the "hard" combat missions, between those
willing and able to pay the price and bear the burdens of alliance
commitments, and those who enjoy the benefits of NATO
membership—be they security guarantees or headquarters
billets—but don't want to share the risks and the costs.

—Secretary of Defense Robert Gates,
closing speech to NATO ministers, June 2011

NATO has not disappeared as a military alliance, and neither its years nor
its days seem to be numbered, differing from predictions by realists like
Waltz and Mearsheimer. On the contrary, the alliance is more active than
ever before in its history. Yet we observe that only some states are active
in the sharp end of operations. Today's NATO at a glance exhibits great
variety in political views and behavior. ISAF is viewed as tough peacekeeping by the Germans but as a Counter-Insurgency (COIN) operation by
others.[1] NATO today cannot agree on a common strategic vision because
the assessment of strategic risks remains so divided.

After Afghanistan, NATO is an alliance that the fundamental security contract, Article 5, still underpins and keeps together, but its political
dynamics have changed in major ways. The realities of coalition warfare have
become very clear in terms of the demands for risk-willing, relevant military
capacities. Some European allies participated in ISAF despite high costs in
terms of life and treasure, but many more offered only token participation.
In Operation Unified Protector in Libya in 2011, only a few states carried

the main burden of combat, while many states did not even participate. These two operations underline the fact that the trend started in Kosovo in 1999 is becoming the *general* rule: NATO is a platform for coalitions of the willing and able when it comes to sharp operations, while it continues to be a military alliance whose mutual security guarantee remains its backbone. The question is how burden sharing can be acceptable in terms of equity in such an arrangement, in which the rule and the glue is solidarity, but only some states take risks, incur losses, and carry costs in actual operations. This question is even more pertinent in today's situation, in which the United States no longer wants to lead all operations, and states consequently must contribute because of operational need, not only because by contributing they get "close to the White House." Because this "alliance dependence" has been the major explanation for contributions for many states, as discussed below, the question of whether contributions will disappear if the United States does not lead must be posed. NATO is a platform for coalitions in which the main "pull" has been U.S. beckoning. Absent the latter, will coalitions be possible when the risks are high?

This chapter discusses how burden sharing is to be understood after the Cold War and how it has evolved in recent operations. It then attempts to assess how burden sharing will evolve in an alliance in which the United States is no longer automatically in the lead but is as important as ever.

NATO as a Platform for Coalitions

Given that the Article 5 guarantee is a "public good" in NATO—that is, one that all members enjoy regardless of military contributions—avoiding risky operations seems entirely rational. Yet many states have contributed to ISAF, Libya, and other optional operations. This is a puzzle from the point of view of alliance theory in the realist tradition, which assumes that states remain in alliances in order to balance against and deter threats,[2] but also from the point of view of collective action theory, which would predict that states should free-ride, and that the larger allies would have to carry most of the burden.[3] This has been the case in general with NATO in the Cold War period—the United States has remained the security guarantee. After the Cold War, absent a common threat, one would expect states to refuse the risk and cost of military involvement in faraway lands; where the public goods produced are even less consequential for all NATO members, one expects the free-riding to be even more prevalent. Yet some states opt for extensive contributions to such operations, while others offer only tokens. What accounts for this variation? And why do many states contribute in the first place? The interesting question is why states offer blood and treasure in operations where they have neither a major interest in the outcome nor a decisive impact on it.

Scholars try to classify groups of states and strategic visions present in NATO. Some speak of four groups of states, with the United States in a class by itself, followed by Britain and France, then states such as Denmark, Canada, the Netherlands, Poland, and perhaps Norway, and finally Spain and Italy. This classification is based on the degree of willingness to take risks and make relevant military contributions to operations like ISAF. Yet there are divisions among states regarding the strategy for NATO, the most common of which is between the "globalists" and "traditionalists."[4]

One can discern groups of states also in other international organizations, for example in the EU, where the inner core in security policy is made up of the contributing states to any one mission but is led by France and Britain.[5] Multitier NATO is a consequence of the lack of a common strategic vision: the globalists want NATO to operate as a global police force, whereas the traditionalists want the alliance to remain in-area and deter attacks from there. Noetzl and Schreer describe the "traditionalists" as reversal-oriented, "comprising Central-European countries, favoring an alliance still focused on Article 5, based on the perception of a resurgent Russian threat. After all, the functioning of collective defense was their primary reason for joining the Alliance."[6] Norway and France could be added to this group. These states argue that NATO must concentrate on its regional role as a defense alliance and not evolve into a global actor.

Despite the classification into two or more groups of states in NATO, these states all have to face up to the fact that the United States is the main actor. NATO without a real U.S. commitment is a Potemkin village. The interesting question is therefore not whether NATO should be described in terms of two, three, or four groups of states, but whether the alliance can function in the long run with only some states being "willing and able" to contribute to global operations. At what point does the unequal burden sharing become too unbearable? Further, how can the United States be kept interested in NATO if European allies are reluctant to share the burden? From the great variation among member-states in geopolitical position and interest, it is clear that national interest in keeping the United States involved in NATO also varies a great deal. This upsets the alliance dependence "equation" because there is no automaticity in following the U.S. lead any longer, and even less so in following a British or French lead in an operation, such as in Libya. In that operation Germany even abstained on the vital Security Council resolution and did not contribute to the operation. Poland, a key pro-American ally, also refrained. This very "variable geometry" underlines two points: member-states in NATO today have totally different national interests in security policy; and absent U.S. leadership, many states will not contribute to a coalition operation.

"Keeping the Americans In"

International organizations (IOs) do not collapse or dissolve. They persist, with rare exceptions like the Council for Mutual Economic Assistance (CMEA), which was abolished, and the Western Union, which was absorbed into the EU in 2002. But IOs wax and wane, they become more or less important, and some are marginalized into oblivion. The Organization for Security and Co-Operation in Europe (OSCE) is an example of an IO that plays a very minor role in international security today. Many UN organizations are in the same situation. Performance, often through being "used" by states as platforms for action, is the decisive factor. The question is therefore whether the United States finds NATO useful for its global security purposes. As one commentator put it, "the real danger comes from within—from European reluctance to pay for its own defense and from growing U.S. indifference towards what Washington sees as feckless allies."[7]

Former U.S. secretary of defense Robert Gates voiced major criticism of the European allies in June 2011 when he said that some states—Germany, Spain, and Poland—should contribute more, above all, to the Libyan operation. He also spoke of "free riders."[8] Because he was leaving office, he allowed himself to state publicly what diplomats normally say in bilaterals, but the gist of the criticism is the same: the allies do not carry their share of the burden, neither in terms of defense spending, 75 percent of which is currently provided by the United States, nor in terms of military contributions to operations. The "crisis literature" on NATO is ubiquitous, vide the delightful study by Wallace Thies, who designates Henry Kissinger as the record holder in diagnosing transatlantic crises for six decades now.[9] Currently, however, there is a new salience to American complaints because of two factors: economic crisis in the United States and a new generation of U.S. politicians who have no history or experience in Europe.[10]

The classification of NATO states as "globalists" and "traditionalists" presents a logical problem. There is no reason to assume that small- and medium-sized states will seek to play global security roles—they never have, and they are simply too small to do so. The primary security concern for these states is in-area and will remain so. Concern about Article 5 and regional European security will always remain the key interest of most European states in NATO. They can only operate globally with niche capacities, "plugged" into the military operations run by the United States and large states like France and the United Kingdom. The dichotomy between "traditionalists" and "globalists" is logically flawed, also in a realist logic.

Today, for the first time in history, small states have become actors on a global scale. Before World War II, small states mostly tried to stay neutral; they had no place at the table at international conferences, and great powers dominated the state system, especially in security policy. Only after that war did the many multilateral organizations emerge that today "populate" international politics, where small states formally have an equal status with large ones.

The NATO alliance was "frozen" as an actor throughout the Cold War, and the role of small- and medium-sized states was basically to defend their own territories. Expeditionary warfare was undertaken on a regular basis by France and the United Kingdom, as exceptions in Europe. The point is that only *after 1990* can we start to assess the fruitfulness of alliance theories and security and defense hypotheses about the political dynamics of NATO. During the Cold War there was one scenario that was not optional: all European states were part of the same invasion plan, and there was little choice in security matters once a country became a member of NATO.

One can assume that "keeping the Americans in" is the key objective for Europeans today as well, but this is much more difficult now than during the Cold War. From the perspective of realism in IR theory, one must ask what the Americans need NATO for, and the answer in realist terms is centered on security interests. In this respect, there are bases in Europe useful to the United States; Europeans make some military contributions to operations, and Europe keeps its own region peaceful. When applying realist logic, we see that it is rational for Europeans to contribute to global operations in order to keep the United States interested in NATO. It is also evident that the United States has less interest in NATO than the Europeans do; they are the *demandeurs*. But one must add that this is so only under a strict realist logic. If one considers political legitimacy important, it is clear that a NATO operation has more legitimacy than a U.S. operation, especially if there is a UN mandate. And if one considers political influence on Europe important, then NATO is the main channel for the United States into Europe. Thus, for general foreign policy reasons, NATO is of great importance to the United States.

Burden Sharing in Sharp, "Optional" Operations

The question of burden sharing has always been important in NATO—it has resulted in a "crisis literature" on NATO[11] and has acute relevance today, because the United States will cut its defense budget over a ten-year period and is no longer automatically willing to lead military operations. The Libya mission, Unified Protector, is a case in point. The United States did not want to lead it but was forced to "lead from behind" because the allies lacked some of the necessary capacities: "shortages in allied intelligence-gathering, aircraft, aerial refueling tankers and precision-guidance kits for bombs proved that the U.S. remained the back-bone of NATO-offensives."[12] Thus, even if Europeans are politically willing, as they were in this case, they may not be militarily able.[13]

It is not easy for a government to contribute to sharp operations when the national interest is unclear and both the end state and end date are also. Nothing can "backfire" as quickly as deployment of one's own forces. What is heroic and acclaimed one day is often the object of devastating criticism the next. From the Iraq and Afghan wars, there are reports of U.S. and Canadian politicians who tried to avoid media coverage of their countries' losses and domestic debates about dangerous deployments. One's own losses are increasingly harder to accept for politicians seeking reelection. Both President George W. Bush and Prime Minister Tony Blair experienced tremendous domestic problems over Iraq. Kosovo was almost unbearably difficult for NATO governments, because their publics demanded changes and recalls, detailed information on military choices and strategies, and so forth.

Burden sharing in NATO today is thus very difficult for governments. Allies expect just burden sharing in terms of carrying risk, whereas domestic publics are in "deep peace" mode and not sympathetic to national causalities or political causes in faraway lands. What can a government do about this dilemma? It has to "deliver" in two arenas, at home and internationally, where the demands are conflicting and even in opposition to each other. Governments have to make painful choices. This is why the modern burden-sharing "equation" is so difficult for states: they must take risks and suffer losses of their own soldiers in wars that are not in their own national interests in a traditional sense.

The "alliance dilemma" formulated by Glenn Snyder in 1984 says that a state in an alliance needs to navigate between being entrapped with the hegemonic ally or abandoned by the same.[14] Today this dilemma is characterized by fear of abandonment rather than entrapment.[15] There was a direct dependence between the United States and European allies in the Cold War; therefore allies could be certain that they would not be abandoned. But as bipolarity has given way to a more multipolar system today, and the threat has become diffuse and variously interpreted, "abandonment outweighs entrapment fears."[16] Burden-sharing "variables"—the type of contribution—differ in importance between the Cold War and the present. Money, sometimes referred to as "checkbook" diplomacy, is always important, as is political support in the form of political contributions to operations. But in the sharp military operations that have developed after the Cold War, from Bosnia to Kosovo and now Afghanistan, the key asset is *military relevance and risk willingness*.

General Sir Michael Jackson (2009) argues:

> The Americans have always been wary of multinational forces, and perhaps understandably they regarded ISAF with a jaundiced eye, because it was mainly . . . composed of European troops and, as ever, hindered by the various national caveats—they can't do this, they must do the other, they can't fly at night. These caveats are there because European governments are particularly nervous of the political effects of military risk-taking, not least when casualties are concerned. Britain has always been less sanguine in this regard.[17]

In their books on burden sharing in NATO, Cimbala and Forster argue that willingness to accept casualties and to engage in sharp fighting without caveats is the defining characteristic of burden sharing in NATO after the Cold War. At present NATO does not share a common vision; national governments pursue their own agendas, they argue, and "these interests and policies, including national caveats around the use of force have deflected European attention and threaten to separate the alliance into tiers."[18] The main problem for European governments is accepting the risk of casualties: "The distribution of risk—measured by troops in the field, location relevant to hostilities, and the willingness to accept the social and political effects of casualties—has perhaps become the most critical and divisive part of burden-sharing."[19]

The authors relate how the first Iraq war marked a change in this regard. At the time the Germans mainly contributed money, which led to dismay and criticism, albeit not in public. A NATO commander is reported to have said that "they pay, we die."[20] Conversely, Jordan's military contribution to this war gave it major political influence. There is, say these authors, a hierarchy of contributions to operations, and today this burden-sharing hierarchy is topped by risk willingness and able troops. The military contribution must be real in war-fighting terms, and the home government must be willing to accept risk and casualties in wars that are nonexistential.

Work by Ringsmose on burden sharing during the Cold War and in the present supports this conclusion:

> [T]he new security environment has changed the burden-sharing debate in three important ways. Firstly, beginning in the middle of the 1990s, the debate's centre of gravity has shifted from the input side to the output side of national defense equations. Secondly, the alliance's embrace of a new set of roles challenged most European member countries with a hitherto unfamiliar need for sending military forces into harm's way . . . consequently the burden-sharing agenda has been dominated by risk-sharing issues . . . thirdly, the security benefits spawned by NATO's new missions are closer to being pure public goods than those produced by its traditional activities.[21]

The more security is a public good, the higher the incentive for free-riding, as mentioned in the beginning of this chapter. Yet all NATO states and others want to contribute to ISAF, the best example of a challenging mission. But as we will see, their contributions vary widely. Risk willingness is a very scarce good. Thus, states want to be seen in Afghanistan, but the kind of burden they are willing to bear varies a lot. In the Cold War, cost was the key burden-sharing variable: "The percentage of GDP—the defense burden—was undoubtedly the most important measure from 1949 to 1989."[22]

The reduction in the importance of cost contributions came with out-of-area operations. Ringsmose recalls the Japanese and German monetary contributions to the 1991 Gulf War, which "did not earn them much applause internationally" because "check-book diplomacy came to be associated with free-riding and unwillingness to share the risks of military action."[23] Those states that seek U.S. security guarantees, such as those in Eastern Europe and to some extent Norway, are likely to contribute risk-willing military capacity. Further, states that seek closeness to the United States for general foreign policy purposes, like Denmark and the United Kingdom, will also do so. In other states, governments have different priorities.

To sum up, the present challenge to NATO states in Europe is not only to contribute and show solidarity with the United States, but also to take responsibility for security and defense policy in lead roles, as in Libya. Moreover, this challenge comes at a time of deep budget cuts and where risk willingness is part of burden sharing. Military contributions must be professional—that is, expeditionary and ready for combat.

The burden-sharing "equation" today demands contributions in kind that are militarily relevant and risk willing. The scholarly literature suggests that alliance dependence matters most as an explanation of contributions, and this raises the important question of what will happen if the United States is no longer in the lead in operations. Will contributions continue? Or will domestic politics predominate?

Let us now consider some recent data from a selection of NATO allies.

Examples of Alliance Dependence: Denmark, Norway, and Canada

Denmark, Norway, and Canada are interesting countries in this context because they are traditionally loyal allies in NATO's "inner circle" but have showed illustrative variations in contributions to ISAF and Libya operations.

Denmark has been contributing consistently, "punching above its weight" in both operations with a good margin. It has been fighting in Helmand as well as in Libya, but the interesting issue is that Denmark used to be a "footnote" country in NATO for many years. In this regard, it was similar to Canada, which "made it a national brand to usually stick to peace operations. . . . [T]his falls into the long tradition of foreign policy where former PM Lester Pearson played a grand role."[24] This "peace nation" image was also cultivated by Norway, and the Left-Socialists, in a coalition government starting in 2005, made for important caveats in Afghanistan.[25] Yet in Libya, Norway contributed much on the sharp side. In all three cases, there is evidence of real change toward sharp contributions. What accounts for this?

Ringsmose has studied the behavior of Denmark, one of the key contributors in coalition warfare both in Iraq and Afghanistan, and found that the key determinant was Danish interest in closeness to Washington. Denmark has no geopolitical security calculus to consider, surrounded as it is by NATO states. The Danish decision to get rid of its submarines testifies to this.

Denmark strongly supports U.S. policy, to the point of being one of the most loyal supporters and contributors to U.S.-led coalitions. Although it was known as a "footnote" country in NATO in the 1980s, there was a clear change of strategic culture in Denmark from 1990 onward, a result of an explicit effort by political leaders.[26] It was clearly very important to Danish politicians that the country be regarded as a good ally, and the Danes have contributed risk-willing, relevant military forces to both ISAF and Libya.

Ringsmose argues that for Norway, its geopolitical relationship with Russia determines coalition contributions, whereas the main point for

Denmark is general foreign and security policy.[27] Thus, the perception of the importance of alliance dependence may not be related to national security concerns, contrary to realist theory. Jason Davidson's study shows that perception of security interests, as well as national prestige, plays an important role in decisions made in national capitals.[28] But these two variables are hardly in opposition to alliance dependence in my view; they should rather be seen as covarying with alliance loyalty.

For Norway, the ISAF case was an "eye-opener." It turned out to be much more warlike than previous operations. This happened while Norway had developed more and more of a "peace culture" domestically, as a view of itself in the world. In a report from the Norwegian Institute of International Affairs (NUPI) in 2007, H. Leira and colleagues define this self-image: "Norway as a peace nation, Norway as a humanitarian giant, and Norway as the best friend of the UN."[29]

Norway contributed sharp capacities to Operation Enduring Freedom (OEF), most notably special operations forces (SOFs), who fought in Helmand with the Americans. These contributions were opposed by the Left-Socialists (SV), and when this party became part of a new center-left government in 2005, it impacted contributions to ISAF. The SOFs in Afghanistan were a particular problem for SV, and the Norwegian government refused two NATO requests for such troops; eventually the SOFs who went to Afghanistan were not allowed to go south. The academic literature on this concludes that keeping the government together trumped the Labour Party's initial priority of accepting NATO's request:

> [T]he focus for the government's Afghanistan policy . . . developed into keeping the government together. SV was given concessions with regard to Norwegian contributions to Afghanistan. This did not lead to a radical change in Norwegian Afghanistan-policy, but definitively to an adjustment of it.[30]

This finding is corroborated by Ida Maria Oma, who concludes her study on the impact of the SV in this issue thus: "[T]he hypothesis that it has not been possible to contribute entirely as desired by NATO because of the need to keep the government together, is clearly brought out. . . . The Labour Party has had to accept influence from SV in security policy."[31]

In 2009 a new Stoltenberg government came into office, this time without much power for the SV partner. The Labour Party returned to its traditional role as leader in security policy and conducted a policy close to that of NATO and the United States. Norway had "become familiar with using military power": in 2003 politicians were appalled when Norwegian planes dropped bombs, yet in 2011 the same planes dropped six hundred bombs on Libya, and politicians were applauding.[32] Likewise, in 2011 war-fighting by special operations forces was celebrated, and they were decorated with the highest military honor for the first time since World War II, while the politicians a few years before had refused to recognize their heroism and preferred to talk about humanitarian issues. Norwegian strategic culture has changed in the last few years, and the catalyst for change has been the war in Afghanistan. As we have seen, domestic politics played a key role in the first Stoltenberg government in which SV influenced Norwegian NATO policy. But this was an exception to the main policy line, which is based on the geopolitical calculus that Norway needs the U.S. security guarantee in the north.

In the Canadian case, the sharp contributions to ISAF in Helmand are explained by alliance loyalty. Because of criticism of the United States for its war in Iraq, tensions were rising between the two countries. Canada sided with France and Germany on Iraq. This caused anger in Washington. In 2005 Canada decided to send sharp combat forces to Helmand, a surprising decision given the "peace nation" image and soft power foreign policy that both Norway and Canada have maintained. The scholarship on this particular decision strongly suggests that the relationship with the United States was of paramount importance. The CHOD, General Hillier, was keen to arrive at such a decision, but the main reason was the political need to "redress the balance" with the United States.[33] There was a need to show its neighbor that Canada was a loyal ally in NATO.[34] The communication director for Prime Minister Paul Martin, the liberal Canadian PM at the time, stated: "[T]his matters to the White House. . . . [T]hings that matter to the White House cannot be taken lightly, because these guys take it personally . . . so we really have to evaluate a decision that runs counter to the White House."[35] Canada has lost many lives in Helmand, fighting alongside the Americans, British, Dutch, Australians, and French.

Conclusion

If alliance dependence is such an important motivation for contributions, why should states contribute if the United States does not lead in a given operation? The answer lies in the fundamental need for Europe to keep NATO alive, which implies that the United States has a keen interest in Article 5 and the alliance. It demands that Europe carry more of the burden and that European allies continue not only to contribute, but also to accept responsibility for leading operations. This demand can be seen as a sine qua non for NATO to continue as the deterrent and security guarantee that it is today. If Europeans do more, the United States will also do its part. This "new deal" in NATO will have to function if the United States is to continue taking the same interest in the alliance as previously.

One may object that there will not be a need for new international operations after ISAF and Libya. Syria does not seem to attract any political willingness. This objection presupposes that NATO plans which operations it will undertake. It does not. "Events, my dear boy, events" was Harold Macmillan's reply when asked what determines international politics. Events determine where NATO goes—no one ever planned to be in sharp operations in Bosnia, Kosovo, Afghanistan, or Libya.

There is, however, not necessarily a clear connection between U.S. interest in NATO and the degree of contributions by European allies. One can assume that the United States will take an interest in keeping NATO intact as a *regional* alliance. But today NATO cannot deter by sitting inside its borders. It can only deter by being able to act where there is a need to act. Security issues are not only territorial; they are increasingly global. Moreover, the United States has pointed out that Europe must take care of its regional security problems itself—whether in Bosnia, Kosovo, or Libya. As we know, the former two issues were "resolved" only when the United States took a decisive lead, and in Libya it was indispensable. NATO as we know it and want it to be—an alliance that deters—therefore depends on military ability to both coerce and fight. There is thus no avoiding contributions, perhaps even bigger contributions to operations in which Europeans take the lead than to ones in which the United States calls for contributions. Put the other way around, in operations that the United States is not leading, is it likely that Europeans will rise to the occasion and both lead and contribute? We have seen how important alliance dependence is as an explanation for contributions. When this logic disappears, or is at least weakened, can we expect reluctant Europeans to come forward?

NOTES

    1. Timo Noetzel and Benjamin Schreer, "NATO's Vietnam? Afghanistan and the Future of the Atlantic Alliance," *Contemporary Security Policy* 30, no. 3 (2009): 529–47.
    2. Kenneth Waltz, *Theory of International Politics* (New York: McGraw Hill, 1979); Wallace J. Thies, *Why NATO Endures* (Cambridge: Cambridge University Press, 2009).
    3. Mancur Olson and Richard Zeckhauser, "An Economic Theory of Alliances," *Review of Economics and Statistics* 48, no. 3 (1966): 266–79.

4. Noetzel and Schreer, "NATO's Vietnam?"

5. Janne Haaland Matlary, *European Union Security Dynamics in the New National Interest* (Basingstoke, UK: Palgrave Macmillan, 2009).

6. Matlary, *European Union Security Dynamics*, 216.

7. Philip Stevens, "NATO's Long Drift Towards Irrelevance," *Financial Times*, September 23, 2011, http://www.ft.com/cms/s/0/5bd18646-c744-11df-aeb1-00144 feab49a.html#axzz2ljXQUgwj.

8. U.S. Department of Defense, "Secretary of Defense Speech: The Security and Defense Agenda (Future of NATO)," As Delivered by Secretary of Defense Robert M. Gates, Brussels, Belgium, Friday, June 10, 2011, http://www.defense .gov/speeches/speech.aspx?speechid=1581.; see also Robert Gates, "NATO Strategic Concept Seminar (Future of NATO)" (speech presented at the National Defense University, Washington, DC, February 23, 2010), http://www.defense .gov/speeches/speech.aspx?speechid=1423.

9. Thies, *Why NATO Endures*.

10. U.S. officials, interviews with author, Washington, DC, April 2011.

11. Thies, *Why NATO Endures*.

12. T. Shanker and E. Schmitt, "Seeing Limits to 'New' Kind of War in Libya," *New York Times*, October 21, 2011; see also Ellen Hallams and Benjamin Schreer, "Towards a 'Post-American' Alliance? NATO Burden-sharing after Libya," *International Affairs* 88, no. 2 (2012): 313–27.

13. See Janne Haaland Matlary and Magnus Petersson, *NATO's European Allies: Military Capacity and Political Will* (London: Palgrave Macmillan, 2013).

14. Glenn Snyder, "The Security Dilemma in Alliance Politics," *World Politics* 36, no. 4 (1984): 461–95.

15. Snyder, "Security Dilemma in Alliance Politics," 484.

16. Snyder, "Security Dilemma in Alliance Politics," 484.

17. Mike Jackson, *Soldier: The Autobiography* (London: Bantam Press, 2007).

18. Stephen J. Cimbala and Peter K. Forster, *Multinational Military Intervention: NATO Policy, Strategy and Burden Sharing* (Burlington, UK: Ashgate, 2010), 154.

19. Cimbala and Forster, *Multinational Military Intervention*, 154.

20. Cimbala and Forster, *Multinational Military Intervention*, 198.

21. Jens Ringsmose, "NATO—a Provider of Public and Collective Goods" (University of Southern Denmark, 2011), http://www.ecprnet.eu/MyECPR/proposals /reykjavik/uploads/papers/1028.pdf.

22. Ringsmose, "NATO," 324.

23. Ringsmose, "NATO," 328.

24. C. Rouleau-Dick, "Why Was Canada Involved in Kandahar: An Analysis" (unpublished manuscript, University of Oslo, 2012).

25. See Matlary and Petersson, *NATO's European Allies*, chapter on Norway.

26. Håkon Lunde Saxi, "Defending Small States: Norwegian and Danish Defense Policies in the Post-Cold War Era," *Defense and Security Analysis* 26, no. 4 (2011): 415–30.

27. Jens Ringsmose, "NATO Burden-Sharing Redux: Continuity and Change after the Cold War," *Contemporary Security Policy* 31, no. 2 (2010): 319–38.

28. Jason W. Davidson, *America's Allies and War: Kosovo, Afghanistan, and Iraq* (New York: Palgrave Macmillan, 2011).

29. H. Halvard Leira et al., *Norske selvbilder og norsk utenrikspolitikk* (Oslo: NUPI, 2007).

30. Erik Bøifot, "Det norske militære engasjementet i Afghanistan: Idealisme eller egeninteresse?" (master's thesis, The Norwegian Defense University College, Oslo, 2007), 64 (author's translation).

31. Ida Maria Oma, "Internasjonal militær deltagelse" (master's thesis, University of Oslo, 2008), 99.

32. Øistein Espenes and Karl Erik Haug, "Norge er blitt vant til å bruke makt," *Norsk luftmakt 100 år* (2012): 42, http://www.forsvarsforening.no/images/blader /2012-2/s42-44.pdf.

33. Bill Schiller, "The Road to Kandahar," *Toronto Star*, September 8, 2006; Stephen Saideman and David Auerswald, "Comparing Caveats: Understanding the Sources of National Restrictions upon NATO's Mission in Afghanistan," *International Studies Quarterly* 56, no. 1 (2012): 67–84.

34. Janice Gross Stein and Eugene Lang, *The Unexpected War: Canada in Kandahar* (Toronto: Viking Press, 2007).

35. Quoted in Schiller, "The Road to Kandahar."

Chapter 5

The Alliance and the Credibility of Extended Deterrence

Helga Haftendorn

At its November 2010 summit in Lisbon, Portugal, NATO's member states adopted a new strategic concept.[1] The deliberations both preceding[2] and following the adoption included a substantial debate about deterrence and the role of nuclear weapons in NATO's strategy. For two decades this issue had been all but absent in a NATO preoccupied by its engagement on the one hand in partnership and expansion, and on the other in crisis response and peace support operations. While many reasons may be identified behind the debate's reemergence, at least partly it resulted from a broader shift away from the almost exclusive focus on out-of-area operations that marked NATO for most of the 2000s. As the issue of collective defense and traditional security challenges moved up the political agenda in NATO, so did the issue of deterrence.

The debate in NATO on deterrence has been ongoing since the Cold War; it focuses on the credibility of extended deterrence and the reassurance of countries at risk. Basically, "deterrence is a form of bargaining which exploits a capability for inflicting damage to such a level as to truly cause hurt far greater than defeat."[3] In the early days of the alliance, the big gamble was whether America's partners could trust that the United States would risk New York and Chicago for Frankfurt and Hamburg—the latter major cities in the country through which the "Iron Curtain" was running. The allies had to put their faith in an alliance of so far unproven worth, rather than defect and save their skin by negotiating for a special deal with the Soviets. The credibility of the U.S. nuclear umbrella was demonstrated during the Berlin and Cuban crises, even more so as it was supported by significant U.S. conventional forces in Europe serving as a trip-wire. After the end of the East-West conflict and the collapse of the Soviet Union, questions arose about the future of NATO and what function deterrence should serve when there was no longer a need to deter Russia.

The issue of the credibility of deterrence consists of three more specific debates. The first concerns political priorities of member states and resource allocation between territorial defense and out-of-area missions. It was initiated by allies with a common border and/or history with Russia, such as the Baltic States and Poland. They requested that the alliance again put more emphasis on regional deterrence and home defense. They wanted to be covered by NATO contingency plans and offered host-nation support arrangements. The United States, though generally quite responsive to the requests of the new members, nevertheless argued for expanding the alliance's global reach and improving its readiness for out-of-area interventions. While some alliance members saw NATO's involvement in Afghanistan as an exceptional case, the United States—and to some degree Great Britain and France as well—at the time considered it a model mission for NATO in a globalized world. Thus, the first debate is on NATO's role, reach, purpose, and capabilities as they relate to its core goal of deterring any open or clandestine military aggression. Given their history and geography, the United States and Germany became the main antagonists in this debate.

The second debate focuses on the function of nuclear weapons in NATO strategy and the connection between armament and disarmament. European politicians have called for a withdrawal of the approximately two hundred remaining U.S. tactical/nonstrategic nuclear weapons (NSNW) in Europe. The weapons no longer serve any realistic military function, the politicians argue, but rather hinder nuclear arms control.[4] For many of the smaller members, however, these weapons are essential elements of extended deterrence; if they are to be withdrawn, they should not be reduced unilaterally, but rather be made part of a multilateral arms control deal with Russia. This second debate deals with NATO's military instruments essential for extended deterrence.

This second debate relates to the uncertainties about the credibility of Article 5 and how a potential threat against NATO members can be successfully deterred, or—in the unlikely case deterrence fails—how they can be defended. The debate shows that deterrence has a lot to do with psychology and perception; it is based on a combination of perceived resolve and available capabilities. Since NATO's founding, nuclear weapons have been seen as an umbrella protecting the security and territorial integrity of all alliance members. Reassurance was provided through the existence of U.S. strategic weapons that were coupled with Europe's defense through forward-deployed tactical nuclear weapons and regionally based U.S. conventional forces. However, as protection was never taken for granted, NATO endured a number of crises that had their origins in doubts about the credibility of extended deterrence.

The third debate deals with the political aspects of extended deterrence. Should NATO prioritize the military dimensions of extended deterrence or reset its relations with Russia, treating it no longer as a latent threat but as a political partner? After U.S. president Barack Obama had pushed the reset button with Russia,[5] it took a while before Russia's Western neighbors were willing to enter into a more constructive relationship with Moscow. They needed assurances that the alliance had adequate capabilities to protect them in the case of a new threat to their security and territorial integrity. But did NATO have the potential to do so, or was it—in Walter Lippmann's words—"insolvent," meaning that its commitments outweighed its resources? Can NATO cope with the challenges it is confronted with, military and other? Or, in order to control the necessary military and political capabilities, does NATO need to intensify cooperation with nonalliance partners and other institutions, such as the EU and the UN?

In this chapter, after a look at the history of extended deterrence, I analyze the three debates laid out above and how they have impacted extended deterrence. I look into the ambivalence of NATO's role and tasks after the end of the East-West conflict and ask what function the alliance is now serving. Further, I discuss the political aspects of extended deterrence and the degree to which it is compatible with cooperation with Russia and China. I also ask whether NATO still needs its traditional, strong reliance on nuclear weapons and whether deterrence without nukes is possible. Finally, I discuss whether NATO's "Deterrence and Defence Posture Review" (DDPR) process has yielded credible answers to the challenges of a fundamentally changed international environment. The basic question thus is what deterrence stands for and involves today.

Cold War Deterrence: A Series of Credibility Gaps

When NATO was founded in 1949, its initial function, according to Lord Ismay, was to keep the Russians out, the Americans in, and the Germans down. After West Germany joined the alliance in 1955, it became a partner in the common defense of the West and was in turn protected by NATO's forward deployed forces and America's nuclear umbrella. First doubts about the credibility of deterrence surfaced when for economic reasons—"to get more bang for the buck"—the Eisenhower administration opted for a strategy of massive retaliation.[6] It put more emphasis on nuclear weapons and less on its conventional forces. European allies had difficulties, however, building up conventional armies as large as NATO defense plans called for.[7] The result was a perceived conventional weakness that lowered the nuclear threshold. In other words, NATO expected it would quickly exhaust its conventional options and be forced to use nuclear weapons to prevent defeat.

Two events combined to cast deep doubts on the wisdom of the new U.S. nuclear strategy and the political credibility of deterrence. One was the effects of "Carte Blanche," NATO's first air-based nuclear exercise in Europe, which targeted much of the (German) territory that the alliance was supposed to protect. The other was the advent of Soviet long-range weapons capable of reaching the American homeland. Would the United States, under the conditions of the "balance of terror,"[8] be willing to risk New York or Chicago for the sake of Frankfurt or Hamburg? These lingering doubts left the allies searching for ways and means to make deterrence more credible.

To the first challenge—nuclear annihilation—the Germans, who clearly saw themselves as most affected by the new strategy, reacted by demanding a finger on the nuclear safety catch. The United States responded by calling for a substantial conventional buildup of NATO forces to withstand a major Warsaw Pact attack and thus to avoid a nuclear exchange that would cause catastrophic damage to allied territory. But given NATO's conventional inferiority, could the United States be relied on to respond to a limited Soviet incursion with a nuclear response? To restore the credibility of nuclear deterrence, the European partners demanded a hand on the nuclear trigger also, either by building their own nuclear forces (the United Kingdom and France), by jointly owning a multilateral nuclear force, or by participating in joint nuclear planning.

In the early 1960s the Kennedy administration and Secretary of Defense Robert S. McNamara were concerned about the West's heavy reliance on nuclear weapons and wanted to build up credible conventional alternatives in case a small-scale conflict were to erupt in Europe. Nuclear weapons were to be transformed from a "sword" into a "shield" for safeguarding deterrence. These plans made the allies very uneasy, because they were afraid that the United States wanted to build a firebreak between its strategic deterrent and the conventional forces stationed in Europe.

They demanded that tactical nuclear weapons be deployed in the European theater, providing a strong link between the American nuclear forces and the inferior regional conventional posture. To contain the proliferation of nuclear weapons, however, Washington wanted to discourage NATO members from attempting to overcome their nuclear dilemma by having a finger on both the trigger and the safety catch of nuclear weapons. Instead of helping them acquire nuclear hardware, the United States suggested that they participate in nuclear planning in a newly formed Nuclear Planning Group. But agreement was only reached when France had left the alliance's integrated military structure. In 1967, after difficult negotiations, NATO adopted a new strategy of flexible response that based deterrence on a triad of conventional, tactical nuclear, and strategic nuclear forces.[9]

Another test of the credibility of the NATO deterrent occurred when the United States and the Soviet Union reached a settlement on a set of bilateral arms control agreements, notably the Strategic Arms Limitation and Anti-Ballistic Missile Treaties of 1972. Was Washington shifting its attention away from deterring to cooperating with Moscow? In a sophisticated and highly fortuitous maneuver, arms control and détente on the one side, and defense and deterrence on the other, were blended in the Harmel exercise.[10] Foreign Minister Pierre Harmel of Belgium had suggested conducting such a review out of concern that individual détente policies would undermine NATO's coherence. The report yielded an eventually highly acclaimed formula that proclaimed détente and defense to be but two sides of the same coin, and that both should be followed by the alliance. This formula took some of the heat out of European criticism of U.S.-Soviet bilateral arms control agreements that had ignored European partners' concerns and of the opposition to German *Ostpolitik* that in some eyes had been moving too far in accommodating Soviet interests and undermined the U.S. leadership role in dealing with Moscow.

The mid-1970s saw a withering away of the tender bloom of East-West rapprochement. The Soviet deployment of SS-20 medium-range missiles targeted at Central Europe alarmed the public. The German government in particular questioned the wisdom of arms control agreements that seemed to undercut the military balance and weaken deterrence. In his famous speech at the International Institute of Strategic Studies in October 1977,[11] German Chancellor Helmut Schmidt highlighted the emergence of a "grey zone" in Europe as a result of the U.S.-Soviet agreements. He urged Washington to include the Soviet SS-20 missiles in arms control negotiations, such as on Multilateral and Balanced Force Reductions (MBFR), or to close the gap in the balance by other means to restore deterrence.

In turn, U.S. politicians became concerned that the NATO posture was again losing its credibility. Their military developed plans for deploying new tactical nuclear weapons in Europe, such as the neutron bomb. The Carter administration initially regarded the idea of modernizing NATO's nuclear systems as a kind of placebo for its allies. But what started as a process of accommodating rising uneasiness among Washington's partners soon acquired a dynamic of its own. After a fairly inclusive process, NATO came up with a proposal to deploy new Pershing II intermediate-range missiles and ground-launched cruise missiles on allied territory.[12] To make their stationing acceptable to Europe's risk-averse public, the deployment decision was linked to a plan for new arms control negotiations. If Moscow agreed to the West's proposal, reductions in the numbers of new systems would be possible. But the Soviets rather chose to let the deployment proceed and exploit the resulting rifts within the West.

For Washington, the NATO double track decision of December 1979 signaled a Western resolve to stand up to the Soviets. The risk-averse German government, which had initiated the debate about a potential "grey zone" in the center of Europe not covered by deterrence, perceived the decision as a double misunderstanding. Instead of including intermediate nuclear weapons in the arms control dialogue, new longer-range systems were deployed in Europe. Because of their capacity to strike Russian territory, they entailed new risks and could decouple U.S. strategic forces from the defense of Europe. Instead of closing the credibility gap, they opened another one. Nevertheless, the double track decision was a compromise that tried to respect the vital interests of all NATO partners as the Harmel formula had done a decade earlier.

Later efforts to negotiate a double-zero arms control agreement only marginally closed the gap of confidence in deterrence. Much more relevant was the dramatic change in Soviet policy that ended the East-West confrontation and helped overcome the division of Europe. Deterrence in its traditional sense of risking mutual assured destruction had lost its relevance.

The Debate on the Credibility of Extended Deterrence

The collapse of the Soviet Union and the end of the division of Europe brought fundamental changes and broadened NATO's political priorities. The alliance's military posture was no longer directed against a clear and present danger but rather had to cope with a set of ambiguous risks and threats. Mainly to smooth the process of German unification, NATO leaders in 1990 announced that they wished to build a new partnership with all European nations. They emphasized the defensive nature of the alliance and declared that nuclear arms would be relegated to weapons of last resort. In particular, they reached out to Russia and the countries of the East that had been their adversaries during the Cold War and extended them a "hand of friendship."[13] At its Rome Summit in 1991, the alliance adopted a new Strategic Concept that emphasized common defense as NATO's primary function and accepted additional tasks such as peacekeeping, crisis management, and coping with failing states.[14]

NATO's core function was now to consolidate "Europe whole and free." In order to help the alliance adapt to a changed international environment, the European security pattern was transformed. A Euro-Atlantic Partnership Council was charged with overseeing the development of dialogue, cooperation, and consultations between NATO and its partners. Russia and Ukraine were invited to enter into cooperative relationships with the alliance; joint institutions for consultation and engagement in cooperative activities were established.[15] With the Partnership for Peace (PfP) Program, launched in 1994, a military dimension was added to the relationship between the alliance and its partners. For those former Warsaw Pact countries that wished to become NATO members, the alliance offered an open-door policy. In 1999 it accepted the Czech Republic, Hungary, and Poland as new members of the alliance. With this step, it started on the road toward enlargement into Central and Eastern Europe; by 2013 its membership had increased to twenty-eight states. The PfP Program was also used to establish flexible relationships with those states that because of political or geographic reasons were not candidates for membership—at least in the short term.

The September 11, 2001, terrorist attacks on the United States were a huge political watershed; they ushered NATO into a new era. Without much argument, the alliance decided to support the United States in its fight against terrorism and activated Article 5—the treaty's collective defense clause—for the first time in its history. The alliance members joined America in combating Al Qaeda and participated in ISAF in Afghanistan. Under the impact of the terrorist challenge, NATO further redefined its military role.

At the 2002 Prague Summit, the alliance took significant steps to strengthen its political and military ability for intervening in regions outside of Europe and North America. It embraced the tasks of fighting terrorism, global conflict management, and worldwide projection of power. On fighting terrorism and preparing for global conflict management,

NATO renounced the geographical limitations of its theater of engagement, the NATO Guideline Area, as specified in Article 6 of its founding document.[16] Home defense was relegated to a secondary priority. The new tasks, however, required different military forces with greater combat effectiveness and interoperability.[17] These far-reaching decisions caused disagreement among the member-states on the methods and means that the alliance should employ to achieve its ends. The controversy centered on the questions of when, and under what circumstances, military force should be used. The U.S. strategy was more interventionist, including preemptive actions, than most Europeans wished it to be; the latter instead championed a more guarded approach and wanted to retain NATO's core defensive role. These divergences widened when U.S.-led coalition forces invaded Iraq without a UN mandate.

To combat terrorism the classical instruments of deterrence—strong nuclear and conventional capabilities—were largely ineffective. How could the West deter a nonstate actor such as a terrorist network that lacked any formal structures or specific geographical location and was united by a strong belief in the superiority of the Islamic creed? Was it enough to threaten retaliation on their host country? Initially, U.S. and ISAF forces were able to hunt down Al Qaeda and its Taliban supporters in Afghanistan and to install a pro-Western government in Kabul headed by President Hamid Karzai; however, that government never gained full political control of the country. In spite of some progress in rebuilding an Afghan civil society, after more than ten years of campaigning the alliance had to admit that its forces were not able to pacify the region and install a participatory democratic government. At the end of 2011 NATO governments announced that by 2014 the alliance would withdraw its combat units and hand over the task of guarding the country's and the population's safety to the Afghan forces.

Afghanistan, the threat of an Iranian nuclear bomb, the unrest in the Arab world known as the "Arab Spring," and the civil war in Syria carried the message that the alliance was heavily affected by political and security developments beyond its borders. The members harbored different priorities for when and where NATO should intervene. The United States and Great Britain considered expeditionary missions among the core tasks of the alliance and wanted to enable NATO to successfully discharge these with enhanced military capabilities. The Anglo-Saxon position was strongly opposed by the Central and Eastern European states that bordered on Russia, such as the Baltic States and Poland. With strong and living memories of the historical threat from Moscow, and uneasy about perceived

Russian aggressiveness, they prioritized home defense. Still another group, including Germany and Norway, argued that NATO should focus more on regional security, though they were less worried about the occasional bouts of Moscow's belligerence—such as the Russian intervention in Georgia in August 2008 and Moscow's support for Syrian president Bashar al-Assad. Yet in most cases they were prepared to support out-of-area missions when Western security was at stake and these were authorized by the UN Security Council. This relaxed attitude changed in the case of Ukraine. Russia's involvement in the east of the country and on the Crimean Peninsula, leading in March 2014 to a referendum on joining Russia, caused deep concern in and strong negative reactions from neighboring countries, especially Poland and the Baltic States. In spite of their criticism, NATO members were nevertheless careful not to become involved in a military conflict with Russia.

At the 2010 Lisbon Summit the heads of state and government confirmed that NATO's core functions were to ensure collective defense, prepare for crisis management, and contribute to common security. The alliance confirmed that Article 5 of the Washington Treaty remained firm and binding. This was thought of as an act of reassurance, especially for those members that saw themselves in need of alliance protection, such as the Baltic States. The summit passed a "Lisbon Package" that was to enable NATO to increase its capabilities for expeditionary missions; expand existing anti-ballistic-missile systems; improve defense against cyber-attacks; and modernize information, intelligence, and decision-making structures. To meet the new "hybrid threats" and nonconventional challenges facing the alliance, NATO was called on to strengthen its nonmilitary instruments.[18] The 2008 global economic crisis not only challenged solidarity among alliance members but also made the acquisition of additional capabilities highly doubtful. In addition, it directed attention away from military matters and toward economic and social challenges. Generally, alliance leaders at the Lisbon Summit papered over their differences on the future role of nuclear weapons, burden sharing, the balance between armament and disarmament, and relations with Russia. To help resolve at least some of the most acute disagreements, they asked the North Atlantic Council (NAC) to review NATO's overall posture in deterring and defending (in the DDPR) against the full range of threats to the alliance in view of the evolving international security environment.[19]

The alliance's DDPR was to provide answers to the deep conflict among its members on political-military priorities regarding out-of-area operations and regional defense. It was further to create a firm foundation for NATO's new missile defense policy.[20] To fill the gaps highlighted in the DDPR, while taking account of the financial squeeze in most member countries, Secretary General Rasmussen proposed a "smart defense initiative"[21] that was discussed at the NATO Chicago Summit in 2012. The three components of smart defense were prioritization of national capabilities; cooperation—that is, pooling of capabilities among allies; and specialization in critical capabilities (and withdrawing from others). In this way European partners were to become equipped to better respond to U.S. burden-sharing requests.

However, it came as no big surprise that none of the divisive issues confronting the alliance was resolved. Yet the DDPR did provide updated information regarding ballistic missile defense and discussed possibilities for nonstrategic weapons stockpile reductions. Regarding missile defense, the report announced that NATO had achieved an "interim capability." It further stated that "in a spirit of reciprocity, maximum transparency and mutual confidence, it will actively seek cooperation on missile defense with Russia." So far, however, nothing has come out of this; as a gesture of protest, newly reelected Russian president Vladimir Putin did not attend the May 2012 Chicago Summit. Regarding nonstrategic weapons, the alliance has tasked the appropriate committees to develop concepts for ensuring the broadest possible participation of allies in sharing arrangements, "including in case NATO were to decide to reduce its reliance on non-strategic nuclear weapons based in Europe."[22] The Central and Eastern European states needed to be assured that deterrence remained credible.[23] During the 2014 Ukrainian crisis, NATO reconfirmed this pledge.

The Function of Nuclear Weapons and Deterrence

The second debate resulted from the uncertainties about the credibility of Article 5 of the NATO charter and on how a potential threat against members could be deterred efficiently, or—in the unlikely case deterrence failed—how they could be defended. Since NATO's founding, nuclear weapons had served to protect the security and territorial integrity of all member-states. Reassurance was provided through the existence of a U.S. strategic force that was coupled with Europe's defense through forward-deployed tactical nuclear weapons and regionally based conventional forces.

In a dinner speech in Tallinn on April 22, 2010, U.S. secretary of state Hillary Clinton outlined "five principles" that should guide NATO's approach to nuclear weapons:

[A]s long as nuclear weapons exist, NATO will remain a nuclear alliance;

As a nuclear alliance, sharing nuclear risks and responsibilities is widely fundamental;

A "broad aim is to continue to reduce the role and number of nuclear weapons" while "recogniz[ing] that in the years since the Cold War ended, NATO has already dramatically reduced its reliance on nuclear weapons";

Allies must broaden deterrence against the range of twenty-first-century threats, including by pursuing territorial missile defense; and

In any future reductions, our aim should be to seek Russian agreement to increase transparency on non-strategic nuclear weapons in Europe, relocate these weapons away from the territory of NATO members, and include non-strategic nuclear weapons in the next round of U.S.-Russian arms control discussions alongside strategic and non-deployed nuclear weapons.[24]

For many of the smaller members, nuclear weapons are essential elements of extended deterrence. When the East-West conflict had subsided and U.S. nuclear weapons as well as NATO conventional forces were reduced, Poland and the Baltic States were concerned that deterrence was weakening to an unacceptable degree. In their view U.S. nuclear weapons continued to play an important reassurance role by symbolizing the "coupling" of American and European security. To strengthen the credibility of extended deterrence, they wished to reinforce their military links with America and requested that the United States base some troops and preposition military material on their territory, as it had done in Germany during the Cold War.

Other European states felt that they did not need to worry about a military attack. Their leaders instead called for a withdrawal of the approximately two hundred remaining U.S. nonstrategic nuclear weapons in Europe (mainly free-fall bombs, many of them under a dual-key rule), arguing that these no longer served any realistic military purpose, but rather hindered nuclear arms control.[25]

This controversy caused a broad debate on the functions of nuclear weapons in NATO strategy and the linkage between armament and disarmament. Should the alliance continue to base its strategy on a mix of strategic, tactical, and conventional forces even though the threat of a nuclear or conventional attack had mostly dissipated? Or should it reduce its nuclear role and "seek the peace and security of a world without nuclear weapons"—as had been proclaimed by President Barack Obama in his 2009 Prague speech and recommended by a number of elder statesmen on both sides of the Atlantic?[26] Other politicians expressed similar views, among them German foreign minister Guido Westerwelle, who for domestic reasons became one of the main proponents of a withdrawal of all nuclear weapons from Europe.

Even without any political prodding, NATO is on the path to disarmament by default. Several European delivery systems are approaching retirement. When the German nuclear-capable Tornado and the Belgian and Dutch F-16 aircraft reach the end of their life spans, their successor models are not necessarily wired for nuclear missions. These NATO partners may then give up their nuclear role. Meanwhile, the United States will upgrade its nuclear posture in Europe by modernizing the existing nuclear bombs to give them greater accuracy, along with the deployment of the stealth F-35 Joint Strike Fighter. This development will hurt nuclear burden sharing if no new formula is found and weaken the credibility of extended deterrence.

Most allies, however, oppose any unilateral withdrawal of the remaining nonstrategic nuclear weapons in Europe. In 2010 France and Great Britain agreed on a defense pact with a strong nuclear element that leaves hardly any room for abandoning nuclear weapons once and for all.[27] Other Europeans are skeptical about a non-nuclear NATO and consider the European-based systems an important element of extended deterrence and an essential link to the U.S. strategic nuclear posture. Alliance members also argue that any withdrawal or reduction of the forward-based nuclear systems should only take place in the framework of an arms control agreement in which Russia reduces equal numbers of its NSNW and agrees to a stringent verification mechanism. All NATO members have endorsed the new Russian-American Strategic Arms Reduction Treaty ("New START," signed in 2010) and have called for resuscitating the treaty on conventional forces in Europe.

Though the United States is in favor of NSNW negotiations, it has recognized that an agreement will be difficult to achieve. In a turnaround of history, the regional balance between Russia and the West has completely changed. During the Cold War the West was very concerned about the Warsaw Pact's conventional superiority and tried to counterbalance it with advanced nuclear weapons. Today the tables have turned: Russia has a large number of nuclear weapons that offset its decaying conventional forces, while—so far at least—NATO can rely on superior conventional capabilities. Thus, only under exceptional circumstances will Russia give up what it sees as its last line of defense against aggression, as well as the basis of its claim to superpower status. A way out of this dilemma might be to start with steps increasing the mutual transparency of nuclear weapons' deployment and to include NSNW in more general negotiations on nuclear arms limitation, aiming for subceilings on both sides.[28]

Any discussion of NATO's nuclear role needs to take into account that the United States is also recalibrating its military capabilities. The Pentagon's Strategic Guidance of January 2012 takes note of the need to counter terrorism and irregular warfare; it pledges that the United States will continue to build and sustain capabilities appropriate for these challenges. American forces should be able to deter and defeat aggression from any potential adversary. Credible deterrence will "result from both the capabilities to deny an aggressor the prospect of achieving his objectives and from the complementary capability to impose unacceptable costs on the aggressor."[29] Planning envisages forces that are able to counter any state's aggressive objectives in one region by conducting a combined arms campaign across all domains—land, air, maritime, space, and cyberspace. The United States wants to be able to project power into areas where its access and freedom to operate are challenged.

On nuclear weapons, the Pentagon has outlined a new policy in its 2010 Nuclear Posture Review.[30] It assumes that the changes in international relations—the end of the Cold War, new advances in the technology of ballistic missile defense, and America's superior conventional capabilities—will allow it to significantly lower nuclear force levels and reduce the reliance on nuclear options. Instead, the non-nuclear elements, including a forward U.S. conventional presence and an effective theater ballistic defense, will take on a greater share of the deterrence burden. The United States will retain a capability to forward-deploy nuclear weapons on bombers but shift the emphasis to long-range strike capabilities. With de-emphasizing the nuclear element in U.S. strategy, defense planners took notice of President Obama's agenda for reducing nuclear dangers while simultaneously advancing American security interests. But the report clearly states that as long as nuclear weapons remain in existence, the United States will maintain a safe, secure, and effective nuclear arsenal.

As a consequence of the Pentagon's reappraisal and its emphasis on a strategy of denial, the alliance has decided to acquire a missile defense system. After difficult discussions among members, NATO resolved to build an "Active Layered Theater Ballistic Missile Defense" system (ALTBMD) that should protect both alliance forces and territory.[31] Some Europeans, though, are skeptical about a BMD system, which they see as a further obstacle to disarmament and a burden on relations with Russia. When they supported the NATO decision regarding BMD, they did so for reasons of alliance cohesion. Some in the disarmament community also hope that an effective BMD system will allow for a full withdrawal of nuclear weapons from Europe. Yet their attempt to establish a link between the construction of a BMD system and steps toward arms control foundered on French and U.S. opposition. Allies may practice a new form of burden sharing in sharing the costs of missile defense.[32]

As a consolation prize for European disarmament buffs, NATO created a Weapons of Mass Destruction Control and Disarmament Committee and mandated it to advise the Council on arms control.[33] To appease concerns in Paris and London about circumscription of their military capabilities, NATO emphasized that the British and French national nuclear forces were to remain significant for deterrence and defense. Because Turkey objected to naming Iran as a source of potential threat and a motive for building an alliance BMD system, it was left up in the air against which threat this system was directed. Ankara also wanted to participate in the system's command and control arrangements and requested that these be located in Izmir, not Ramstein, Germany, as had been originally planned.[34]

As long as nuclear weapons exist, NATO will remain a nuclear alliance. To keep extended deterrence credible, NATO leaders have to cope with the problem of tying together the various strands of nuclear policy into a coherent alliance policy. Regarding the role of nuclear weapons, they have to take care that solidarity and cohesion of the alliance are not undermined. They will also ask how NATO can contribute to the goal of reducing, and potentially eliminating, nuclear weapons.[35]

Political Aspects of Extended Deterrence

The third debate deals with the political aspects of extended deterrence. After the end of the Cold War, allies were aware that NATO was not only a military alliance, but also a political security system spanning the Atlantic, and that the nonmilitary aspects of deterrence had gained in importance. To meet the new threats and unconventional challenges, NATO needed to strengthen its nonmilitary instruments.[36] The alliance thus created new organizational units to cope with new threats, for example, for improving defense against cyber-attacks and modernizing its information, intelligence and decision-making structures. Regarding cyber-attacks, a debate has ensued about whether these may trigger an Article 5 military response or should only be dealt with by political and technical means. As they may become more intrusive and sophisticated—think of "*stuxnet*"[37]—without adequate countermeasures at hand, NATO becomes more vulnerable.

In the fight against terrorism, the alliance drew on the support of members' police forces and other domestic agencies. Opposing the United States, the Europeans recommended that NATO should not take on new responsibilities such as safeguarding energy security and dealing with environmental issues. But will the increased focus on hybrid threats strengthen alliance cohesion and the credibility of deterrence, or will the gaps in this approach discredit NATO and prevent quick reaction?

All NATO members share a conviction that closer cooperation with Russia is a precondition for international peace and security and for coping with challenges such as nonproliferation and unrest in Afghanistan, Iran, Syria, and Ukraine. With its invitation to Moscow to participate in the construction of a European BMD system, the alliance wanted to open a new chapter in its relations with Russia. At the Lisbon Summit, Russian president Vladimir Medvedev accepted this invitation on the condition that Moscow be treated as an equal partner.[38] In contrast, NATO—and above all the United States—felt that the fundamental decisions on BMD should be taken within NAC and not in the NRC with Russia present at the table. The Kremlin was not very interested in developing a joint BMD position with NATO members, and nothing came of the invitation.

Because of its size and stature, Russia inevitably will play a prominent role in shaping the Euro-Atlantic security environment. NATO members have applauded Moscow's willingness to support the air and land transport of withdrawing forces from Afghanistan and to oppose terrorism, piracy, and the proliferation of nuclear weapons. Some concern has been voiced about Russia's attempts to intimidate neighboring states politically and economically. The Baltic States, sharing a common border with Russia and hosting large minorities of ethnic Russians within their borders, watched with apprehension when President Obama announced that NATO wanted to establish a more constructive partnership with Moscow. Shocked by the Russian intervention in Georgia, which seemed to be the writing on the wall, a group of former political leaders and intellectuals from Central and Eastern Europe sent an open letter to the U.S. administration criticizing it for pursuing a "Russia First policy vis-à-vis Eastern Europe."[39] The Baltic States felt like sheep sitting next to a big bear whose aggressiveness was well known, though they were told that by now the bear has become quite docile. In any case, they want to hedge against any recurrence of Russian belligerence and have therefore called for strengthening regional defense. Many Western observers, though, found it difficult to sympathize with the sensitivity of Baltic politicians. To some extent, however, their situation resembles that of West Berlin during the Cold War, when the Germans had little alternative other than to place their trust in extended deterrence.

To implement the Comprehensive Approach heralded in the new Strategic Concept and to make up for its conventional deficiencies, NATO needs to strengthen civil-military cooperation. The most obvious partner is the EU, which has broad experiences in civil reconstruction and municipal administration.[40] To assure complementarity between NATO and the EU, the alliance needs to forge a comprehensive and cost-effective approach for stabilizing missions.[41] The alliance needs to cooperate with partner states and other institutions. It will further need to strengthen routine and crisis consultations with the members of the Partnership for Peace, the Euro-Atlantic Partnership Program, the Mediterranean Dialogue, and the Istanbul Cooperation Initiative. In view of declining financial resources, implementing Rasmussen's "smart defence concept"[42] will not be easy. For some allies, a pooling of capabilities and specializing in critical elements while withdrawing from others will infringe on their autonomy and sovereignty. A weak common posture will, however, undermine the credibility of extended deterrence.

Special emphasis is placed on transatlantic cooperation. The alliance shall continue "to serve as a transatlantic means for security consultations and crisis management along the entire continuum of issues facing the alliance."[43] NATO is the only contractual link between North America and Europe; it remains *the* essential venue for these functions and carries out the common security and defense commitments of its members. This reflects both the political and military dimensions of the alliance and merits all attention in light of the diversity of today's security risks and the wide-ranging positions of the organization's current membership. For this reason, Article 4 of the NATO Treaty, the consultation clause, should receive more attention; suitable (declaratory) policies should also be developed. This is seen as another precondition for making deterrence credible.

Conclusions

The concept of deterrence originated in the political environment of the Cold War. Its purpose was to prevent an attack on the United States and its allies, especially one involving nuclear weapons. But what do deterrence and extended deterrence mean since the end of the East-West conflict, 9/11, and the Russian annexation of the Crimean Peninsula, and does NATO still perform a credible deterrent role?

If the alliance still has a deterrent function, it is due to the adaptability of NATO to changing international situations and altered national priorities. Though the alliance continues to be challenged worldwide, the discouraging experience of its engagement in Afghanistan has cooled members' previous enthusiasm for significant out-of-area commitments.

The "new" risks and challenges vary in origin and impact. International terrorist groupings, whether linked to Al Qaeda, radical Islamists, or national irredentists, constitute asymmetric threats that are difficult to cope with. The traditional response of counterstriking with military means is inadequate for combating small groups fighting for religious beliefs and radical ideologies. This strong focus on nonstate terrorism may also obscure other, more dangerous possibilities. Many politicians and publics continue to see Russia and China as latent threats; they attribute to them the capability to seriously harm alliance nations and their interests.

A new theater of conflict may be space and cyberspace. NATO and the United States rely heavily on space for communication and surveillance (e.g., with spy satellites) and protection (with BMD systems) that are highly vulnerable to attack. For some ten years the Chinese military has developed methods to harass the West in a high-tech, space-based war.[44] Thus the question arises: What kind of deterrence is conceivable and can serve as a stabilizing factor? More efficient than deterrence by punishment will be deterrence by denial, by making space objects more resilient.

With the agreement on a "Deterrence and Defence Posture Review" report,[45] NATO leaders at their 2012 Chicago Summit accepted a thorough review of NATO's role and posture on defense and deterrence. Nevertheless they were not able to solve several divisive issues and reach a consensus on a credible NATO political-military posture. Trying to make ends meet and reestablish the credibility of deterrence, the Chicago Summit leaders adopted a concept of "smart defense." As technology grows more expensive, especially for space and cyber defense, and military budgets are under great pressure, allies can only obtain key capabilities if they work together on developing and acquiring them jointly.[46] Along with this economizing approach, ministers have announced putting in place a new and leaner command structure. Critics, however, warn that this new approach may lead to a much looser alliance, to a "NATO á la carte."[47]

The urgency for regional and home defense has also changed. In general, alliance members today do need less protection against an open military attack, but they feel more exposed to terrorism or cyber harassment; they strive to acquire protection against these kinds of threats. Their vulnerability has been demonstrated by the crippling of the Estonian IT system for twenty days in 2007 and the *stuxnet* cyber worm targeted at the control and command systems of Iranian nuclear enrichment plants. Under NATO auspices, the Cooperative Cyber Defense Center of Excellence has been built in Tallinn—but will it and the U.S. National Security Agency (NSA) be able to devise adequate protection and deterrence strategies to fend off attacks on allied electronic installations? And will they balance effective control with respect for the civil liberties of countries' populations?

Over time, as I have argued above, doubts about the credibility of extended deterrence have changed. No longer are NATO members primarily concerned that in case of an emergency allies will not come to their support with superior military forces. Instead, to meet the challenges of terrorism and attacks in space and in the cyber world, the alliance is developing new means and methods for protection. As deterrence now has even more to do with psychology than with military forces, politics will play an increasingly important role. Resolve has become more relevant than capabilities.

In most cases, however, deterrence by denial will be more adequate and acceptable to the population than deterrence by punishment.

To the degree deterrence by punishment is replaced with deterrence by denial, the role of nuclear weapons for other than worst-case scenarios decreases. For protecting the integrity of territory and the well-being of populations, deterrence must be blended with strategies of negotiation and integration. As an alternative to deterring potential adversaries, NATO wants to encourage them to respond positively and be ready for cooperation. The Conference/Organization on Security and Cooperation in Europe has sometimes served as a positive historical example. Blending strategies of denial with cooperative moves will also respond to the aversion of many politicians and publics against a world resting on mutual vulnerability—not by chance, but willingly.[48]

NATO will not be considered insolvent as long as it continues adapting to the new challenges it is confronted with, to the changing priorities of member states, and to the changed meanings of deterrence. If Europe and America remain a single security space, many elements of deterrence—though in different forms and with a reduced reliance on nuclear weapons—will thus survive the end of the East-West conflict.

NOTES

All Web sites last accessed in November 2013.

The author wishes to thank Paal Sigurd Hilde for his thoughtful suggestions and his help in revising this chapter.

1. North Atlantic Treaty Organization, "Active Engagement, Modern Defense: Strategic Concept for the Defense and Security of the Members of the North Atlantic Treaty Organization" (adopted by Heads of State and Government in Lisbon, November 19, 2010), www.nato.int/cps/en/natolive/official_texts_68580 .htm; "Lisbon Summit Declaration" (issued by the Heads of State and Government participating in the meeting of the North Atlantic Council in Lisbon, November 20, 2010), www.nato.int/cps/en/SID-D603755F-789DEF72/natolive/official _texts_68828.htm.

2. North Atlantic Treaty Organization, "Comprehensive Political Guidance" (endorsed by NATO Heads of State and Government on November 29, 2006, Riga, Latvia), http://www.nato.int/cps/en/natolive/official_texts_56425.htm; *Nuclear Posture Review Report (NPR)* (Washington, DC: U.S. Department of Defense, April 2010), www.defense.gov/npr/docs/2010 nuclear posture review report.pdf; North Atlantic Treaty Organization, *NATO 2020: Assured Security, Dynamic Engagement; Analysis and Recommendations of the Group of Experts on a New Strategic Concept for NATO* (Brussels: NATO Public Diplomacy Division, May 17, 2010), http://www .nato.int/cps/en/natolive/official_texts_63654.htm.

3. Thérèse Delpech, *Nuclear Deterrence in the 21st Century. Lessons from the Cold War for a New Era of Strategic Piracy* (Santa Monica, CA: The Rand Corporation 2012), 6.

4. "Letter to Secretary General of NATO from Five Foreign Ministers," February 26, 2010, www.armscontrol.org/system/files/Letter%20to%20Secretary%20 General%20NATO.pdf. See also Sidney D. Drell and James E. Goodby, "Nuclear Deterrence in a Changed World," *Arms Control Today* (June 2012), www.armscontrol .org/act/2012_06/Nuclear_Deterrence_in_a_Changed_World.

5. See Comments by Kiera McCaffrey, "Pushing Reset Button Won't Be Easy for Obama, Russia," *The Hill*, July 3, 2009, thehill.com/homenews/administration /49330-pushing-reset-button-wont-be-easy-for-obama-russia. With Russia granting asylum for the American whistle-blower Eduard Snowden and, in return, President Barack Obama canceling his meeting with President Vladimir Putin, we observe a new cooling of American-Russian relations, even more so after the Ukrainian crisis.

6. North Atlantic Military Committee, "Decision on MC 14/1, 9 December 1952" (Strategy of Massive Retaliation), in *NATO Strategy Documents, 1949–1969*, ed. Gregory F. Pedlow (Brunssum: SHAPE, 1997), 193–228.

7. North Atlantic Treaty Organization, "Medium Term Defense Plan" (Lisbon Force Goals), July 1, 1954, in *NATO Strategy Documents*, ed. Pedlow, 115–77 (177).

8. Albert Wohlstetter, "The Delicate Balance of Terror," *Foreign Affairs* 37, no. 2 (1959): 211–34.

9. North Atlantic Military Committee, "Decision on MC 14/3, 16 January 1968" (Strategy of Flexible Response), in *NATO Strategy Documents*, ed. Pedlow, 345–71.

10. North Atlantic Treaty Organization, "The Future Tasks of the Alliance" (The Harmel Report), Brussels, December 13–14, 1967, in *NATO Handbook: Documentation* (Brussels: NATO Office of Information and Press, 1999), 194–201.

11. Helmut Schmidt, "The 1977 Alastair Buchan Memorial Lecture," *Survival* 20, no. 1 (1978): 2–10.

12. U.S. Diplomatic Mission to Germany, "The Double Track Decision on Theatre Nuclear Forces" (presented at Special Meeting of Foreign and Defense Ministers, Brussels, December 12, 1979), in *NATO Handbook: Documentation*, 202–5.

13. "Declaration on a Transformed North Atlantic Alliance ('The London Declaration'), Issued by the Heads of State and Government Participating in the Meeting of the North Atlantic Council, July 6, 1990," in *NATO Handbook: Documentation*, 271–76.

14. "The Alliance Strategic Concept," Rome, November 8, 1991, in *NATO Handbook: Documentation*, 281–99; "The Alliance's Strategic Concept," Washington, April 23–24, 1999, *NATO Handbook: Documentation*, 406–29.

15. "Founding Act on Mutual Relations, Cooperation and Security between NATO and the Russian Federation," Paris, May 27, 1997, in *NATO Handbook: Documentation*, 127–38.

16. "The North Atlantic Treaty," Washington, April 4, 1949, *in NATO Handbook: Documentation*, 35–39.

17. North Atlantic Treaty Organization, "Prague Summit Declaration" (issued by Heads of State and of Government Participating in the NATO Meeting at Prague, November 21, 2002), www.nato.int/docu/pr/2002/p02-127e.htm.

18. North Atlantic Treaty Organization, "Active Engagement, Modern Defense"; "Lisbon Summit Declaration."

19. "Lisbon Summit Declaration." Following up on this mandate, NATO instituted a DDPR process that reported to the 2012 NATO Chicago Summit. See North Atlantic Treaty Organization, "Deterrence and Defence Posture Review," Chicago, May 20, 2012, www.nato.int/cps/en/natolive/official_texts_87597.htm.

20. "Delaying Decisions: NATO's Deterrence and Defence Posture Review," NTI, May 11, 2012, www.nti.org/analysis/articles/delaying-decisions-natos -deterrence-and-defense-posture-review/.

21. See Bastian Giegerich, "NATO's Smart Defence: Who's Buying?," *Survival* 54, no. 3 (2012): 69–77.

22. "Deterrence and Defence Posture Review"; see also Daniel Painter, "NATO Summit: Deterrence and Defense Review," American Security Project, american securityproject.org/blog/2012/nato-summit-deterrence-and-defense-posture -review/ (last edited May 22, 2012).

23. North Atlantic Treaty Organization, "Summit Declaration on Defence Capabilities: Toward NATO Forces 2020," Chicago, May 20, 2012, www.nato.int /cps/en/natolive/official_texts_87594.htm.

24. U.S. Secretary of State Hillary R. Clinton, speech presented at Tallinn NATO Foreign Ministers Meeting, April 22, 2010; see Oliver Meier, "NATO Chief's Remark Highlights Policy Shift," Arms Control Association, www.armscontrol .org/act/2010_05/NATO.

25. Five foreign ministers to Secretary General of NATO (letter), February 26, 2010, www.armscontrol.org/system/files/Letter to Secretary General NATO.pdf; Arn Specter, "Five NATO States Want U.S. Nukes Out of Europe," *OpEdNews.com*, February 19, 2010, www.opednews.com/Diary/Europe-Wants-US-to-Remove -by-arn-specter-100226-272.html; Ralf Neukirch, "Berlin Takes on Washington: German Foreign Minister Pushes for NATO Nuclear Drawdown," *Spiegel*

Online, February 25, 2010, www.spiegel.de/international/germany/berlin-takes-on
-washington-german-foreign-minister-pushes-for-nato-nuclear-drawdown-a-680
174.html.

26. The White House, Office of the Press Secretary, "Remarks by President Barack Obama," Hradcany Square, Prague, Czech Republic, April 5, 2009, www.whitehouse.gov/the_press_office/Remarks-By-President-Barack-Obama-In-Prague-As-Delivered; "A World Free of Nuclear Weapons, Arguments from a U.S. 'Gang of Four': George Shultz, William Perry, Henry Kissinger and Sam Nunn," *Wall Street Journal*, January 4, 2007, http://online.wsj.com/article/SB116787515251566636.html. These remarks were echoed in Germany by Helmut Schmidt, Richard von Weizsäcker, Egon Bahr, and Hans-Dietrich Genscher in "Für eine atomwaffenfreie Welt," *Frankfurter Allgemeine Zeitung*, January 9, 2009, www.aixpaix.de/atomwaffenfrei/4dtstatesmen.pdf and www.nytimes.com/2009/01/09/opinion/09iht-edschmidt.1.19226604.html. For similar statements see Global Zero Initiative, www.globalzero.org.

27. UK Ministry of Defence, "UK-France Defense Cooperation Treaty Announced," November 2, 2010, www.gov.uk/government/news/uk-france-defence-co-operation-treaty-announced--2.

28. Hans Binnendijk and Catherine McArdle Kelleher, "NATO Reassurance and Nuclear Reductions: Creating the Conditions," in *Reducing Nuclear Risks in Europe: A Framework for Action*, ed. Steve Andreasen and Isabelle Williams (Washington, DC: NTI, 2011), www.nti.org/media/pdfs/NTI_Framework_Chpt5.pdf.

29. U.S. Department of Defense, "Sustaining U.S. Global Leadership: Priorities for 21st Century Defense," January 5, 2012, www.defense.gov/news/Defense_Strategic_Guidance.pdf.

30. *Nuclear Posture Review Report (NPR)*, U.S. Department of Defense, April 2010, www.defense.gov/npr/docs/2010nuclearposturereviewreport.pdf; U.S. Department of Defense, "Report on Nuclear Employment Strategy of the United States Specified in Section 491 of 10 U.S.C.," June 12, 2013, www.globalsecurity.org/wmd/library/policy/dod/us-nuclear-employment-strategy.pdf.

31. Robert Golan-Vilella, "NATO Approves Extended Missile Defense," *Arms Control Today* (December 2010), www.armscontrol.org/act/2010_12/NATO_MissileDefense.

32. Trine Flockard, "Hello Missile Defence—Goodbye Nuclear Sharing?," *DIIS Policy Brief, Defence and Security* (November 2010), subweb.diis.dk/graphics/Publications/PolicyBriefs2010/PB2010-nov-Flockhart-Goodf-Bye-web.pdf.

33. Oliver Meier, "NATO Sets up Arms Control Committee," Arms Control Association, www.armscontrol.org/act/2011_04/NATO; "NAC Taskings to the WMD Control & Disarmament Committee," www.armscontrol.org/system/files/DEU_F_WP.pdf.

34. See "Turkish, French Presidents Row over Iran at NATO Summit," *Hürriyet Daily News*, November 21, 2010, www.hurriyetdailynews.com/n.php?n=gul-sarkozy-spat-tops; "Turkey Unshielded from NATO Debate," *Hürriyet Daily News*, November 21, 2010, www.hurriyetdailynews.com/default.aspx?pageid=438&n=nato-summit-flares-up-new-round-of-turkey-centered-negotiations-2010-11-21.

35. Simon Lunn, "Questions and Issues for NATO," in *Perspectives on NATO Nuclear Policy*, Fondation pour la Recherche Stratégique, Etudes & débats, No. 03/2011, www.frstrategie.org/barreCompetences/proliferations/doc/ED_201103 .pdf.

36. See Supreme Allied Command Transformation, "Findings and Recommendations," in *Multiple Futures Project: Navigating Toward 2030* (Norfolk: Supreme Allied Command Transformation, April 2009), 8.

37. See Alard von Kittlitz, "Stuxnet und der Krieg, der kommt," *Frankfurter Allgemeine Zeitung*, December 4, 2010, 3.

38. North Atlantic Treaty Organization, "NATO-Russia Council Joint Statement," Lisbon, November 20, 2010, www.nato.int/cps/en/natolive/news_68871 .htm.

39. Radio Free Europe, "Open Letter to the Obama Administration from Central and Eastern Europe," July 16, 2009, www.rferl.org/content/An_Open_Letter _To_The_Obama_Administration /1778449.html.

40. See Philipp Rotmann, *Built on Shaky Ground: The Comprehensive Approach in Practice*, NATO Defense College Research Paper no. 63 (Rome: NATO Defense College, December 2010).

41. See Sven Biscop et al., *What Do the Europeans Want from NATO?*, Institute for Security Studies Report no. 8 (Paris: EU, 2010), www.iss.europa.eu/uploads /media/Report_8-What_do_Europeans_want_from_NATO.pdf.

42. See Bastian Giegerich, "NATO's Smart Defence: Who's Buying?," *Survival* 54, no. 3 (2012): 69–77.

43. North Atlantic Treaty Organization, *NATO 2020*.

44. See Thérèse Delpech, *Nuclear Deterrence in the 21st Century. Lessons from the Cold War for a New Era of Strategic Piracy* (Santa Monica, CA.: Rand Corporation 2012), 146–47. NSA's electronic intercepts are also seen as a major threat to citizens' right to privacy and states' autonomous decision making.

45. North Atlantic Treaty Organization, "Deterrence and Defence Posture Review."

46. North Atlantic Treaty Organization, "Summit Declaration on Defense Capabilities."

47. See, for example, Nikolas Busse, "Zeitenwende für die Nato," *Frankfurter Allgemeine Zeitung*, May 22, 2012, 1.

48. Delpech, *Nuclear Deterrence in the 21st Century*, 140.

Chapter 6

When Virtue Is Deceptive

A Critical Look at NATO's Comprehensive Approach

Sten Rynning

NATO, like Odysseus in the ancient world, is struggling to return home after war. Where Odysseus returned from the war for Troy on Andalusia's edge, NATO is returning from "security assistance" in the heart of Asia, in Afghanistan. In both instances the fatigued soldier is beset by dangers and lured by deceptive attractions that could destroy him. Odysseus had to overcome witches, sirens, loving nymphs, and angry gods to make it home to Penelope. He prevailed thanks to godly intervention, but also good fortune. Thus, if Odysseus knew how to charter a course between Scylla and Charybdis, it was because Circe, a witch, told him how to do so, because she had fallen in love with the hero.

NATO is not so lucky. It does not know what the monsters and whirlpools of the future look like, and there is no loving Circe to offer guidance. Moreover, there is no Atlantic Penelope—no safe haven that can serve as a lodestar in turbulent times. Yet there is hope of a sort for the Atlantic alliance as it embarks on its journey: scholars working on the alliance may not possess the bewitching magic of Circe, but their observations should provoke new thinking and clarify the political choices that alliance leaders must make.

It is the conclusion of the analysis offered here that NATO is attracted to a project of inner contradictions: that NATO, whenever it moves into operation outside its territory, must bring together the full menu of civilian and military instruments to ease the pain of the conflict and help bring about desirable outcomes. This project has become NATO's Comprehensive Approach. It has long roots stretching back to the crisis management operations of the 1990s and a great deal of intuitive appeal. It obviously takes broad shoulders and many and varied tools to rebuild other nations, whether in Bosnia, Kosovo, Afghanistan, or elsewhere. And the effort to work with the center of gravity of international organization, the UN Security Council, confers legitimacy. In short, the Comprehensive Approach is apparently what NATO needed from day one in Afghanistan, and it is what it needs in the future: a broad, civil-military toolbox defined in partnership with a wide variety of countries and organizations.

The inner contradiction is plainly visible in Afghanistan, however. Comprehensive Approaches are slow in coming and leave broad and bloody campaigns dangerously adrift. Some might dismiss the Afghan case as deviant: good theory but wrong theater. That would be foolhardy. Afghanistan illuminates a general problem: Comprehensive Approaches have abundant intuitive appeal but contain no strategy of action. Such an approach ties people and organizations together but does not tell them what will happen when the grid locks. It is bereft of the political leadership that can question the feasibility and rationale of the campaign, which in the case of Afghanistan concerns the decision to build up the "Bonn republic" that resulted from the Bonn conference in 2001. The problem in Afghanistan has not been one of insufficient comprehensive action but rather of insufficient leadership in questioning the political viability of this republic, which has to do with Afghan corruption but also the privileging of personal relations over the development of political institutions and, relatedly, the missing effort to reconcile with Taliban forces. As these issues are intractable, it is not surprising that Afghan leaders have skirted them. More surprising is the reluctance of NATO nations. Rather than critically evaluating the purpose of their mission, NATO nations and partners have preferred to invest in the Bonn republic as outlined in the "Afghan Compact" and "National Development Strategy." The levels of money, manpower, and firepower put on offer have surged accordingly. In essence, it has proven easier and less controversial to ramp up on resources (means) than to address the viability of the deal made in Bonn back in 2001 (ends). That is poor strategy, obviously, and it appears to be a generic challenge in comprehensive actions.

The operational inclusion of multiple actors—with multiple ways of doing things and multiple interests—precludes a critical review of ends, because an end above reproach is a precondition for the campaign's much-wanted "unity of effort." In Afghanistan this end became the Bonn republic; in Libya in 2011 it became the "responsibility to protect" civilians. Neither of these offers a view of how international efforts (means) can connect to feasible political bargains for stability in these countries (ends). It is a simple question of strategic capacity, even though strategy in practice is hard to do. In consequence, NATO should face the requirement for globalized networking with sanguine thinking and develop and protect its capacity to make hard political decisions—not only under duress in campaigns but also in regard to the emerging architecture of consultative partnerships.[1] It is a question of clarifying the utility of networks to the alliance rather than networking in the belief that connections confer purpose.

New NATO: Global and Political

The basic and entirely reasonable contention in NATO's Brussels headquarters is that if the collective organization—the decision-making council and the remainder of the political-military (pol-mil) organization—does not address the main concerns of the capitals, NATO has no future. NATO leaders therefore periodically agree to major upgrades, which then become focal points for alliance renewal and indeed transformation. The London Summit of June 1990 promised a new NATO for a new continent; the Berlin North Atlantic Council meeting of June 1996 NATO-EU synergy; the Washington Summit of April 1999 a capable security organization; the Prague Summit of November 2002 "transformation" in almost every respect to counter terrorism; and finally, the Lisbon Summit of November 2010 heralded yet another new and globally focused NATO.

The latest surge in NATO transformation is rooted in the conviction that NATO must become both more global and political.[2] It is appropriate because the main threats—from international terrorism to proliferation and cyber security—are inherently global and overwhelmingly political in character. To create and nourish this surge, NATO leaders have sought to present this "new NATO" in opposition to the NATO of 1991–2010. It takes considerable imagination to thus lump twenty years of post–Cold War NATO into one image that somehow stands in contrast to a new and more global and political alliance, but imagination is the stuff of politics.

The internal balance of viewpoints among allies traditionally poses a challenge to drivers of NATO reform. Typically, some allies labor for change, others resist, and reform grinds to a halt. Reformers have for the past couple of decades been the allies with stakes outside allied territory, led by the United States and supported by a host of allies located on or close to the Atlantic seaboard. Other allies may be Atlantic minded but are located in proximity to past and present threats—from Russia to the Middle East—and are therefore overwhelmingly concerned with NATO's geographical "approaches." Global and political NATO as a key priority or an appendix—this is the controversial question. The divide has *not* significantly impacted the making of a more networked and extroverted alliance, however, and there are several distinct reasons for this.

First, NATO's main stake in the fight against terrorism—the Afghan ISAF campaign—is the next best thing to an Article V operation. True, it is not strictly an Article 5 operation—that would be the surveillance mission in the Mediterranean, Operation Active Endeavor—but NATO's vast efforts in Afghanistan are intrinsically tied to the September 11, 2001, attacks on the United States that in the first place provoked NATO's activation of its Article 5. In effect, therefore, Afghanistan belies the earlier idea that out-of-area was non-Article 5 and therefore of less value to the alliance. In fact, "out-of-area" has become a misnomer now that NATO views its Article 5 commitment outside geographical constraints.[3]

Second, the security environment is dominated by various transnational threats that deny validity to old categories of thought. The Strategic Concept of NATO details a number of these threats, from the proliferation of weapons of mass destruction as well as conventional weapons to terrorism, trafficking, extremism, and cyber attacks.[4] The post–Cold War alliance members—traditionally proponents of regional NATO—have been affected by these threats as much as other allies.

Finally, the military means with which NATO must work are one and the same: expeditionary forces capable of deploying out of their home countries and sustaining themselves abroad. This goes for the defense of Turkey or Norway as well as for intervention in Afghanistan or Sudan. It provides for conceptual stability in the domain of military planning, allows NATO to use contingency planning to reassure worried allies (i.e., in proximity to Russia), and furthermore allows NATO to channel organizational energy into the opening of planning procedures to nonmilitary and non-NATO organizations. It enhances NATO's operational impact and serves the "cooperative security tasks" outlined in the Strategic Concept.[5]

If long-standing cleavages within the alliance did not play out as could have been expected in regard to "new NATO"—NATO 3.0—it could be because change was rooted in two decades' worth of reflection and critical debate that, following some turbulence, resulted in a real consensus for change by 2009–2010. It was always clear from the beginning of the terrorist age, in 2001, that NATO would have to globalize to remain relevant. The decade of the 1990s had made it clear that crises cannot be solved with military means alone, and the 2002 Prague Summit prolonged the debate on missions, partners, and capabilities, but now in the context of global terror and NATO's "transformation." However, change proved easier to announce than to implement. At the Riga Summit in November 2006, two important symbols of frustrated desire for improvement were evident. One related to the Strategic Concept, which was widely felt to be in need of revision but was hostage to disagreement. NATO settled for a Comprehensive Political Guidance, which, as the name indicates, was fairly strong on military guidance but weak on political principles. The other symbol related to the Comprehensive Approach, which NATO for the first time recognized as a necessity, promising to seek civil-military cooperation and partnership with other institutions. However, the text providing for this approach was convoluted even by NATO standards, reflecting suspicion among key allies that some were trying to expand the alliance into domains where they would rather not see it go.[6]

Still, for all the controversies and stalled planning, NATO's agenda was increasingly defined by global and political imperatives. President George W. Bush pushed an agenda of liberty that knew no borders, but this was controversial. NATO awaited the dying days of the Bush presidency before it could agree to begin the revising of its strategic purpose. It would pull NATO in a global direction, but hopefully now without all the controversy.

NATO kicked off the revision with a short and crisp declaration issued at the 2009 summit. The declaration quickly dealt with the European scene and then focused attention on global interconnections: new security challenges, strategic distance, and new partnerships.[7] This was followed by an advisory expert group headed by Madeleine Albright, which presented its advisory conclusions in May 2010 and observed NATO's balance between "assured security" at home and "dynamic engagement" in the world, but also concluded that if NATO always had the former, it needed more of the latter. It would require NATO to greatly expand its partnership policy, to which the expert group dedicated a full section, and "at all levels" to prepare for "integrated civil-military missions."[8] What followed from this "dynamic engagement" vision was NATO's new Strategic Concept in November 2010, the cornerstone of "NATO 3.0."

I shall have more to say about the Strategic Concept later. At this point we should take note of the momentum this more global and political vision had gathered up through the 2000s, overcoming the severe crisis of confidence inspired by the "War on Terror," and how it got anchored in new strategic thinking in late 2010. The sum total is a certain experience and sense of purpose that make it all the harder to argue in opposition to new NATO. Yet by way of an Afghan reality check, a note of caution is warranted.

An Afghan Reality Check

Afghanistan is a window on the Comprehensive Approach because it inspires that approach and has become a critical test bed. Admittedly, Afghanistan fits the adage Winston Churchill ascribed to Russia—a riddle wrapped in a mystery inside an enigma—and it may not be the ideal test for the Comprehensive Approach policy. However, the Western campaign there reveals flaws that are general and therefore fundamentally worrisome.

The flaw becomes apparent when we regard the vehicle of civil-military cooperation and delivery on the ground—the provincial reconstruction teams (PRTs). They are in their terminal phase given the transition to Afghan leadership and ownership, which will be completed by the end of 2014. The PRT experience reveals the following lessons: the Western allies lacked a concept of intervention and simply picked up what was already there; they could not manage to establish effective mechanisms of coordination once on the ground, which is to say develop the concept; and they leave Afghanistan without an uncontested concept to build on in the future. Some improvements were made along the way, as we shall see, but the consistent lack of integrated thinking must in no small part be attributed to a wide and wavering strategic framework.

NATO came into Afghanistan thinking that the mission was one of "security assistance" to the government. There simply was no NATO concept for delivering civil-military services—security, governance, and development; NATO was security focused and moreover assumed a benevolent environment, even as the need to expand the mission geographically was fairly well understood. The PRTs became a stepping-stone for the alliance in the fall of 2003, as it had to design a policy for moving the ISAF campaign out of Kabul. The only model on the ground was the American one, invented during the early phase of the Afghan campaign—the PRT. Germany provided the bridge between this model and NATO when in October 2003 it agreed to become the lead nation of ISAF's expansion and take over the American PRT in Kunduz. In the course of 2004 and 2005 the PRTs became the NATO/ISAF campaign's acclaimed leading edge.

It is curious to note that the communiqué of the July 2010 Kabul conference, the occasion for agreeing to transition and thus foreseeing the end to the combat mission by 2014, makes no mention of the PRTs at all. However, the PRTs remained important for the international community and also as stepping-stones for transition. The transition strategy presented and agreed to at the Kabul conference—as defined in the transition paper "Inteqal"—builds on PRTs. It foresees a four-stage process beginning with full civilian leadership in all PRTs and ending with Afghan ownership.[9] The PRTs were thus designated containers for Afghan capacity building, if all goes according to plan.

Moreover, the PRTs continue to matter for the lessons one can learn from the campaign. To a degree they are symbols of NATO adaptability; after all, what was foreign to NATO in 2002 soon became an operational centerpiece. However, some issues must be kept in mind. NATO's operational centerpiece in many ways continued to be military operations. This happened because the insurgents were smart and because NATO forces were ill prepared for their resilience and generally were too few for the job. Moreover, the civilian organizations that could take the development-governance lead did not appear, and meanwhile NATO/ISAF combat missions kept growing. Finally, NATO allies and partners never found a way to meaningfully coordinate their PRTs. The international-Afghan Joint Coordination and Management Board (JCMB) that from 2006 on was to drive the implementation of the National Development Strategy proved woefully inadequate. Later improvements should be placed in a larger context that begins with the PRT itself.

The PRT concept originated in the ranks of the first American troops deployed to Afghanistan in 2001–2002. These first troops brought with them certain limited means to do "quick impact projects" that by way of civilian engagement would create safe zones for the armed forces. As it became apparent that more things needed doing and that civilian engagement was an end in itself, the American forces shifted to a territorially focused organization—whereby forces would be concerned with stability within their "area of operation" as much as with chasing bandits—that invited a new approach to civil-military coordination on the ground. This at first became joint regional teams and then the PRT.

The improvements that later came about concern the establishment of the PRT Steering Committee in early 2008 and the reinforcement of NATO's Senior Civilian Representative (SCR) in Afghanistan in early 2010. The committee was a response to an obvious vacuum of coordination and the dysfunctional joint international-Afghan board; the reinforced SCR was a response to NATO's wider engagement in the transition strategy that the Obama administration was driving. These measures never really lifted the PRT concept above the military mold from which it had emerged, though. The SCR track came late. The reinforced SCR post—which was in British hands from January 2010 to October 2012, with Simon Gass taking over from Mark Sedwill in mid-April 2011, and then in Dutch hands, with the appointment of Maurits Jochems—was important in shaping the PRT component of the "Inteqal" strategy. However, the transition train soon picked up such speed that coordinated PRT development became nearly impossible. Past the Kabul Summit of 2010, the overriding issue was transition more than coordination, quite simply.

Looking further back, PRT steering was good in theory but ineffective in practice, and the fault lay at the strategic level of operations. First of all, the PRTs were nationally owned and operated, and NATO never got command of them. The allies investing in PRTs were therefore to a great extent free to shape their individual teams idiosyncratically, leaving the hard work of coordination to a NATO-run chain of command without experience and real prerogatives.[10] The security forces of the PRTs fell under the chain of command, it should be noted, but national caveats and an untested and incomplete concept of operations made central command difficult. National ownership of PRTs continued to bedevil the operation, moreover. The reinforced SCR could have done more to drive the "Inteqal" strategy had he had more say over the PRTs, but he did not, of course. He was left with two PRTs highly receptive to his agenda, the ones in Helmand and Kandahar, and with various PRTs whose agendas were compatible with the "Inteqal" strategy in many ways but whose missions and operations were defined primarily in a national context.

The second dimension of the strategic problem concerns relations among, notably, NATO, the UN, and Afghan president Karzai. Everyone has wanted to be in the lead, and no one has trusted the others to lead effectively, to put it bluntly. NATO and the UN did come together in late 2007 around the idea that the NATO SCR and the UN Special Representative should be fused into a single and effective mechanism of civilian coordination—the equivalent of a development czar. Paddy Ashdown was the designated appointee. However, fearing strong intervention, President Karzai vetoed the idea, which then collapsed.

The new UN Special Representative instead became Kai Eide. He saw it as his task to provide the coordination that had been on the table in 2007 and had resulted in the Steering Committee. However, Eide saw it as his mission to oppose the campaign's "militarization," and he never managed to organize a working relationship with the military mission, ISAF. The proposal for coordination he developed in the latter half of 2008 was laborious and tended to engender ISAF hostility. When Eide moreover could not mobilize resources from UN headquarters, the plan fell apart. The baton was passed to President Obama, who took office in January 2009 and in the course of that year engaged in two major Afghanistan policy reviews. The PRTs did not at any point figure prominently in these reviews. Rather, the military and civilian surge that President Obama led was militarily channeled through ISAF/NATO but otherwise mostly through an enhanced American Kabul embassy. The United States moved into the lead, and other actors, whether in NATO or the UN, settled for influencing American—in addition to Afghan—decision making.[11]

What lessons can one draw from this experience? One is that the Comprehensive Approach never took off in Afghanistan. There has been much talk and some degree of improved coordination, but the blueprint for coordinated and integrated action remains largely a blueprint. Another is that the slow pace of improvement is due to a lack of strategic understanding between the major capitals and headquarters (i.e., the UN, the EU, and NATO), which in turn raises the question of whether the work in progress will ever be completed.

Dispute and disagreement between NATO capitals account for the weak footing of the original ISAF PRTs. They were in effect designed to work according to the wishes and assumptions of a majority of NATO allies, not according to reality on the ground. At some point allied relations improved, but NATO-UN relations then deteriorated. The two organizations had a turbulent history that fueled a degree of mistrust, and in late 2008 it proved impossible for the two General Secretaries—Jaap de Hoop Scheffer and Ban-ki Moon—to have their organizations come together in principle.[12] In practice, on the ground things were no better because UNAMA-ISAF relations turned sour on the issue of Eide's approach and plan for coordination.

Afghanistan as a window on the problems inherent in the Comprehensive Approach thus calls attention to deep-seated political problems that must be dealt with for the approach to work. In a NATO lens one is led to ask two questions: How solid in terms of political alignment is NATO's internal understanding of the Comprehensive Approach? What can NATO do to improve this understanding and thus its capacity for action? The next two sections deal with these questions.

Comprehensive Approach Origins: Necessity Barely Trumps Division

A review of the origins of the Comprehensive Approach reveals that NATO was never firmly united around the idea. It emerged from a variety of operational experiences, political designs for influence, and a measure of distrust that proved hard to dissipate. Riga was where NATO committed to the idea, as we saw, in 2006. Afghanistan was a strong driver because the ISAF campaign had at that point moved into the south and east of the country, and everyone knew that trouble was brewing. NATO's Operational Plan foresaw combat-like situations, and NATO/ISAF rules of engagement were in the spring of 2006 adapted accordingly. There was disagreement between the allies moving down south and those watching from the north and west, but everyone agreed that an immense and combined security-development-governance challenge awaited ISAF. It made sense, therefore, to invite the wider international community to take part in the effort.

The Balkan missions of the 1990s, notably the IFOR/SFOR experience in Bosnia, which began in December 1995, and the KFOR experience in Kosovo, which began in 1999, had prepared the groundwork. NATO's mission mind-set changed as it engaged in crisis management in addition to "real" war. However, the alliance in the Balkans was there to do security only; it left development and governance issues to the UN and the EU and was famously restrained in the search for war criminals, whose arrest might advance new governance but also momentarily upset security. In Kosovo in June 1999, NATO sought to hand off the operation quite quickly to the UN. This was partly to compensate for the fact that the alliance had fought the air war without an explicit Security Council mandate, but it also reflected the alliance's discomfort with broad and comprehensive missions.

Between Kosovo and Riga the ground for change was prepared inside the alliance, but it was also clear that change would not be easy. One problem was coordination. Individual NATO nations had not stood idly by but had begun the development of national approaches to the comprehensive challenge. Everyone had been prodded into action by the Balkans; others were pushed further by their early engagements in Afghanistan and then also Iraq. The outcome was a multiplicity of "comprehensive" planning.

This complicated matters because collective work could not start from scratch. A compromise among "best" but disparate practices was necessary. Naturally the allies who had advanced the farthest in the domain were those who most keenly felt the heat of Afghan war—the United States, Great Britain, the Netherlands, Canada, and also Denmark. They all invested in the civil-military bedrock of the ISAF campaign—the PRTs—and sought to derive lessons learned.

The door was not simply wide open for these allies, because in Brussels politics mattered. Some allies, led by Germany, were uncomfortable with the military intrusion into a civilian domain they knew well. Other allies, led by France, worried about political prerogatives. If NATO gained a civilian dimension, it might come at the expense of the EU, which France hoped would develop an autonomous security capacity. It would take a double round of agenda setting and considerable delay before political conditions clarified to the point where NATO actually developed a policy on the issue. This still did not mean that NATO could implement a Comprehensive Approach; this was the vision. It merely meant that NATO agreed to work on it.

Agenda setting first came from the aforementioned small but engaged ally, Denmark. In 2004 the Danish government wrote to the Secretary General of NATO to enlist his support for a major initiative, which then resulted in the organization of a high-profile Comprehensive Approach (then labeled Comprehensive Planning and Action, CPA) conference in Copenhagen in June 2005. It was now on NATO's agenda. However, the momentum soon stopped.

Conditions in Denmark partly account for this. The project was not sufficiently integrated across the defense and foreign ministries—which was ironic, of course, given the emphasis of the Comprehensive Approach—and subsequent to the conference the major drivers were located in the defense ministry (which needed the initiative to help the soldiers), whereas the foreign ministry, the NATO policy lead, pushed the break (perceiving the many problems in the alliance) and wanted other allies to step in and take the lead.

The alliance patron, the United States, was not particularly willing. It had its own concepts—Effects Based Operations (EBO), COIN, and S&R—and needed to sort them out before buying into a NATO CPA. There were many other items on NATO's agenda, moreover, all captured by the "transformation" agenda defined in Prague in 2002. NATO needed new and stronger expeditionary forces, and it needed to develop "usability" goals to drive this process forward. Developing a civilian dimension might easily detract from the effort and sow new seeds of confusion.

The head of NATO, Secretary General de Hoop Scheffer, could have picked up the CPA following Copenhagen and become its entrepreneur. However, at this point he was about two years into his tenure as Secretary General, bruised by the Afghan mission. He had run a high-profile diplomatic campaign to have allies step up to their own Afghan commitments and commit forces. This was no easy task, and de Hoop Scheffer had to be insistent and at times adopt a high profile. Some referred to his campaign as "name and shame"; he himself has referred to the repeated use of the "begging bowl" to get the alliance into gear. [13]

The experience of leading NATO through 2004–2005 and ISAF's expansion had thus been particularly difficult, and the last thing the

Secretary General needed in 2005–2006 was another intractable issue on his agenda. In consequence, and to protect the Secretary General, his private office declined following Copenhagen to put the CPA on his desk. In short, it was up to the member-states to drive the process. The issue was not formally on NATO's agenda; there was no "tasking" to lead the international staff, and there was no consensus or silence that reluctant nations would have to break in order to raise objections. The latter had it easy, therefore. France, Germany, and Belgium were in the lead in the opposition, and they could effortlessly control the occasional roundtable discussion inside the headquarters.

The game changer between Copenhagen in June 2005 and the Riga Summit in November 2006 was Afghanistan. Given the bloody reality of moving into Afghanistan's south and east, it became impossible not to address comprehensive cooperation among NATO, the UN, and others. The big nations therefore moved. A French-American compromise can be read into the Riga text. The United States gained NATO initiative, having accepted the "comprehensive" language, and France gained NATO's promise not to invade EU territory. This was the second round of agenda setting, this time in formal terms.

It took another year and a half for NATO to develop a policy, the Comprehensive Approach Action Plan adopted at the Bucharest Summit in April 2008. The interim was marked by the three principled positions already noted: the American desire to activate NATO, the French reluctance to move NATO into new domains, and the German fear that security policy might be militarized. Secretary General de Hoop Scheffer became a policy advocate through this process, which was natural given the Riga formal tasking. His position was forceful, and he emerged as a strong advocate for the view that NATO could not do everything on its own; it was dependent on broad cooperation. NATO remained a security organization; its business was not development and governance. He thus protected NATO as a security agent, and he became instrumental in engineering the comprehensive agenda of Bucharest, which, as discussed in the preceding section, now has blossomed into a global and political agenda for NATO.

The slow progress on the CPA shows that policy engineers such as a small ally or the Secretary General can only do so much; the big allies retain the power to move the alliance. The action plan of Bucharest in 2008 resulted in comprehensive planning inside the NATO organization, but the underlying policy purpose was not there. Everyone could subscribe to "cooperation," but there was not one predominant view of what it meant. This helps explain why the Comprehensive Approach made no real imprint on the Afghan campaign. The question is therefore whether the allies can come to a new and firmer agreement that involves partners and anchors the Comprehensive Approach in solid political soil. If not, comprehensive action will remain a hope, which is a dangerous foundation for military operations.

Beyond Hope? Preconditions for a Real Policy

I begin this forward-looking assessment with the 2010 Strategic Concept, which involves three tasks: collective defense, security through crisis management, and cooperative security. They are placed on a par but entail distinct modes of operation. In respect to crisis management, NATO emphasizes its willingness to actively engage with other actors "before, during and after crises to encourage collaborative analysis, planning, and conduct of activities on the ground."[14] From this follows the principle that NATO will be *in the lead* when the going gets rough but otherwise act in a *supporting* role.[15]

In today's hybrid wars, phases are difficult to distinguish and resources hard to come by, so NATO takes the further step of outlining a set of new initiatives:[16]

> Intelligence sharing and doctrinal development;
> A "modest" civilian crisis management capability within NATO to man-
> age activities until they can be transferred to other actors;
> Enhanced integrated civilian-military planning;
> Enhanced capability to train local security forces;
> A capability to identify and train civilian specialists from member states
> made available for rapid deployment; and
> Intensified political consultations.

Behind this agenda of change lies a policy crisis. NATO wants to develop a "modest" organizational capability, because it has not been able to rely on cooperation with others in Afghanistan and also because its PRT coordination was insufficient. A crisis at headquarters-to-headquarters level, principally among NATO, the EU, and the UN, has led NATO to beef up its own organization. NATO wants to transfer the lead to these organizations as soon as possible—which forms part of the Franco-American dialogue on this issue—but everyone can see the deeper policy crisis. Thus, even the detractors of NATO activism in this domain have come to acknowledge that it must prepare civilian specialists from within its own ranks for rapid deployment, though this is framed as a voluntary initiative.

NATO's ambition to train local security forces runs in the same complicated vein. These forces are the ultimate ticket home for NATO—because it is the security lead and merely acting in support of development and governance. We should not be surprised that NATO allies do not want to leave this return ticket in the hands of others—say, in the hands of other regional organizations or a UN agency. Even so, the training of other forces forms part of the greater complex of "security sector reform," which if applied in its full logic requires the kind of networked action that is the theory of the Comprehensive Approach.

There is thus tension between building a capacity to gain leverage, on the one hand, and making investments in tools that by nature are networked, on the other. This tension cannot be overcome, but it can be alleviated. It will require greater investments in NATO's own leadership capacity, which is to say capacity to mobilize its own resources, shape security thinking across the NATO-EU divide, and clarify the alliance's own strategic priorities. I look at these preconditions in turn.

The NATO Organization

NATO continues to be a primarily military organization, which is capped off with an international staff and political leadership. To get the Comprehensive Approach going within its own ranks—to really develop a new "operational culture"[17]—NATO must change its own ways: it must make civil-military coordination an organizational standard, anchor civil-military planning in a visible unit, and encourage its people to develop the career profile that NATO needs.

Civil-military coordination is best promoted as an organizational standard if the divide between the International Staff (IS) and the International Military Staff (IMS) is erased and the civilian and military staffers are integrated up and down the lines of policy and operational planning. This idea was on the table in 2010 but did not gain sufficient traction, and it is in any case open to question about exactly how such major organizational reform should be carried out. Still, it seems a precondition for changing the organizational mind-set.

Another related precondition is to establish a NATO equivalent of the UK Stabilization Unit.[18] It should become host to new doctrinal development, just as it should be responsible for civil-military planning and training—all of which are emphasized in the Strategic Concept. It should liaise with member-state units, because member-states provide the forces, thus becoming an internal hub of alliance development, and it should provide fast-track career opportunities to attract the best and brightest and become an engine of cultural change.[19]

If NATO does not create such mechanisms for changing its own mindset and developing real organizational planning and training capacities, it will not effectively gain a capacity for action. This capacity is important not only for NATO's operational weight, but also as a means for aligning the national interagency policy packages that are under development and in refinement.

Of course it is possible that NATO will renege on its ambition and go back to its predominantly military ways. The 2011 intervention in Libya was perhaps an indicator thereof: all military action, no comprehensive stability operation. However, this is tantamount to setting itself up for failure. Air wars are very limited policy instruments that do not clean up the mess on the ground (they are either followed by local turbulence, as in Libya, or by long-term stability operations, as in Kosovo). Unless NATO plans on being the air wing or perhaps navy of some other organization, it will want to develop this expeditionary capacity to connect land force to stabilization and training. These operations are inherently difficult, but the proper response is organizational development as outlined here, and then political clarification, to which we now turn.

NATO-EU Relations

European allies are challenged by a number of geopolitical developments, in particular by turmoil in North Africa and the Middle East, as well as the U.S. decision to lower its security engagement in Europe. The United States is not abandoning Europe, but it is cutting its forward deployed forces—among them two combat brigades—and upgrading its focus on Asian geopolitics. This shift should cause Europeans to clarify their priorities, including NATO-EU relations.

If comprehensive action hitherto has lacked political direction, it is important that NATO-EU controversies do not linger to undercut the operations that Europeans manage to launch in response to these external challenges—that political direction in Europe be clarified. This does not have to involve a consensus on Europe's future, which is not possible to achieve, but it should involve a more pragmatic approach to institutional relations and then also an enhanced diplomatic effort to establish some foreign policy priorities that cut across NATO and the EU. North Africa is where this effort should begin. In 2011 NATO bombed Colonel Qad-dafi's Libyan regime out of power; in 2013 France led a coalition into Mali to counter a fundamentalist surge that threatened to install a new radical regime; and the wider Sahel region continues to be plagued by conflicts over identities and resources. These conflicts cut across borders, so much so that the intervention in Libya helped engender the turmoil that enabled the Mali surge, which necessitated a renewed intervention and ended up pushing extremists back into neighboring countries.[20] It is possible to cast the net wider still. Al Qaeda and its affiliates may look to the Sahel as a pre-ferred area of operation because they have been pushed out of Afghanistan, Pakistan, and the Arab peninsula, save for pockets in Yemen.

NATO-EU relations enter into this because the same set of member-states must confront these challenges, and because one of the pivotal states is Turkey. Turkey is a member of NATO but a controversial candidate for the EU, and combined with the Cyprus issue it has created institutional gridlock. NATO's Secretary General sought at one point in 2009–2010 to solve issues by stealth—by entering into practical security agreements and gaining Turkey's association with the European Defence Agency—but the effort came to naught. It is an issue of high politics. Turkey is active in the wider region—it has engineered a regional dialogue on Afghanistan, the Istanbul process; it resisted the interventions in Libya and Mali; and it has become an active opponent of Bashar al-Assad in Syria's civil war—and will continue to oppose the idea that "Europe" can run foreign affairs outside due consideration of Turkey's priorities. This goes for EU foreign policy and also European-led NATO, as in Libya. Moreover, given the aforementioned trends in the region, the Turkish-American relationship is likely to remain a priority for Washington.

The key for Europeans will be to focus on these issues *outside* institutional confines. Given the intractable nature of these problems and the difficulty of improvising policy, the temptation will be strong to fall back on institutions. This temptation is to remain focused on the world as it looks from within NATO and the EU, respectively, which will reveal different empha-ses on geopolitics and multilateralism, and then pretend that differences can be smoothed over by way of organizational partnering and networking. It would be the Comprehensive Approach without political priorities, and it would be a rerun of what has happened in Afghanistan. Europe should begin with priorities, and to establish them it will be necessary to engender foreign policy debate across borders and institutions. This can only happen incre-mentally, and with difficulty, one might venture, but a common NATO-EU initiative to foster such debate could be a place to start.

NATO's Strategic Mind-Set

Major military operations will require the involvement of the United States, given the state of military affairs in Europe, so NATO will continue to remain an operational cornerstone. The two preceding sections touched on NATO's organization and its European dimension, respectively. This section discusses the question of political agreement across the Atlantic. Afghanistan illustrated the dangers of lacking such agreement when undertaking military operations: the operation divides into separate parts (i.e., ISAF vs. OEF), and the ambition to enlarge the scope and resources of the campaign becomes the best way to avoid questions related to its purpose (i.e., the Comprehensive Approach as bad strategy). NATO can deliver strategy, both in the matching of ends and means and in the ability to adjust operational course in response to conditions on the ground, but this presupposes Atlantic coherence.

It has become a truism that to win a fight, you must know yourself and your enemy. One might add that in the day and age of comprehensive action, you should know not only yourself and your enemy but also your partners. Be that as it may, the challenge is to define the interests that one has at stake in an operation so that they can serve as a strategic anchor when complications arise and outsiders call for expanded investments. It is possible that NATO interests can be reconciled with that of the wider international community, but it will require this kind of reflection on interests.

Does NATO know itself well enough to define its own interests? The Strategic Concept and the Expert Group's report that prepared it provide ambiguous answers. There is a definite sense of process—as in NATO moving from being regional and military to becoming global and political. But there is little sense of being. The obvious answers to what NATO *is* do not appear in these official texts: it could be NATO as the West, the Atlantic Community, or a Liberal Democratic club. It is not difficult to understand why NATO eschews the challenge of defining its political core: it is hard to do for an alliance of twenty-eight nations. It is not only that the allies are in doubt; they also worry about outside repercussions. The Western label might antagonize China and Russia, the Atlantic label could be interpreted to exclude Poland and other Central European nations, and non-NATO liberal democracies such as Australia might question NATO's appropriation of the liberal label. Thinking in terms of process is diplomatically sanguine, because it leaves sore spots such as these to be massaged.

Like the EU, NATO is not about to reach consensus on its basic purpose. NATO is a geopolitical patchwork stitched together by experience and national interests, and multiple purposes come with this territory. The 2010 Strategic Concept is a case in point. It not only placed three strategic tasks on a par—collective defense, crisis management, and partnering—but placed old and new threats on a par within the collective defense pillar. Still, there are some limits to the elasticity of the alliance, and this is where renewed thinking on "who" the alliance is could take place. One limit concerns the United States and its European engagement. Without it, there would be no Atlantic alliance. Another limit concerns NATO-UN relations and NATO's continuing reluctance to define itself as simply another regional organization under the UN Charter.[21] If it did, it would be subject to UN Security Council oversight and control, and it would cease to be an alliance.

These two dimensions of the Atlantic community define the boundaries within which NATO can define its interests once a crisis emerges and an operation is launched. It is a truism that events drive policy and sometimes drive it off course—which is what British prime minister Harold Macmillan once quipped. NATO will react to events, and events will shape NATO's thinking. Still, as NATO leaders react to these events, they should keep in mind the outer boundaries. The role of the United States in Europe should lead them to think about the nature of an operational partnership—as opposed to U.S. policy defined in isolation and European instincts for criticizing without investing. The role of NATO vis-à-vis the UN should lead it to think about the "international community" as something that is desirable but also bereft of operational leadership, and thus to ponder the extent to which operational stakes are worth international criticism. If they are not, then maybe the operation is poorly defined and should be revised, if not abandoned.

Conclusion

Expeditionary warfare is made up of grueling efforts in the bloody business of coercion and punishment in areas far from home. It is hard to return home from efforts such as these and simply resume business as usual. If this to some degree was possible for Odysseus, it was in no small part due to his wife, Penelope. Besieged by suitors, she kept them at bay with her canny skill in never finishing a certain burial shroud, thus maintaining a home worth its name. For NATO there is inspiration to draw from Penelope's steadfastness and commitment to inner values.

The conundrum of the Comprehensive Approach—and thus the model of connectivity and networked governance that is in vogue—concerns political priorities and leadership. Absent leadership and the identification of political goals, the Comprehensive Approach is simply the full-scale effort to rebuild nations and states top-down and bottom-up. It is beyond the means of everyone, and its pursuit will lead to overstretching and frustration, then in turn to political radicalization. In contrast, leadership comes from knowledge of inner values and the contemplation of the interests they feed in an operational environment. Leadership is to drive comprehensive actions in a certain direction and for a certain purpose.

NATO is a composite of nations, and it does learn lessons the way that individuals or individual nations do. It is not clear what lessons NATO is learning in respect to operations and its Comprehensive Approach. On the one hand, there is a push for more Comprehensive Approach capacity in so far as it has become a strategic priority, with the 2010 Strategic Concept, and in so far as NATO is seeking to embed its expeditionary experience from Afghanistan in new initiatives such as "connected forces" and flexible partnerships. This could signal that NATO post-Afghanistan will retain its Afghan capacity to be on the move and to work with partners. In terms of the theme of this book, it would herald continuity in out-of-area ambitions. However, there is also a push in the inverse direction. In fact, there are two. One is the push for a politically partnered NATO that will help the big NATO nations manage relations with rising powers in Asia in particular.[22] This would be political and global NATO justified by global geopolitics; the NATO of complex crisis management operations would whither on account of the lessons of the travails of land warfare in Afghanistan and also Iraq. Another push is for a return to the alliance's military virtues. This would be the NATO of the Libya operation in 2011: militarily sharp but with no ambition to establish a follow-on "security assistance" mission. It would pull NATO in a regional direction focused on hard threats in the neighborhood, where the other pull of political engagement would globalize NATO, but outside the debate on out-of-area operations.

The Comprehensive Approach became NATO policy because of Afghanistan. There were many lessons from the 1990s that pointed in the direction of comprehensive action, but politically it took Afghanistan and especially the war for Afghanistan's south and east to shake the alliance and open it to a policy initiative. It became a policy initiative in 2006, a policy in 2008, and a strategic task in 2010. If Afghanistan has been so important for this drive, it is possible that NATO post-Afghanistan will let the initiative wither. There are conflicting views on this within the alliance. For now, and as it contemplates its future, the alliance should heed two general lessons that come out of the Comprehensive Approach experience.

One concerns the tendency to compartmentalize issues and argue that the Comprehensive Approach is for crisis management only; if NATO post-Afghanistan will be less focused on such management, there is apparently no need to worry too much about the lessons that comprehensive action is only possible if infused with a distinct set of political priorities and a capacity for adjusting them as the campaign unfolds. However, this is a generic issue of leadership, and it would be a mistake to limit it to crisis management. Leadership—the process through which leading allies have the North Atlantic Council take control of operations—should be inherent to all missions. NATO's lack of collective and strategic leadership in a mission as important as the one in Afghanistan—where NATO's engagement was massive and dangerous for troops as well as the alliance as a whole—goes to show that the problem is general. Moreover, the fact that Western troops are now engaged in security assistance in Mali goes to show that the option of restricting leadership to narrow military engagements such as the one in Libya is really a false one. At the heart of current out-of-area challenges, therefore, lies the difficulty of defining political priorities and being strategic about them.

The second lesson concerns the tendency to see the real problem of interventions as being one of coordination. For instance, in Afghanistan everyone might agree that the goal is a stable, moderate, democratic state capable of providing for its own welfare and security, and the challenge is to have stakeholders coordinate their efforts and "lines of operation." This is largely wrong. The political future of Afghanistan and the future of political relations in the region are precisely not issues of consensus, and underlying disagreement—a type of power politics that feeds the ongoing war—is the condition sine qua non that prevents the intervention from proceeding smoothly. As "transition" gets under way and as post-2014 "partnerships" between Western states and Afghanistan develop, it will become more apparent that the country's basic political bargains remain unsettled. We will observe it in regard to the post-Karzai presidential elections in 2014, the ongoing involvement of Pakistan and India, and the Taliban strategy of combining combat and reconciliation. In short, politics, not process, is what matters most.

There is a great deal of deceptive attraction attached to the Comprehensive Approach. It has been said that in Afghanistan an "elaborate theory" of intervention produced an excessive combination of "courage and grandeur and fantasy."[23] This is an apt description of the belief that networks and partnerships would produce an effective Comprehensive Approach, which they could not. This lesson should not prevent nations or organizations from seeking broad civil-military toolboxes and partnerships, however. Instead, it should lead them to consider the preconditions for successful engagement: the clarification of an end-state that builds on tenable political alignments in the area of intervention as well as the continued engagement of, in this case, Western political leaders in connecting campaign ends and means. NATO would be better prepared for new challenges if its national leaders learned the lesson that intervention is a political art, not a science, and as such is located at the heart of their vocation.

NOTES

All Web sites accessed in November 2013, if not otherwise specified.

This is a revised and updated version of "Of Sirens and Deceptive Virtue: A Critical Look at NATO's Comprehensive Approach," *Studia Diplomatica* 64, no. 2 (2011): 37–56. It is published here with the permission of the journal. For constructive comments along the way the author would like to thank participants in the September 2010 conference in Oslo, "NATO's New Strategic Concept—Finding a New Balance"; the editors of this volume, Paal Sigurd Hilde and Andrew Michta; as well as the anonymous reviewers of the book manuscript.

1. NATO's Strategic Concept of 2010 emphasizes three basic tasks—the defense of the Atlantic realm, crisis management, and partnerships—and the trend post-Afghanistan is that the second of these, crisis management, will be downgraded in favor of policies to counter new threats to the realm, such as cyber threats, and policies to consult more widely, which is partnership. For this type of emphasis see Jamie Shea, "Keeping NATO Relevant," *Carnegie Policy Outlook* (April 2012), http://carnegieendowment.org/2012/04/19/keeping-nato-relevant/acl9. One may question the trend, of course, on the ground that operations always will find a way: Libya is one example hereof, Afghanistan another. For the wider argument that NATO post-Afghanistan needs first and foremost to redefine its Atlantic vision to provide for political leadership, see Sten Rynning, *NATO and Afghanistan: The Liberal Disconnect* (Stanford, CA: Stanford University Press, 2012).

2. Jens Ringsmose and Sten Rynning, eds., *NATO's New Strategic Concept: A Comprehensive Assessment* (Copenhagen: DIIS, 2011); and Arita Holmberg, "The Changing Role of NATO: Exploring the Implications for Security Governance and Legitimacy," *European Security* 20, no. 4 (2011): 529–546.

3. NATO's new Strategic Concept affirms Article V and states: "that commitment remains firm and binding. NATO will deter and defend against any threat of aggression, and against emerging security challenges where they threaten the fundamental security of individual Allies or the Alliance as a whole." North Atlantic Treaty Organization, *Strategic Concept: Active Engagement, Modern Defence* (Brussels: NATO, 2010), paragraph 4.

4. North Atlantic Treaty Organization, *Strategic Concept*, paragraphs 7–15.

5. North Atlantic Treaty Organization, *Strategic Concept*, paragraphs 28–35.

6. The wording of the Riga Declaration is: "Experience in Afghanistan and Kosovo demonstrates that today's challenges require a Comprehensive Approach by the international community involving a wide spectrum of civil and military instruments, while fully respecting mandates and autonomy of decisions of all actors, and provides precedents for this approach. To that end, while recognizing that NATO has no requirement to develop capabilities strictly for civilian purposes, we have tasked today the Council in Permanent Session to develop pragmatic proposals in time for the meeting of Foreign Ministers in April 2007 and Defense Ministers in June 2007 to improve coherent application of NATO's own crisis management instruments as well as practical cooperation at all levels with partners, the UN and other relevant international organizations, Non-Governmental Organizations and local actors in the planning and conduct of ongoing and future operations wherever appropriate" (North Atlantic Treaty Organization, "Riga Summit Declaration," November 29, 2006, paragraph 10, http://www.nato.int/docu/pr/2006/p06-150e.htm).

7. North Atlantic Treaty Organization, "Declaration on Alliance Security," April 4, 2009, http://www.nato.int/cps/en/natolive/news_52838.htm.

8. North Atlantic Treaty Organization, *NATO 2020: Assured Security, Dynamic Engagement; Analysis and Recommendations of the Group of Experts on a New Strategic Concept for NATO* (Brussels: NATO Public Diplomacy Division), May 17, 2010, http://www.nato.int/cps/en/natolive/official_texts_63654.htm, 42.

9. The "Inteqal" paper itself has not been published, but the Prioritization and Implementation Plan regarding the Afghan National Development Strategy, issued at the Kabul conference, contains a detailed overview. See Afghan Government, *The ANDS Prioritization and Implementation Plan, Mid-2010–Mid-2013, Volume I, Kabul International Conference on Afghanistan,* July 20, 2010, 35–37. The "Inteqal" paper, to which the author has had access, is formally entitled "Joint Framework for Inteqal: A Process for Strengthening Peace and Stability in Afghanistan and the Region." A Joint Afghan-NATO Inteqal Board (JANIB) will prepare recommendations for the Afghan government formally in charge of the transition process; see Afghan Government, "Kabul Conference Communiqué," July 20, 2010, http://unama.unmissions.org/Default.aspx?tabid=12279&language=en-US, 2–3.

10. The PRTs have notably differed in respect to command, with some being led by the military and others involving degrees of civilian command, and also in respect to the extent of projects they engage in, with each PRT defining "security sector reform" according to national policy and local Afghan conditions. For the early experience in organizing the Afghan PRTs, see Peter Viggo Jakobsen, "PRTs in Afghanistan: Successful but Not Sufficient," DIIS Report (April 2005), 6, http://subweb.diis.dk/sw11230.asp; and Russel L. Honoré and David V. Boslego, "Forging Provincial Reconstruction Teams," *Joint Forces Quarterly* (January 1, 2007): 85–89. For a more recent evaluation of the entire civil-military organization, including the PRTs, see Joshua W. Welle, "Civil-Military Integration in Afghanistan: Creating Unity of Command," *Joint Forces Quarterly* (1st quarter 2010): 54–60. For a critical assessment of the Helmand experience of Britain, an often-cited innovator in counterinsurgency, see Robert Engell, "Lessons from Helmand, Afghanistan:

What Now for British Counterinsurgency?," *International Affairs* 87, no. 2 (2011): 297–315.

11. See Rynning, *NATO and Afghanistan*, ch. 5 for Eide and ch. 6 for the Obama surge.

12. A declaration of intended cooperation could thus not be entered, even though the two Secretary Generals wanted it. What they could and did do on September 23, 2008, was to sign it as a statement of intent on behalf of the Secretary Generals: "Joint Declaration on UN/NATO Secretariat Cooperation." It was a rapprochement, but a weak one. The declaration was not made public but has leaked and can be googled.

13. Jaap de Hoop Scheffer, interview with author, February 1, 2010.

14. North Atlantic Treaty Organization, *Strategic Concept*, paragraph 21.

15. NATO's policy is to be "prepared and capable to manage ongoing hostilities" and then to be "prepared and capable to contribute to stabilization and reconstruction," see *Strategic Concept*, paragraphs 23–24.

16. North Atlantic Treaty Organization, *Strategic Concept*, paragraph 25.

17. Jamie Shea, "A NATO for the 21st Century: Towards a New Strategic Concept," *Fletcher Forum for World Affairs* 31, no. 2 (2007): 43–55.

18. Peter Viggo Jakobsen, "NATO's Comprehensive Approach after Lisbon: Principal Problem Acknowledged, Solution Elusive," in *NATO's New Strategic Concept*, ed. Ringsmose and Rynning, 83–90.

19. Jakobsen, "NATO's Comprehensive Approach," 83–90.

20. On these dynamics, see Samuel Laurent, *Sahelistan* (Paris: Seuil, 2013).

21. On this history, see Lawrence Kaplan, *NATO and the UN: A Peculiar Relationship* (Columbia: University of Missouri Press, 2010).

22. Zbigniew Brzezinski, "An Agenda for NATO," *Foreign Affairs* 88, no. 5 (2009): 2–20.

23. Rory Stewart and Gerald Knaus, *Can Intervention Work?* (New York: Norton, 2011).

Chapter 7

Lean, Mean Fighting Machine?

Institutional Change in NATO and the NATO Command Structure

Paal Sigurd Hilde

The institutionalized nature of NATO sets it apart from most other alliances, both past and present.[1] Beginning in the early 1950s, the institutionalization of the North Atlantic Treaty alliance made it into the NATO we know today—it added the *O* in NATO. The end of the Cold War and the dissolution of both the Warsaw Pact and the Soviet Union removed the perceived threat that had spurred the formation of the alliance. It also removed the core raison d'être for NATO's institutional structures: to coordinate preparations for and command the collective defense against an attack from the East. Instead of ending in the dustbin of history, however, NATO and its institutions proved adaptable.

In the early 1990s the institutional strengths of the alliance provided an important basis for the allies' decision to take the alliance out-of-area rather than out of business. One of the most recent examples of this decision is Operation Unified Protector over Libya in 2011, in which most allies saw utilizing NATO's unified command structure as the only viable alternative to a U.S.-led operation.[2] NATO's institutions have also remained relevant to tasks other than operations. The emphasis in recent years on bringing NATO's attention back home—that the alliance must be "in-area or in trouble"[3]—has also focused on NATO's institutional strengths, notably on its command structure.

There are two essential institutional elements in the NATO we know today. One is the permanent, intra-alliance consultation mechanism in the North Atlantic Council in Permanent Session, chaired by the Secretary

General and supported by the International Staff. The second is the stand-ing, multinational NATO Command Structure (NCS). The NCS sets NATO apart from other international organizations with a security focus, such as the UN and EU; both the latter have institutionalized political consultation but no comparable military command and control capability. Moreover, the NCS is the single biggest element of NATO's institutional structure. Both these aspects make the command structure a natural focus for a study of institutional change in NATO.

This chapter has two aims. The first is to analyze the drivers behind the reforms the NCS has undergone since 1990. I identify three drivers of change as the most important and explore them in some detail: military requirements, political ambitions, and cost cutting. Of the three, the chang-ing military requirements that have resulted from NATO's expanding role in out-of-area operations have been the overall most important driver in shap-ing the organizational setup of the NCS. Political ambitions—that is, specific political demands made by both individual and groups of member-states—have simultaneously served as both drivers and inhibitors of change. The final driver, cost cutting, has unsurprisingly driven the most visible aspect of change: the reduced size of the NCS. While the aim to reduce costs has been evident since the first round of post–Cold War reforms, cutting costs has become increasingly important as an aim unto itself. With the sovereign debt crisis placing austerity at the top of most NATO members' political agendas, the pressure to reduce the cost and size of NATO's institutional structure—to make it a "lean, mean fighting machine"—is likely to continue.

In the second part of the chapter I analyze the actual and potential conse-quences of the reduction in the size of the NCS. In the late 1980s the NCS consisted of about 24,500 personnel in seventy-eight headquarters. The structure adopted in 2011 has 8,800 personnel in thirteen headquarters. This represents a reduction of about 64 percent in two decades. By comparison, the core staff of the European Commission alone has grown from 15,429 in 1989 to 23,964 in 2011—a growth of about 64 percent.[4] What does the considerable reduction in the size of the NCS—and NATO's institutional structure per se—entail for NATO? I analyze actual and potential conse-quences from a practical perspective and from the point of view of IR theory.

Drivers of Change: The Evolution of the NATO Command Structure

Although the North Atlantic Treaty was signed on April 4, 1949, NATO as we know it today came into existence only two years later. The catalyst for change was the Korean War, which persuaded the United States to both commit itself to the defense of Europe and push for unity of defense efforts. Notably, the U.S. "attitude toward a command structure for Europe changed from reluctance to strong advocacy."[5]

The establishment of the NATO Command Structure was a tale of strong national preferences, rivalry between member-states, and even personal ambitions.[6] While the major commands were in place by 1952, structuring and geographically distributing subordinate commands proved challenging. The European command, Allied Command Europe (ACE), was fully in place only with the creation of the Danish-German Baltic Approaches command in 1962. After a substantial reform following the French withdrawal from NATO's military structure in 1966, however, the command structure remained essentially unchanged until the end of the Cold War.

The end of the Cold War meant for NATO the beginning of a period of more or less constant adaptation and reform. The NCS was no exception. Since 1990 it has gone through a series of major reforms, decided through at times intense negotiation in four periods: 1991–1992, 1994–1997, 2002–2003, and 2010–2011. In the following sections I analyze these reforms from the perspective of the three drivers of change identified above: military requirements, political ambitions, and cost cutting.

Military Requirements

Military requirements denotes the changing requirements placed on the NCS by the allies. Overall, the political decisions that gradually expanded NATO's role in out-of-area operations—from Bosnia through Kosovo to Afghanistan—have been the single most important driver in the post–Cold War transformation of the NCS. The first round of reforms, decided in 1991–1992, only reduced the size of a command structure still geared toward meeting the Cold War threat.[7] It quickly became evident that more radical reform was needed. Apart from increasing NATO engagement in supporting out-of-treaty-area peacekeeping, the allies also decided to support the building of what came to be known as the European Security and Defense Identity. Notably, this included a European ability to conduct crisis response operations using NATO assets.[8] Both these ambitions required a more flexible and deployable command structure. At the January 1994 Brussels Summit, the allies thus set in motion a new round of NCS reforms before the structure decided in 1991–1992 was fully in place.[9]

The chosen vehicle for giving the command structure mobility and flexibility, for both NATO- and EU-led operations, was the Combined

Joint Task Force (CJTF) concept.[10] As I discuss below, the task of implementing this concept and establishing consensus on a new NCS in general proved arduous. Apart from CJTF, the 1994–1997 reforms, which were finally implemented in March 2000, reflected a clear reorientation in several respects. Most important was that the most likely security challenges the alliance was likely to face, even in the worst case, would involve NATO's response being regional collective defense, not full mobilization and war.[11] This change in threat perception created a further impetus for flexibility in all parts of the NCS, in that the purely military distinction between Article 5 and non-Article 5 operations was blurred.

The November 2002 Prague Summit set the third round of NCS reform in motion. It represented a watershed. The changing military requirements resulting from "reduced static defence needs" and "NATO's increasingly proactive approach to crisis management demanded" were, in the eyes of Air Vice-Marshal Andrew Vallance, "dramatically reinforced by the paradigm shift in the strategic outlook in the wake of 9/11."[12] The new structure involved the creation of a single strategic command for operations, Allied Command Operations (ACO), and a functional strategic command, Allied Command Transformation (ACT). ACT was to be a driver of transformation in the alliance. In ACO, three new operational level commands replaced two regional commands. The new HQs were to be flexible and generic and thus able to assume command of a NATO, or EU, operation anywhere. The number of tactical level commands was cut drastically.[13]

The new structure was supposed to reach Full Operational Capability (FOC) in 2006. This goal was not reached.[14] Again a further reform effort was launched before the previous one had reached fruition. In June 2006 NATO defense ministers endorsed the start of a new, major review of the peacetime personnel structure of the NCS, a Peacetime Establishment Review (PE Review) that eventually spanned three years. For reasons I return to below, motivated partly by important changes in military requirements, some allies tried to make the review into a full-fledged reform. This effort did not succeed, though some significant changes were implemented.

In November 2006 the Riga Summit adopted the strategic guidance document "Comprehensive Political Guidance." Unlike the 1999 Strategic Concept, which referred to out-of-area operations in a Euro-Atlantic context, "Comprehensive Political Guidance" took a global perspective on NATO's role in crisis response operations.[15] Moreover, the same June 2006 meeting of defense ministers that set the PE Review into motion also adopted a new level of ambition for NATO. The 2006 version of "Ministerial Guidance," the document that provided political guidance for NATO defense planning (until 2011, when it was replaced by "Political Guidance"), changed NATO's military level of ambition from three large Major Joint Operations (MJO) in the 2003 version, to two MJO and six smaller joint operations (SJO).[16] Overall, the emphasis changed from a few large to several smaller operations, and from operations on or around NATO territory to operations at a strategic distance. For the command structure, the PE Review reflected this change in emphasis in the all-but-official abandonment of the CJTF in favor of a new concept based on small, easily deployable headquarters, termed Deployable Joint Staff Element (DJSE). All in all the NCS was to field four such DJSEs, with two more to be fielded by the NATO Force Structure (i.e., mainly multinational headquarters available to NATO)—fulfilling the six SJO requirement.[17]

Pressure for radical reform increased with the onset of the financial crisis in 2008. The 2010 Lisbon Summit gave final endorsement to a plan for a new, substantially smaller NCS proposed by a Senior Officials' Group[18] in September 2010. As I discuss below, the allies gave the Secretary General the task of tackling the most difficult question in NCS reforms: the geographic location of commands.[19] At their meeting in Brussels in June 2011, NATO defense ministers approved the agreement hammered out by the Secretary General and thus decided the final shape of the new command structure.[20]

In the 2010–2011 round of reforms, the pressure from allies such as Poland, the Baltic States, and Norway served as a counterforce to the pressure for increased out-of-area, crisis response capability that had dominated in previous rounds.[21] As Danielsen and Widerberg outline in chapter 1, these allies sought to ensure NATO's relevance for and ability to deal with security challenges on and around NATO's territory. They were motivated by the shift in Russian foreign and security policy from 2006 to 2007. For the NCS, this shift has in essence entailed an increased emphasis on contingency planning and in-area collective defense exercises, as well as the introduction of a geographic focus for the operational commands. At the time of writing, the unfolding events in Ukraine seem likely to give further impetus to this change in emphasis.

Overall, however, the military requirements embodied in the NATO level of ambition described above remain in force and thus serve to structure the organization of the NCS. The new NCS abandons the short-lived DJSE concept in favor of making the operational commands themselves deployable. It also shifts more of the burden of providing deployable command facilities to the NATO Force Structure.[22] Moreover, the NATO operation over Libya in spring 2011 reinforced a concern that had emerged early in 2011 about the capability of the NATO air command and control structure. The requirement for robustness was instrumental in the modification of the air commands of the model approved in Lisbon, in the final NCS structure adopted in June 2011.[23]

Political Ambitions

The consensus principle requires that all member-states approve all major decisions in NATO. In this sense, politics—the process of hammering out consensus among allies on NATO's development and tasks—is inevitably the ultimate driver of and obstacle to change. In this context, however, *political ambitions* denote the narrower and often ulterior political considerations that may play a significant role in shaping NATO decisions. Two key examples in the case of command structure reform are analyzed below. The first is the struggle over how NATO was to make command and control assets available to the Western European Union (WEU; the EU's "military arm" from 1991 to 1999) and later the European Union directly. The second is the question of the NCS's "geographic footprint"—the geographical location of NATO's commands.

The political tug-of-war over how European-led operations should be enabled using NATO's command and control and other resources has been the focal point of a protracted political dispute beginning in the 1990s. For much of the post–Cold War period, the main protagonists have been France and the United States, with Turkish sniping from the sidelines increasingly taking over the role as key obstacle in the mid-2000s. The crux of the dispute may be described as follows. Particularly in the early 1990s, France wanted truly independent European military operations using NATO assets. The United States favored Europe's taking on larger defense responsibilities. However, it wanted to retain overall control over the use of NATO assets also in WEU-led operations, as many of these included U.S. personnel and materiel put at NATO's disposal.[24]

As noted above, the allies adopted the CJTF concept as the vehicle for allowing the use of NATO assets in European-led operations. A breakthrough was announced at a foreign ministers' meeting in Berlin on June 3, 1996, later giving its name to the Berlin Plus framework.[25] Only at the 1999 Washington Summit, however, did final details fall into place.[26] The Berlin Plus framework was activated by an exchange of letters between NATO and the EU in March 2003, only to see Turkey block its further use after the admission of the Greek part of Cyprus into the EU in May 2004.[27]

The dispute over EU access to and use of NATO's command assets has been the most visible and most studied political dispute connected to the

NCS. The most persistent and debilitating political aspect of NCS reform, however, has been opposition to the closure of headquarters. As Rob de Wijk observed about reforms in the 1990s: "National considerations regarding the maintenance of one or more headquarters on national territory played an important, if not decisive, role in a number of countries."[28]

The issue has marked NCS reforms in recent years as well. As noted above, some allies and senior NATO officials sought to make the 2006–2009 PE Review into a new round of fundamental NCS reform. This did not succeed, as some member-states, notably in the south of Europe, blocked the review from changing either the geographical footprint or the status of existing commands. As the SHAPE historian Gregory W. Pedlow concluded in 2010:

> [E]fforts by SHAPE in recent years to reduce the number of headquarters by eliminating unneeded component commands and thus achieve in this manner the manpower cuts mandated by the nations have proven unsuccessful, due to national desires to retain a NATO headquarters on their territory, even if the SHAPE thinks the headquarters is no longer needed. As a result, SHAPE has been forced to result to "salami slicing" of all headquarters . . . reducing their effectiveness, while having to retain headquarters for which there is no longer a military requirement.[29]

The importance of the geographic footprint was evident also in the 2010–2011 reforms. As noted, in the declaration from the Lisbon Summit the NATO Secretary General was given the task of facilitating a "final decision on a new NATO Command Structure, including its geographic footprint" by June 2011.[30] Some differences between the structure approved at the Lisbon Summit and that finally adopted in June 2011 clearly show the significance of member countries' political ambitions regarding the NCS's geographic footprint.[31] The introduction of a land component command in Izmir, Turkey, is the clearest example of this. Even the United Kingdom, which had long taken a tough line on cutting costs in the NCS and other NATO issues, argued in favor of keeping the NATO maritime command in Northwood. As Defense Minister Liam Fox stated in June 2011: "As one of the leading contributors to NATO operations it is only right that NATO retains a command presence on British soil. Agreement on this matter was a fundamental objective for the UK Government."[32]

Cost Cutting

Budget constraints were a challenge for NATO also during the Cold War. In the early years the aim of rebuilding the economies of Western Europe led NATO members to underline the need to build their military strength "without endangering economic recovery and the attainment of economic stability, which constitute an essential element of their security."[33] Later the introduction of the strategy of flexible response again brought budgets into focus, as "modernized conventional forces are far more costly than nuclear, and are becoming more expensive."[34] A cursory search conducted by this author does not suggest, however, that during the Cold War the NATO Command Structure was the target of calls for rationalization.[35] One reason might have been that the gradually increasing focus on conventional forces in NATO required greater, not less, volume in the NCS.

With the end of the Cold War, the NCS soon became the target of cost-cutting efforts. The initial cuts in the NCS, like the extensive cuts in NATO members' nuclear and conventional forces, were a logical consequence of the disappearance of an imminent conventional threat to NATO; they were a peace dividend. An ambitious goal was set for the first round of reforms in 1991–1992:

> We are streamlining existing structures and procedures and we will continue with our efforts to achieve further savings in order to make best use of future scarce resources. . . . When these changes are implemented, the reductions in the number and size of NATO military headquarters will achieve manpower savings in the order of 20%.[36]

This emphasis on reducing the cost of the NCS remained a key motivation in the following rounds of reform. Meeting in Berlin on June 13, 1996, NATO defense ministers concluded that "[a]daptations should not be driven only by savings but every attempt should be made to reduce running costs."[37] Eventually the 1994–1997 reforms entailed only a modest reduction in the number of major headquarters. The communiqué from December 1997 announcing the final agreement claimed "a reduction from 65 headquarters at present to 20 in the proposed new command structure."[38] This reduction was, however, almost fully a result of the removal—the disassociation—of a large number of fourth-level, tactical headquarters. Many of these were NATO headquarters only in name and would not actually close given their national tasks.[39] Moreover, these tactical commands had already lost their right to receive NATO infrastructure funding, so their removal from the NCS resulted in little actual cost savings.[40]

The reforms set into motion by the 2002 Prague Summit brought substantial cuts. The Summit gave the task of providing "the outline of a leaner, more efficient, effective and deployable command structure" to a Senior Officials Group (SOG) comprising senior representatives from all member countries.[41] When alliance defense ministers approved the SOG's report on June 12, 2003, they did so with the expectation that "[t]he streamlined structure will be more effective, and is expected to yield cost and manpower savings."[42] Indeed, in its report the SOG had set the ambitious target of a 30 percent cut in NCS personnel numbers.[43] This aim became a *leitmotif* for the 2006–2009 PE Review.

In February 2009 the NAC finally endorsed the recommendations of the second and final phase of the PE Review. While smaller in terms of personnel, the recommended structure was only partly cheaper. Individual member-states have to cover the cost of their own officers working in NATO commands. Thus, a reduction in PE numbers mainly reduces the member states' expenditures, hardly NATO's. While the former was an important aim, so was a reduction in common funded expenditures. Given that no headquarters could be closed, and that the establishment of new deployable elements required investments in communications equipment and additional civilian technicians (who are paid by NATO, not member-states), the new NCS became more expensive. With a global financial crisis unfolding, pressure for more radical reform quickly emerged with force.

More than any previous round, the aim of cutting costs marked the fourth and latest round of NCS reform in 2010–2011. At the informal defense ministers' meeting in Istanbul in February 2010, U.S. secretary of defense Robert Gates came out forcefully in favor of a reform of NATO structures, including the NCS.[44] He gained support for tasking Secretary General Rasmussen with presenting a proposal for cuts by the June ministerial. This was followed by a nine member-state initiative, including the United States, the United Kingdom, Germany, and France, presented in April 2010. Their initiative called for an NCS that was "affordable, scalable, and able to support deployable operations" and required that "the number of headquarters should be reduced substantially" and the number of personnel should be "significantly less than 10,000 . . . (towards a 7,500 level)."[45]

To fulfill his February tasking, Rasmussen turned to the chairman of the Military Committee and the commanders of the two strategic commands, earning the group the nickname "twelve-star committee." It presented its proposals for drastically cut structures to NATO defense ministers in June 2010. The models, A and B, were 7,500 and 9,500 strong, representing personnel cuts of 43 and 28 percent, respectively. Instead of accepting either of these, however, the ministers again appointed an SOG to hammer out an agreement.[46]

In its report, the new SOG proposed a "geographically unconstrained" model for a new NCS. Both the meeting of defense and foreign ministers in Brussels in October 2010 and the Lisbon Summit in November subsequently endorsed the report. Overall, the number of personnel was to be about 9,000, compared to about 13,900 in 2010—representing, as the Lisbon Summit declaration put it, "a significant reduction in the number of headquarters and a manpower saving of 35%, representing almost 5,000 posts, or more, if and where possible."[47]

In the following fixing of the geographic footprint in the spring of 2011, the SOG model had to yield to both military and political considerations, as outlined above. Though this resulted in a somewhat larger number of headquarters and personnel, the allies reached the target of around 9,000 personnel, with 8,800 in the new structure,[48] by shifting some positions over to NATO's agencies. Although this makes the changes somewhat of a numbers game, the emphasis on keeping personnel numbers on target also evinces the significance of cost cutting as a motivation. Similarly, while actual savings again fell short of what many hoped for, this does not detract from the significance of the initial motivation.

Perspectives on the Shrinking NCS

As noted in the introduction to this chapter, the NCS has been reduced by about 64 percent in size since the 1980s. What does such a major reduction in size mean for NATO? In this section I analyze two perspectives on this question. First, I take a practical perspective to highlight the effects on day-to-day operations and NATO's overall military ability, and on the loss of the NCS as a training ground. Second, I use a theoretical perspective to assess the potential consequences of institutional weakening based on the significance afforded institutions in IR literature. Finally, I contrast these actual and potential costs with expected cost savings.

In terms of the day-to-day workload, there is little evidence to suggest that the NCS struggled significantly with meeting the high operational tempo NATO saw in the late 2000s, although the workload was clearly unevenly shared.[49] This is despite—and this is a crucial point—the fact that the level of actual manning for many years consistently was at 80–85 percent—or basically the fully manned personnel size of the structure adopted in Lisbon. Evidence thus suggests that with some synergy gained from concentration at fewer sites, even a much smaller NCS should be fully able to run all ongoing NATO operations. With the ISAF operation in Afghanistan mission ending, the operational tempo is also likely to decrease significantly.

The reduction in the size of the command structure obviously entails a reduction in NATO's overall capacity to lead military operations. Without doubt the latest round of reform shifts more of the burden of fulfilling NATO's still valid 2006 "Level of Ambition" to force structure and national headquarters.[50] The practical implications of this are probably limited, however, both because NATO will continue to use mission-specific HQs ("composite HQs," like ISAF HQ and KFOR HQ) and because member-states, notably the United States, are able to fill gaps. However, it does raise the question of what NATO's Level of Ambition really is.

The short-term, day-to-day impact of the major cut in the NCS agreed upon in Lisbon thus seems small. What about longer term, practical effects? Linguistic skills, cultural differences, varying emphasis on and quality of military education, and political caveats are factors that will prevent the NCS from becoming optimally efficient. This argument for redundancy is even more convincing if one adds that the NCS is a key arena for leveling out such differences—for fostering interoperability. Military academies teach the skills of the NATO trade; NATO doctrine, planning and operational procedures, and so on; and often the NATO lingua franca, English. However, being taught in an academy is a far less intensive experience than learning by doing in a multinational NATO command. This is important for officers from all NATO countries but particularly for those from new member-states with often different military traditions and procedures. Longer term, cutting the size of the NCS may thus hurt NATO interoperability and the overall integration of member-state military forces. As one scholar noted: "Multinationality is not needed for military purposes: 'multinationality in NATO is a tool of integration, not efficiency.'"[51]

The existence of large NATO HQs in operations, such as the massive ISAF HQ, has made this challenge less acute. Indeed, two decades of close and extensive multinational NATO operations have fostered an unprecedented degree of interoperability, both in the field and in terms of command and control. The likely reduced operational tempo in NATO with the end of the ISAF operation in 2014, however, means allies must maintain this gain by other means. To address this challenge, Secretary General Rasmussen launched the Connected Forces Initiative (CFI) in February 2012.[52] The May 2012 Chicago Summit adopted CFI as a component of a larger "Defense Package."[53] Stressing the role of exercises, the CFI is important, yet even regular exercises cannot fully stop the likely decrease of interoperability after the end of ISAF. As a permanent structure involving day-to-day cooperation throughout the year, the NATO Command Structure is clearly better suited to perpetuate important aspects of interoperability at the headquarters level.

Thus, while the short-term, practical consequences of a reduced command structure are likely small, the longer-term ones may be significant. I now turn to what insight academic theory might provide about the potential costs of shrinking the NCS.

NATO's supposed imminent or inevitable death has been a recurring theme in the media and policy-oriented and academic writings about NATO.[54] While doomsday prophecies were not infrequent during the Cold War, they multiplied after its end. From a realist perspective, as Robert B. McCalla observed, "an alliance that sees its primary threat shrink or disappear will be less cohesive, leading to eventual irrelevance or breakup."[55]

Despite such prophecies, NATO has endured. This has led scholars to seek to explain why NATO has fared so differently than most other alliances in history. Most fundamentally, many argue, with Wallace J. Thies, that NATO is different from seemingly similar, prior alliances in being an alliance of democracies. "The Atlantic Alliance," Thies argues, "was intended to be a permanent alliance among liberal democratic states."[56]

From a theoretical perspective, as Zoltan Barany and Robert Rauchhaus argue, "[a]t the end of the Cold War, neo-liberal institutionalists were optimistic about NATO's future. Their confidence sprang from their view that NATO differs from traditional alliances in at least two important ways."[57] One of these ways is basically the argument presented by Thies on the wider political basis of NATO. More important from our perspective, however, Barany and Rauchhaus argue that NATO is "unlike most military alliances" in that it "is highly institutionalized."[58]

In its most simple form, the institutional approach holds that organizations will fight for their own survival. While one should not dismiss the significance of lobbying by NATO officials, such a simple explanation seems insufficient. As McCalla argues: "Despite the appearance of organizational strength, the particular structure of NATO and the nature of its day-to-day interaction actually make for a weak bureaucracy."[59] This argument about insufficiency holds also if one considers the bureaucracy with a stake in NATO's survival as not limited to NATO's own organization. Celeste A. Wallander claims: "Anyone familiar with the foreign-policymaking apparatus of countries such as Germany and the United States knows that NATO's existence has shaped departments and procedures within national foreign and defense ministries."[60]

More sophisticated institutional approaches emphasize other facets of institutions than their propensity to fight for survival. One is a cost-benefit approach. As Wallander has argued:

> Institutional maintenance entails costs, but these costs are generally lower than those involved in creating new institutions. . . . Other things

being equal, then, the more institutionalized a security coalition, the more likely it is to persist in the face of change in its environment.[61]

In other words, "[u]sing existing institutions, even if they are sub-optimal, makes sense when the alternatives are too costly or risky."[62] "NATO has persisted after the Cold War," Wallander continues, "not merely because it exists (the sunk-cost argument), but because its Cold War institutional form included specific assets for achieving transparency, integration and negotiation among its members, and because it developed general assets that could be mobilized to deal with new security missions."[63] In particular, Wallander emphasizes that NATO's military cooperation "enabled members' military to work together as complex and multipurpose organizations, not merely as military instruments to blunt a Soviet attack."[64] "Most importantly," she continues, "NATO's multinational integrated military command and the interoperability of its member's forces provided a general organizational capability" that could be adapted to a changing environment.[65] Thus, Wallander wrote in 2000, the "integrated command structure as a general asset is crucial to understand why NATO—and not other institutions, such as the UN or the Western European Union (WEU)"—was chosen "for post-Cold War military missions in Europe."[66] Or as Barany and Rauchhaus argued from a different perspective in 2011: "[T]he unique organizational attributes of NATO, and its proven track record, are very important for understanding why the alliance was the preferred vehicle for advancing American interests."[67]

Adherents of the constructivist approach to international relations have also generally taken a more optimistic view of NATO's survival. Basing his argument on Karl Deutsch's work on security communities, Thomas Risse-Knappe claims that "the Western Alliance represents an institutionalization of the transatlantic security community based on common values and a collective identity of liberal democracies."[68] Risse-Knappe argues that the key dimensions for "alliances and cooperative institutions among democracies" are "the degree of institutionalization of the community and the extent to which collective identities have developed among its members."[69] Values and identities are important, as "the fundamental agents in international politics are not states but individuals acting in a social context—whether governments, domestic society or international institutions."[70] The setting they work in shapes the opinions of such individuals. Thus, as Robert B. McCalla states, "those who support the regime [the international institution constitutes the core of] are more likely to do so because they value the regime, not because their jobs are at stake."[71] This is the case not only for those working in international institutions, as "internal incentives for norm compliance" also form "as domestic actors develop a stake in the regime and regime norms become part of individual belief systems on the part of officials and even the public."[72]

Both Wallander's neoliberal institutionalist and Risse-Knappe's constructivist approaches, briefly outlined above, emphasize the significance of institutions in NATO's survival. Though their perspectives differ, both conclude that a more extensive institutional structure is likely to be more conducive to institutional survival than a less extensive one. In Risse-Knappe's framework an extensive institutional structure serves to socialize more individuals into the norms and identity of the institution. In Wallander's perspective, greater institutional assets result in the benefits of perpetuating an institution being greater than the maintenance costs. As a third scholar frequently quoted above, Robert B. McCalla, observes: "[W]here the organizational development of an alliance is high, we would expect the impact of the loss of a threat on an alliance to be mitigated and hence slowed."[73]

Given that the long-term cost of cutting the size of the NCS seems potentially great both from practical and theoretical perspectives, the pertinent next question is: What will NATO member-states save, in monetary terms, from the Lisbon cuts? The savings will come in two forms: on the common funded NATO budget (Military Budget and NATO Security Investment Program) and on officers working in the NCS. The member-states carry most costs associated with having officers in the NCS, including wages, benefits, and some travel expenses. In essence, the common funded expenditures on the NATO Command Structure are limited to running, maintaining, and upgrading headquarter facilities; the wages and benefits of international civilians (most civilian employees in NATO structures are paid by NATO); as well as some expenditures connected to training, exercises, and operations. Compared to the personnel expenditures of member-states, common funded costs are small.

The average cost of having personnel in NCS varies greatly among member-states, depending on the officers' wages and benefits.[74] For the sake of argument, let us assume the average cost of an NCS officer is €100,000. The cut of 5,000 positions would then theoretically result in savings of €500 million (if all associated costs, including the wage of the officers, could be cut). Actual savings will be much lower, mainly because the pre-2011 NCS was far from fully manned. Adding a further €200 million in annual savings in common budgets (running costs and investments) and other national costs, theoretical total annual savings from the Lisbon reforms could be €700 million. Compared to total NATO defense spending in 2010 of about €212 billion (USD 275 billion) in NATO-Europe and €830 billion (USD 1.08 trillion) including North America, the saving amounts to 0.33 percent of total NATO-Europe and 0.08 percent of total NATO defense spending.[75] Even given the massive cuts in defense budgets seen in later years, savings from NCS still represent far less than 1 percent of NATO defense spending.

Conclusion

I have argued in this chapter that military considerations, political ambitions, and cost cutting have been the main drivers behind the evolution of the NATO Command Structure after the end of the Cold War. While all three factors have been important throughout the period, they have had somewhat different functions. Military requirements have been the key driver behind the increased flexibility and deployability of the NCS. In other words, they have shaped how the headquarters in the NCS are structured and used. Political ambitions have given direction to, but also inhibited, the change driven by military requirements. Finally, cost cutting has by far been the main, though not the sole, driver toward a smaller NCS. Moreover, the relative significance of cost cutting has increased to the point where it constituted the single most important factor behind the reforms adopted in 2010–2011.

I have also argued that whereas the short-term, practical implications of cutting the size of the NCS seem limited, the longer term negative effect on, notably, interoperability may be significant, as the NCS constitutes an important training ground for alliance officers. When one considers that even the most optimistic savings from cutting the NCS amount to a mere fraction of a percent of NATO defense spending, even from a practical perspective a long-term and broad cost-benefit analysis seems unfavorable.

If one adds the institutional perspective on NATO's survival, the long-term picture becomes even bleaker. From this point of view, reducing the size of NATO institutions, among which the NCS today still is the largest, means cutting the very structures that have served to keep NATO vital. Depending on one's specific focus, a smaller NCS means fewer officers socialized into supporters of NATO, or a reduced sunk cost and organizational capability—the present value—of NATO. While a strong argument may be made against overemphasizing how institutions in themselves serve to perpetuate NATO, to say that such arguments carry no weight clearly seems mistaken.

Why then do NATO members push for, or at least accept, such heavy-handed cost cutting? One answer clearly lies in the present "age of auster-ity." This argument is insufficient, however, as this crisis has also led to an increased emphasis on multinational cooperation on defense. From this point of view, it is a paradox that the Lisbon Strategic Concept stressed the need to "develop and operate capabilities jointly, for reasons of cost-effectiveness and as a manifestation of solidarity," yet simultaneously the Lisbon Summit reduced cooperation in the NCS.[76]

An important reason that the NCS has become the target of cost cutting seems to be that many member-states see its day-to-day benefit, in terms of the challenges NATO faces, as limited. Despite various ambitious plans for making the NCS more deployable and flexible, the command structure has had a limited role in ongoing operations. Some of the countries push-ing hardest for cuts will continue to do so as long as they perceive that the NCS gives few or no practical benefits in operations. They will continue to push for the NCS to become a "lean, mean fighting machine." Operation Unified Protector in Libya in 2011 served to rectify this image somewhat, as the NCS led that operation from its static locations. However, in the eyes of the cost cutters, the new structure adopted in Lisbon must prove its opera-tional value, in both "out-of-area" operations and "in-area" planning, train-ing, and exercises—if it doesn't, they will continue to call for cuts. While a "NATO on the cheap" may seem politically desirable now, such a policy disregards the other important, nonoperational roles of the NCS described above. It will also weaken the foundation that makes NATO what it is today: its organizational structure, and the command structure in particular. Over the longer run, this is a question of the survival of the *O* in NATO. While NATO may survive in a shape not dissimilar from that of the period from 1949 to 1951, it will become more like a traditional alliance than it is today; like a traditional alliance, but without a unifying threat.

NOTES

All Web sites last accessed in November 2013 unless otherwise noted.

I would like to thank the NATO and national officials at NATO Headquarters, both present and former, who generously supported my research by agreeing to be interviewed.

1. The only similar cases were the Warsaw Pact and to some extent the UK–U.S. alliance during World War II.

2. See, for example, Nicholas Watt, "Setback for Nicolas Sarkozy as NATO Wins Command of Libyan Campaign," *The Guardian*, March 24, 2011, http://www.guardian.co.uk/politics/wintour-and-watt/2011/mar/24/libya-nato.

3. Dan Hamilton, "NATO Summit I: In Area, or in Trouble," *International Herald Tribune*, October 26, 2006, http://www.nytimes.com/2006/11/26/opinion/26iht-edhamil.3668151.html.

4. Koen van den Heuvel, Unit HR.A.1, Workforce Planning, Organizational Structures and Metrics, Directorate-General for Human Resources & Security, European Commission, e-mail message to author, June 7, 2012. The figures are as of December 31, 2011. Including all "contract agents, local agents, special advisers and agents under national law," the 2011 figure would be about thirty-three thousand. The author is grateful to Mr. Koen van den Heuvel for providing the workforce data.

5. Gregory W. Pedlow, "The Politics of NATO Command, 1950–1962," in *U.S. Military Forces in Europe: The Early Years, 1945–1970*, ed. Simon W. Duke and Wolfgang Krieger (Boulder, CO: Westview Press, 1993), 19.

6. See Pedlow, "The Politics of NATO Command." For simplicity, the currently used term NATO Command Structure will be used throughout this paper. Historically, different terms have been used, with Integrated Military Command Structure being the most common.

7. See Rob de Wijk, *NATO on the Brink of the New Millennium: The Battle for Consensus* (London: Brassey's, 1997), 76–77.

8. North Atlantic Treaty Organization, "The Rome Declaration," November 8, 1991, points 6–8. All NATO documents referenced here may be found at www.nato.int.

9. North Atlantic Treaty Organization, "Brussels Summit Declaration," January 11, 1994, points 8–9.

10. North Atlantic Treaty Organization, "Brussels Summit Declaration," points 4–8. On CJTF see, for example, Charles Barry, "NATO's Combined Joint Task Forces in Theory and Practice," *Survival* 38, no. 1 (1996): 81–97.

11. On this see de Wijk, *NATO on the Brink of the New Millennium*, 100.

12. Andrew Vallance, "A Radically New Command Structure for NATO," *NATO Review* (Fall 2003), http://www.nato.int/docu/review/2003/issue3/english/military.html. Air Vice-Marshal Vallance was responsible for NCS implementation at SHAPE from 2001 to 2004.

13. On the reform see, for example, "NATO's Command Structure: The Old and the New," http://www.nato.int/ims/docu/command-structure.htm.

14. Details on the 2006–2009 PE Review and 2010–2011 reforms are based mainly on a number of anonymous interviews conducted at NATO HQ (among the IS, IMS, and national delegations) in June and October 2010 and March and June 2011.

15. North Atlantic Treaty Organization, "Comprehensive Political Guidance," November 29, 2006; North Atlantic Treaty Organization, "The Alliance Strategic Concept," April 24, 1999.

16. Ministerial Guidance was a classified series of documents. The still valid Level of Ambition from the 2006 version is, however, referred to in, for example, North Atlantic Treaty Organization, *The Secretary General's Annual Report 2011*,

12, http://www.nato.int/nato_static/assets/pdf/pdf_publications/20120125_Annual _Report_2011_en.pdf.

17. See North Atlantic Treaty Organization, "The DJSE Concept," http:// www.nato.int/fchd/FCHD/djse-concept.html.

18. The group comprised senior representatives from the member countries, mostly high-level Ministry of Defense officials.

19. See North Atlantic Treaty Organization, "Lisbon Summit Declaration," paragraph 49.

20. See North Atlantic Treaty Organization, "Background on NATO Command Structure Review," 2011, http://www.nato.int/nato_static/assets/pdf/pdf _2011_06/20110609-Backgrounder_Command_Structure.pdf.

21. On the impact on NCS see Paal Sigurd Hilde, "The Strategic Concept and NATO's Command Structure: Shifting Gears?," in *NATO's New Strategic Concept: A Comprehensive Assessment*, ed. Jens Ringsmose and Sten Rynning (København: Danish Institute for International Studies, 2011), 126–36.

22. See North Atlantic Treaty Organization, "Technical Background Briefing on NATO Command Structure," http://www.nato.int/cps/en/natolive/opinions _75353.htm.

23. See note 14.

24. See Lawrence S. Kaplan, *NATO United, NATO Divided: The Evolution of an Alliance* (Westport, CT: Praeger, 2004), 123; de Wijk, *NATO on the Brink of the New Millennium*, 99, 126–27.

25. See North Atlantic Treaty Organization, "Final Communiqué. Ministerial Meeting of the North Atlantic Council," June 3, 1996, point 7.

26. See North Atlantic Treaty Organization, "Washington Summit Communique," paragraphs 4 and 10.

27. See, for example, "EU-NATO Relations: Time to Thaw the 'Frozen Conflict,'" *SWP Comments*, no. 12 (June 2007), http://www.swp-berlin.org/fileadmin /contents/products/comments/2007C12_hof_reyn_ks.pdf.

28. De Wijk, *NATO on the Brink of the New Millennium*, 130.

29. Gregory W. Pedlow, "The Evolution of NATO's Command Structure, 1951–2009," http://www.aco.nato.int/resources/21/Evolution%20of%20NATO% 20Cmd%20Structure%201951-2009.pdf, 15.

30. "Lisbon Summit Declaration," paragraph 49.

31. See note 14.

32. "NATO Defence Ministers Agree New NATO Command Structure, Endorse Decision to Extend Operation in Libya," June 9, 2011, at http://www.fco .gov.uk/en/news/latest-news/?view=News&id=611915482 (accessed May 2012, no longer accessible).

33. "MC 3: The Strategic Concept for the Defense of the North Atlantic Area," October 19, 1949, in *NATO Strategy Documents 1949–1969*, ed. Gregory W. Pedlow (SHAPE, 1997), http://www.nato.int/archives/strategy.htm, 4.

34. Robert W. Komer, "Ten Suggestions for Rationalizing NATO," *Survival* 19, no. 2 (1977): 67.

35. The only reference found was to the cost of moving "NATO's two military headquarters at Rocquencourt and Fontainebleau" in 1966. See "NATO: Who Pays the Bill?," *Time*, April 8, 1966, http://content.time.com/time/magazine/article /0,9171,835273,00.html.

36. North Atlantic Treaty Organization, "Ministerial Communiqué," May 27, 1992, point 10.

37. North Atlantic Treaty Organization, "Final Communiqué. Meeting of the North Atlantic Council in Defense Ministers Session," June 13, 1996, point 8.

38. North Atlantic Treaty Organization, "Final Communiqué. Ministerial Meeting of the North Atlantic Council," December 16, 1997, point 14.

39. On this see Thomas-Durell Young, "Reforming NATO's Military Structures: The Long-Term Study and Its Implications for Land Forces," U.S. Army War College, 1998, http://www.strategicstudiesinstitute.army.mil/pdffiles/pub141.pdf, 8.

40. Young, "Reforming NATO's Military Structures," 17.

41. North Atlantic Treaty Organization, "Prague Summit Declaration," November 21, 2002, point 4b.

42. North Atlantic Treaty Organization, "Statement on Capabilities," June 12, 2003, point 3.

43. See note 14.

44. On this meeting see North Atlantic Treaty Organization, "Allies Agree Budget Package," http://www.nato.int/cps/en/natolive/news_61313.htm?mode=news.

45. "Four Major Initiatives for NATO Reform" (unpublished manuscript, April 2010). The other signatories were the Czech Republic, Denmark, Italy, Netherlands, and Norway.

46. See note 14.

47. "Lisbon Summit Declaration," November 20, 2010, point 49.

48. North Atlantic Treaty Organization, "Reshaping NATO's Command Structure," June 28, 2011, http://www.nato.int/cps/en/natolive/news_75773.htm?selectedLocale=en.

49. This observation is based on conversations with numerous officers serving or having recently served in the NCS.

50. For an overview of headquarters in the NATO Force Structure, see "High Readiness Forces and Headquarters in the NATO Force Structure," http://www.aco.nato.int/page134134653.aspx.

51. Celeste A. Wallander, quoting Charles Kupchan, in "Institutional Assets and Adaptability: NATO After the Cold War," *International Organizations* 54, no. 4 (2000): 727.

52. On this see "Remarks by NATO Secretary General Anders Fogh Rasmussen at the Munich Security Conference Plenary Session on 'Building Euro-Atlantic Security,'" http://www.nato.int/cps/en/natolive/opinions_84197.htm.

53. North Atlantic Treaty Organization, "Summit Declaration on Defence Capabilities: Toward NATO Forces 2020," May 20, 2012, paragraph 11.

54. See Wallace J. Thies, *Why NATO Endures* (Cambridge: Cambridge University Press, 2009), 2–14.

55. Robert B. McCalla, "NATO's Persistence after the Cold War," *International Organizations* 50, no. 3 (1996): 451.

56. Thies, *Why NATO Endures*, 22.

57. Zoltan Barany and Robert Rauchhaus, "Explaining NATO's Resilience: Is International Relations Theory Useful?," *Contemporary Security Studies* 32, no. 2 (2011): 290.

58. Barany and Rauchhaus, "Explaining NATO's Resilience," 290.

59. McCalla, "NATO's Persistence after the Cold War," 460.

60. Wallander, "Institutional Assets and Adaptability," 732.

61. Wallander, "Institutional Assets and Adaptability," 706–7.

62. Barany and Rauchhaus, "Explaining NATO's Resilience," 291.

63. Wallander, "Institutional Assets and Adaptability," 711–12.

64. Wallander, "Institutional Assets and Adaptability," 714.

65. Wallander, "Institutional Assets and Adaptability," 714, 727. While underscoring the significance of U.S. power and policy, Wallander nevertheless argues that U.S. decisions also must be seen as dependent of the existence of NATO's institutional structure. See pp. 730 and 712.

66. Wallander, "Institutional Assets and Adaptability," 725.

67. Barany and Rauchhaus, "Explaining NATO's Resilience," 303.

68. Thomas Risse-Knappe, "Collective Identity in a Democratic Community: The Case of NATO," in *The Culture of National Security: Norms and Identity in World Politics*, ed. Peter Katzenstein (New York: Columbia University Press, 1996), 395.

69. Risse-Knappe, "Collective Identity in a Democratic Community," 397. He sees the EU as the only organization scoring higher than NATO in this sense.

70. Risse-Knappe, "Collective Identity in a Democratic Community," 395.

71. McCalla, "NATO's Persistence after the Cold War," 464.

72. McCalla, "NATO's Persistence after the Cold War," 463.

73. McCalla, "NATO's Persistence after the Cold War," 470.

74. According to figures provided to the author, the average total cost of keeping an officer in the NCS in 2010 was about €180 000 per annum for Norway, €95 000 for the Netherlands, and €74 000 for Romania. These numbers should be taken as merely indicative, as the methods use to calculate them may have varied significantly. The author is grateful to Hans Bakke, Lt. Col. Peter Teeuw, and Col. Mihai Ceausu for their assistance.

75. Based on 2010 figures in *Financial and Economic Data Relating to NATO Defence*, March 2011, http://www.nato.int/nato_static/assets/pdf/pdf_2011_03/20110309_PR_CP_2011_027.pdf. Exchange rate set at 1.3 USD per euro, based on data from http://www.exchange-rates.org/history/USD/EUR/G/M.

76. "Lisbon Summit Declaration," paragraph 37.

Chapter 8

Caught between Strategic Visions

NATO's Rapid Reaction Force

Jens Ringsmose

According to legend, it was NATO's first Secretary General, Lord Ismay, who cogently identified the alliance's principal purpose as one of "keeping the Russians out, the Americans in, and the Germans down." Continued U.S. commitment to Europe was recognized as the key means; deterrence against the Soviet Union and the denationalization of European security politics were the objectives. Despite almost chronic intra-alliance bickering and recurrent crisis, all NATO allies could agree to this basic formula until 1991. The internal Cold War debates were thus always more about *how* to achieve well-established objectives than about *what* exactly should be NATO's raison d'être.

The fall of the Berlin Wall heralded the beginning of more fundamental deliberations about the grand strategy for NATO. No longer did it suffice to address the "how-security" question. In the absence of a substantial and easily identifiable threat to Western interests, the "security-against-what" question moved center stage. Many member-states—and certainly most of the Central and East European newcomers—could straightforwardly identify with the twin objectives fleshed out by Lord Ismay in the 1950s. But others came increasingly to see NATO's future well outside of its traditional remit. Different visions of what should be the alliance's main concerns and geographical focus points thus developed: Should NATO go global or remain a regional organization with regional members and a regional mission statement?

In effect, NATO has been struck by profound strategic confusion as the Atlantic alliance, to a large extent, has become different things to different allies. This is also the central tension that has affected, among many other areas, NATO's rapid reaction force, the NRF. Conceived to be the alliance's major transformational flagship and a powerful cutting-edge military tool deployable to all parts of the globe, the NRF has fallen victim to the strategic schizophrenia currently beleaguering NATO. The response force thus in many ways constitutes a microcosm of the wider debate about NATO's core purposes and the "in-area versus out-of-area" schism.

Besides constituting a microcosm of the post–Cold War alliance, NATO's experiences with the NRF are also illustrative of the opportunities and challenges associated with the pooling of national forces and with defense cooperation in a wider sense. For some years now, "smart defense"—the NATO terminology currently in vogue—has been high on the alliance's agenda, and judging from the political signals from allied capitals (and their respective ministries of finance), it will continue to be so for the foreseeable future. No doubt the pressure for common, or at least coordinated, development, acquisition, and maintenance of military capabilities will increase. To better understand the pros and cons of a more cooperative approach to defense, NATO leaders could do worse than to study the somewhat turbulent history of the NRF. In particular, the story of the alliance's reaction force is instructive of the difficulties related to the sharing of sovereignty. The analysis of the NRF is thus a case that also illustrates what the alliance should expect from a more collaborative future.

This chapter first explains how the NRF evolved from an American brainchild to a fully fledged, multinational, and combined force in less than four years and provides a brief overview of the NRF's main structure. The second section assesses the extent to which the ambitions that originally surrounded the NRF have been met. I also present an outline of the latest incarnation of the response force—the so-called Option Charlie. The main argument proposed in this section is that the NRF has been a qualified failure: although the force has had a transformational impact, lack of troop commitments and disagreements about the force's operational role have largely eroded its credibility. The third and final section takes stock of the ways in which the NATO "in-area" versus "out-of-area" controversies have affected the development and functioning of the NRF. It does so by examining three partly interrelated issues that have been at the forefront in the debate about the NRF: the use of the force in relation to Article 5, when and how to use the NRF, and common funding.

A Brief History of the NRF

The original NRF concept was approved with great enthusiasm by NATO leaders at the Prague Transformation Summit in November 2002. An American initiative proposed to the European NATO members a few months before the meeting in Prague, the concept essentially entailed the making of the type of "strike force that could have deployed to Afghanistan and worked closely with US forces there" during Operation Enduring Freedom.[1] In essence, the initiative was thus conceived to furnish NATO with an agile and robust military tool, while at the same time inducing an expeditionary mind-set among the European allies. NATO-Europe, it was argued, needed to invest in an intrinsically American way of war. Hence, the twenty-five-thousand-strong, predominantly European, "first generation NRF" was designed to be a technologically advanced military instrument, capable of engaging in high-intensity operations across the globe on short notice. If successful, it was expected that the force would help shrink the "transatlantic capability gap" (put so vividly on display during NATO's air war against Serbia in 1999) and in turn alleviate the political fallout of the military lopsidedness between the United States and its junior partners. Revitalizing the alliance at a time of internal crisis was thus the concept's underlying political rationale.[2]

In the NRF construct's first incarnation, the force comprised a reinforced brigade combat team, a combined naval task force, and an air element capable of undertaking approximately two hundred combat sorties per day. In addition to these core components, the force was planned to include a number of smaller niche capabilities, including special forces.[3] By rotating both national troop commitments and NATO assets assigned to the force every six months, the NRF was—and still is—structured to stimulate military transformation. After an initial six to eighteen months of national training, units designated to the NRF undergo another six-month NATO exercise program and a final test before being certified as an NRF force. Only then, the entire multinational force is put on six months' standby, as NRF rotation number "X." Due to critically low national force contributions, the NRF standby period was extended to twelve months in 2012.

It took a while and some tough discussions between NATO's ACO in Mons, Belgium, and the IMS in Brussels before the alliance could announce the NRF's mission statement.[4] But eventually NATO's military authorities concluded that the new force should be prepared to undertake seven generic missions, ranging from deployment as an initial entry force in a hostile environment at the high end of the conflict spectrum to nonkinetic operations such as noncombatant evacuation and consequence management operations at the other end of the operational spectrum. At the Istanbul Summit in 2004, the NATO family formally agreed to the proposed mission set.

From Prague in 2002 to NATO's summit in Riga in November 2006, the force progressed swiftly, at least to a certain point. Beginning in June 2003, NATO's defense ministers approved a so-called Detailed Implementation Plan; the first force generation conference was held in July 2003; in October 2003 NRF 1 was formally launched; and after a number of exercises in late 2003 and 2004, the Secretary General and Supreme Allied Commander Europe (SACEUR), General James Jones, declared the force at Initial Operational Capability in October 2004. About a year later, in September and October 2005, a few NRF elements were for the first time deployed to provide disaster relief in the aftermath of Hurricane Katrina. At about the same time and until February 2006, a more substantial part of the force was used in the disaster relief effort in Pakistan following the October 8, 2005, earthquake. Since then the NRF has not been utilized in "real-world operations."

The NRF was declared to be at FOC at the Riga Summit in November 2006, yet not without considerable difficulties. Until immediately before the summit, the force's manpower quotas (in NATO speak, the Combined Joint Statement of Requirement, CJSOR) were not adequately met. Only with the use of somewhat creative, last-minute measures and accounting did NATO's military authorities manage to meet the objective, allowing Secretary General de Hoop Scheffer to proclaim "mission accomplished" in the Latvian capital.[5]

However, as it became clear in the spring of 2007 that the capabilities offered for the following NRF rotations were critically low, in October 2007 NATO defense ministers agreed to a first revision of the force. Following the suggestions made by SACEUR and the NATO Chiefs of Defense, the alliance adopted a "graduated approach," which was to remain in force until 2010; that is, the NRF's second incarnation. According to this formula, the actual NRF was slimmed down significantly, to about 12,500 troops organized as a core of command and control elements and a number of key enablers, onto which further predesignated elements could be bolted. These supplementary elements were in principle part of the NRF but could be used by nations for other purposes even while they were formally on NRF standby. Without additional force generation the "core NRF" was merely able to conduct the least demanding of the seven generic missions, consequence management.[6]

Assessing the NRF's Performance

To what extent has the NRF met the aspirations set out by national and allied policy makers at the Prague Summit and in subsequent policy papers? Has the force actually fulfilled its twin transformational and operational purposes?

On the positive side, there is little doubt that the NRF has contributed to the modernization and reformation of NATO's Force Structure. Although often ignored because of the somewhat unmerited tendency to focus exclusively on the NRF's operational dimension, the force has most likely generated genuine transformational benefits. Senior NATO officials in Brussels, Mons, and Norfolk (Virginia) ascribe to the NRF an important role in the allegedly successful implementation of the so-called Prague Capabilities Commitments, which obliged NATO members to acquire specific equipment that could improve the alliance's operational capabilities. The Prague Capabilities Commitments were adopted by NATO concurrently with the NRF concept. In some areas, such as defense against chemical, biological, radiological, and nuclear weapons, progress has supposedly been quite remarkable. Moreover—and perhaps more important—the initiative has facilitated a (slowly) developing European acceptance of the need to invest in deployable and sustainable military assets. According to NATO officials, the force has thus been instrumental in instilling an increasingly expeditionary mind-set in several European capitals. Allegedly the concept has even promoted the development of an "embryonic expeditionary strategic culture" within NATO-Europe.[7]

The crux of the issue is whether NATO's operations in Afghanistan and elsewhere undermined the transformational raison d'être of the NRF. Did not Afghanistan become the main driver of reform within the alliance, thereby diluting a key rationale behind an allied reaction force? Does NATO really need a modernizing tool such as the NRF, when real-world operations so obviously compel the alliance to adapt and transform?

There is little doubt that the Afghan International Security Assistance Force (ISAF) has served as an important catalyst for transformation and increased investments in expeditionary capabilities. The often extremely demanding operations in Afghanistan have forced many allies to invest in a fundamentally new way of war.[8] However, relying solely on current and recent operations as engines of transformation would leave the alliance perilously ill-equipped for the future, as it would focus training, organization, and capability development exclusively on ISAF-type operations.

Taking its transformational cue from Afghanistan only, NATO would (despite the tough fighting in the south and east of the country) generate armed forces configured entirely for military undertakings below the threshold of major combat operations and conventional war. Many of the high-intensity capabilities that the NRF is currently adding to the transformation agenda would be missing. This is certainly not a problem if, as some have argued, the effort to turn NATO-Europe's armed forces into something akin to the U.S. military—that is, a military instrument designed for *both* high- and low-intensity operations—is intrinsically misguided. If the types of operations that NATO will have to conduct in the future "will require different capabilities and a different understanding of war from what has to date been advanced through NATO transformation,"[9] then NRF-driven reform is indeed flawed and superfluous. However, if one assumes, as does this author, that the Europeans—and the Atlantic alliance—are better prepared for future challenges with capabilities tailored to conduct high-performance interventions and conventional warfighting in their military inventory, then the NRF still serves an important transformational purpose. Whether that is enough to justify the continued existence of the force partly depends on its operational performance. And this brings us to the more depressing side of the NRF.

Envisioned to be the alliance's high-powered first response to an emerging crisis, the NRF soon proved to be a force in constant need of additional troops and capabilities. Since (at least) 2006 and until 2010, SHAPE's yearly force generation conferences repeatedly failed to source the CJSOR and left the NRF with substantial deficiencies in several areas. This became evident well before the declaration of FOC and the Riga Summit, in the spring of 2006, when NATO conceded that only 82 percent of the force needed was available for NRF 7 to conduct its full range of missions.[10] Confronted with the specter of a humiliating political defeat, Washington, at the request of the outgoing SACEUR, assigned the missing forces (in the shape of an expeditionary strike group) in a last-minute rescue effort at the Riga Summit.[11] The U.S. contribution, of course, had not participated in the NRF's half-year training, and it was never clear exactly which expeditionary strike group had been designated to the alliance's new response force. It is therefore hardly surprising that well-informed NATO officials describe the declaration of FOC in Riga as "completely fictitious."[12]

The FOC announcement, however, was not signaling the end to the NRF's fill rate problems, but rather the beginning. Only eight months after Riga, in the summer of 2007, the new SACEUR, General Bantz

Craddock, informed the Secretary General that the manpower quota for NRF 9 (July 1, 2007, to December 31, 2007) was at an alarming 66 percent. And as the Bush administration—disappointed with the Europeans' troop contributions—had recently announced that there would be no more American gap-filling, there was little prospect of bringing the force to its planned strength in the short run. Moreover, the force generation offers for the following four years had only produced an average fill rate of 47 percent (see table 8.1 for the actual fill rates for NRF 9 to NRF 14). Concluding that the alliance had exhausted the willingness of the member-states to provide sufficient capabilities to the NRF, Craddock deemed the force incapable of conducting even the least demanding of the seven generic missions without considerable risk. He therefore took the rather extraordinary step of rescinding FOC of the NRF. This, of course, was never made public, but in principle—and despite the fact that NATO declared the NRF "a credible force" at about the same time[13]—the force was not at fully operational capability from July 2007 to 2010.[14]

As noted above, the inability to properly resource the CJSOR led to the first revision of the NRF's construction in October 2007 and the adoption of the "graduated approach." Already by mid-2008, however, NATO policy makers had determined that the graduated approach was an unsustainable solution. Again, inadequate fill rates were identified as the key problem. After a fundamental discussion of the concept at their informal meeting in Budapest in September 2008, the ministers of defense therefore tasked the Military Committee and SHAPE with the development of additional options for ensuring the success of the force—that is, the second revision of the NRF within two years of the declaration of FOC.

Various background interviews suggest that SACEUR was in favor of sacrificing the NRF in early 2009. Faced with recurring force shortfalls and the unenviable task of producing gloomy NRF Operational Capability Assessments for the North Atlantic Council every half year, Craddock simply considered it reasonable to put the force to rest. The increasing call for Western troops in Afghanistan only added to the feeling that the NRF was becoming a liability rather than a strategic asset.

TABLE 8.1. Force Contributions for NRF 9 to NRF 14

Rotation	NRF 9 (2007/2)	NRF 10 (2008/1)	NRF 11 (2008/2)	NRF 12 (2009/1)	NRF 13 (2009/2)	NRF 14 (2010/1)	Average
Fill rate (%)	70	74	71	65	61	74	69

Source: Correspondence with senior NATO official, NATO Headquarters, Brussels, April 2010.

At that point, however, too much political capital had been invested in the concept to abandon it. Exhibited as a symbol of commitment and solidarity, the renouncement of the force would have signaled the disarray of a feeble alliance unable to find the capabilities to man a fairly small force. Certainly the low fill rates spawned awful press reports, but the liquidation of the high-profile NRF program would have been little less than a public diplomacy disaster. Thus, what appeared sound from a purely military viewpoint was simply a political impossibility.

In the spring of 2009 Allied Command Operations developed three possible solutions to the NRF's predicaments: Option Alpha entailed only command and control elements and consequently—for all practical purposes—abolishing the entire concept; Option Bravo included a further refinement of the graduated approach, that is, Option Alpha plus a limited number of additional troops and capabilities; and Option Charlie—as we shall see below—proposed a more fundamental restructuring of the force. In late spring the Military Committee endorsed Option Charlie, and at their meeting in June 2009 defense ministers approved this option as well. Implementation was completed in January 2012.

Why has it been so difficult for NATO to generate the required forces for the NRF? There are several probable answers to this question, but most important, the NRF came to life just as the alliance's level of operational activity began to increase drastically as a consequence of NATO taking responsibility for ISAF in the summer of 2003. Missions in Iraq, Kosovo, Lebanon, Chad, and elsewhere—although not to the same extent as ISAF—have also taken their toll on the force pool of NATO member-states. True, when the number of ISAF troops peaked in 2011, there were little more than 130,000 troops in Afghanistan. However, just as a functioning NRF requires the equivalent of three NRFs on standby at any given time, so the ISAF mission involves—at least—three times the number of forces actually deployed at any moment.

On a more fundamental level, however, NATO's inability to man both the NRF and ongoing operations simultaneously reflects the alliance's critical lack of deployable forces. Despite years of transformational efforts, several European member-states are still far from meeting NATO's so-called usability goals, stating that 50 percent of national land forces must be "structured, prepared and equipped for deployed operations" and 10 percent must be "undertaking or planned for sustained operations."[15] Some allies—for example Turkey, Greece, and Belgium—have only restructured their military half-heartedly and partly on the cheap. Given the current economic situation in most NATO nations, there is little prospect of rectifying the imbalance between operational demands and the number of usable forces in the short run.

Another—less influential—reason for the shortage of commitments to the NRF has been the allies' failure to clearly agree on when and where to deploy the force. I return to this issue below, but the conflicting views on how to utilize the NRF were already apparent in 2005 and have remained so to this day. According to NATO officials interviewed by the author in Brussels and Mons, a number of member-states are reluctant to assign manpower and equipment at a time of substantial operational demands because they anticipate that the NRF will never be used. From this point of view, the idle force is little but a drain on already insufficient resources. Allegedly, the United Kingdom and Norway have been prominent members of this category of member-states.

Finally, the NRF's operational viability has in all likelihood been hampered by NATO's long-standing principle of "letting the costs lie where they fall." According to this formula—which has been applied to the NRF since its inception—the expenses of deployment and exercises fall to the nations that have forces on standby for a given rotation. As Spain was painfully taught during the NRF deployment to Pakistan in autumn of 2005, signing up for the rapid reaction force can be a very costly experience. Thus, the "reverse lottery" creates strong disincentives for member-states to make CJSOR commitments.[16]

Option Charlie

Has the alliance's embrace of the revised NRF construct—that is, Option Charlie—provided NATO with a more credible force? That is, in fact, the likely outcome of this most recent restructuring of the force designed with the explicit intention of offering maximum opportunities for nations to participate. What the allies agreed to in June 2009 was essentially the making of a twofold structure consisting of a thirteen-thousand-strong Immediate Response Force (IRF) similar to—but more flexible than—the "core" of the extant graduated approach, and a residual Response Force Pool (RFP). The latter is open ended, and its actual size depends on the number of forces that nations are willing to make available. Significantly, nations and partner countries can contribute forces to the RFP under "flexible terms and conditions," meaning that actual operational commitments to future NRF missions can be made on an ad hoc basis. The IRF comprises predesignated operational and tactical level command and control assets as well as maritime, land, air, and joint response forces. It is not scaled to be a stand-alone force for all but the smallest operations, and in most cases the

IRF will therefore have to be supplemented by national capability commitments made to the RFP.[17]

Perhaps more important, NATO's Secretary General, Anders Fogh Rasmussen, breathed new life into the NRF in early 2012 when he announced that the response force will be a key component of the Combined Forces Initiative (CFI). Realizing that the alliance will need new transformational drivers once the last combat troops have left Afghanistan, this initiative is meant to promote NATO interoperability and drive a continuous process of peacetime transformation. As could perhaps have been expected, the NRF is thus destined to play a more important role when the alliance enters a period characterized by less operational strain.[18]

Also crucial, the NRF's mission statement has been altered to a more generalized description of the construct's fundamental purpose. According to its latest mission statement, the force is destined to endow the alliance with a more flexible tool that can provide "immediate military response to an emerging crisis as part of the Alliance's comprehensive crisis management system for both Article 5 and Crisis Response Operations." The revision is significant, because it allows the NRF to move away from the previously used rigid CJSORs and the Operational Capability Assessments that have served as little more than a mechanism for reporting failure. After the implementation of Option Charlie, SACEUR is no longer required to assess and report to policy makers on whether the force is able to conduct the full range of predefined missions or not. In effect—as one senior NATO official described it—"NATO's self-inflicted fiasco reporting on the NRF will be a thing of the past." Although somewhat creatively, the image of the force has therefore improved as the low fill rates and the associated negative press reports have disappeared. The perceived capability shortfall has thus been "defined away."

To sum up: the NRF has hitherto been a qualified failure. While the initiative has added valuable impetus to NATO's transformational agenda, it has failed to provide the alliance with a credible operational tool. This, in turn, has done little to enhance NATO's public reputation. Although the main reasons for the NRF's lack of success are unlikely to disappear in the near future, the latest revision of the concept might just be the scheme that will make the force a real—and perceived—success.

NRF Issues

Perhaps unsurprisingly, discussions about the NRF have closely mirrored the wider debate about the overall purpose and tasks of NATO in a security environment devoid of a major unifying threat. According to Jeffrey Bialos and Stuart Koehl, "The NRF is a microcosm of these broader considerations—the tensions in the alliance, the different security perspectives and different force doctrines and trajectories—and must be understood in this context."[19] The strategic confusion plaguing NATO has also afflicted the alliance's quick response force. As some member-states perceive Russia as the main threat to their security, while others are more focused on what is generally portrayed as "out-of-area" challenges such as substate actors, failing states, and global terrorism, the NRF becomes a potential instrument for competing security visions. As mentioned above, these competing visions are observable in the intra-alliance exchanges about three key issues: Article 5, the issue of when and where to make use of the force, and common funding.

The NRF and Article 5

Although the NRF was formally designed to be an instrument for both global operations and collective defense, differences over how to balance the two types of missions did not emerge in earnest until the Russian-Georgian conflict of August 2008. President Vladimir Putin's somewhat belligerent speech at the Munich Security Conference in February 2007 did spur concern, but prior to Moscow's assertive show of force in the Caucasus the year after, it was almost instinctively understood that the alliance's new response force was intended for operations beyond the Euro-Atlantic area—not for the defense of allied territory. NATO's expeditionary capabilities, including the NRF, were more or less implicitly linked to non-Article 5 missions. However, Russia's aggressive behavior in "its near abroad" changed the strategic and diplomatic dynamics within the alliance markedly, as some allies increasingly came to see their self-confident eastern neighbor as a principal threat to their national security. A majority of the East European member-states—as well as Norway—therefore began to question the trajectory of globalized engagement embarked on by the alliance after the terrorist attack on the United States in 2001. NATO must, so the argument goes, reorient its focus on Europe, Article 5, and defense against conventional threats to the region.

As a consequence, the alliance is currently split into—at least—two factions: "the globalizers," who hold that NATO should basically transform itself into a hub for global security relationships, and the "Article 5ers."[20] Surely the approaching disengagement from Afghanistan and the lack of appetite for yet another major operation far from the Euro-Atlantic core area will make the issue less salient and the related debates less pointed.

Nonetheless, this is still the most significant line of demarcation within the alliance.

It was within this context that the United Kingdom proposed the creation of a so-called Allied Solidarity Force (ASF) in February 2009. Envisioned as a fifteen-hundred-strong multinational force, the ASF would be a smaller version of NATO's now-disbanded Allied Command Europe Mobile Force-Land (AMF-L), designed to demonstrate alliance solidarity by acting as a tripwire during the Cold War. The unstated—but obvious—intention behind the AMF-L was to have as many flags as possible on the coffins at the start of a conflict, thereby ensuring that NATO's musketeer clause would be activated. The British-proposed ASF, so it seems, was projected to serve a similar purpose. Created within the larger framework of the NRF, the separate solidarity force would thus reassure "those countries that are concerned about being on the border and feel that Article 4 or 5 is important to them."[21] Just like the AMF-L, the ASF—which was planned to comprise personnel from all twenty-eight NATO members—would be a purely political initiative with very little or no military value.

The British proposal received a mixed reception, clearly reflecting the wider debate within the alliance. Most of the Article 5ers, for obvious reasons, welcomed the idea (although with some reservations), while a majority of the older allies have been mostly skeptical about the benefits of such a force. Some nations, including the United States, Canada, and the Netherlands, argued that NATO cannot afford to develop capabilities for collective defense missions only. Others, including France and Germany, have been opposed to the initiative on the grounds that it would further aggravate NATO's already difficult relationship with Moscow. From a military point of view, the Military Committee has resisted the idea, maintaining that the risk arising from such a high level of multinationality would simply be too high. Too many national contributions would render the force highly inefficient. Moreover, neither Washington nor Paris or Berlin sees Russia as a genuine threat to allied security. In fact, not even the proposer—the British government—perceives of Russia as a real danger to the alliance. Background interviews at NATO Headquarters thus suggest that the scheme was ultimately aimed at freeing up more Eastern European troops for ISAF. As indicated by then British defense secretary John Hutton, "Such a force would make it easier for the alliance's new member countries to increase their troop contingents in Afghanistan without fearing [Russian] provocations against them at home."[22]

Without the support of the United States, Germany, France, and the Military Committee, the original ASF initiative gained little traction, and it was soon abandoned. However, unwilling to let the concept die altogether, most of the new member-states and Norway have insisted that the revised NRF should include elements of the ASF scheme and be given a more visible role in collective defense. And so it will. As part of a compromise between the globalizers and the Article 5ers, the "third generation NRF"/Option Charlie will give increased emphasis to its responsibilities in relation to Articles 4 and 5, effectively subsuming the tasks of the proposed ASF into the new construct. In addition to its previous functions, the NRF will be used to "provide visible assurance of the Alliance's cohesion and commitment to deterrence and collective defense," through—among other things—planning, training, and regularly exercising elements of the NRF on the alliance's territory.[23] That was exactly what happened in late 2013, when the NRF exercised in the Baltic countries and Poland as part of the exercise Steadfast Jazz.

Indicative of the new and less "out-of-area"–centric context in which the NRF is functioning is NATO's Strategic Concept from November 2010, which interestingly states that the alliance "will develop and maintain robust, mobile and deployable conventional forces to carry out both Article 5 responsibilities and the Alliance's expeditionary operations, including with the NATO Response Force."[24] Compared to 2006, the force is clearly less intimately tied to a more globalist vision.

When Should the NRF Be Used?

The absence of a clear and common sense of NATO's fundamental purpose has also fueled the debate over when and where to actually make use of NATO's contested response force. Differing threat perceptions and diverging understandings of what the Atlantic alliance's core role should be have thus contaminated and to some extent paralyzed the NRF. One group of allies, the self-described "progressive" or "global NATO" nations, including the United Kingdom, the United States, Canada, and Denmark, has repeatedly called for the employment of the force in Afghanistan.[25] Based on a "use-it-or-lose-it" philosophy, these member-states, all heavily engaged in the most unruly southern part of the Afghan theater, have argued forcefully that if the NRF is not used in real operations, it will lose its credibility and eventually pass away. This is also a point of view adhered to by a few of the member-states calling for an increased in-area focus, such as Norway. In effect, it is argued, the force will become a victim of an excessively constricted interpretation of its potential missions.

While their readiness to use the NRF is partly explained by the deep commitment to the ISAF mission and the worrying situation in southern

Afghanistan, these allies are also motivated by an underlying global view of the alliance's future. They all subscribe—although to different degrees—to the vision of an Atlantic alliance intervening and integrating globally. As the viability of the idea of NATO as a global security exporter has been perceived to be highly dependent on whether the alliance is successful in Afghanistan, the globalizers have been prepared to make use of the force if required—even if the mission is not clearly within the NRF mission set.

Another group of countries, led by France and Germany, has been profoundly opposed to the use of the NRF in Afghanistan—either as a real fighting force when ISAF troops are under pressure or as a reserve bolstering security during elections.[26] They have been so, however, for slightly different reasons. France has repeatedly stressed that the NRF should be a force only for "in extremis" situations (not "an arm of the International Red Cross")[27] and has generally given priority to the transformational benefits of the concept. Berlin has allegedly been reluctant on the grounds that German troops assigned to the force could find themselves involved in high-intensity combat—something that could cause tremendous domestic problems for any German government, given the country's constitution and troubled past. Both allies, however, have argued that using the NRF as an operational reserve would dilute the force's transformational value and its originally intended ability to engage in hard-hitting first-in, first-out operations. As observed by a German senior NATO official: "If we use the force as a reserve it will eat up the NRF."[28] Ostensibly, that is also why Germany and France vetoed using the NRF to create security during the Riga Summit in 2006. The risk of weakening the force's high-performance capacity by using it as a reserve is also acknowledged by allies belonging to the "use-it-or-lose-it" category.[29]

Behind these arguments, however, lies a deep-seated aversion to the vision of a more globally engaged NATO. This was already obvious when Washington launched the NRF initiative in 2002. In the autumn of that year French minister of defense Michele Aillot-Marie commented on the U.S. proposal: "NATO has to keep its original geographical limitation."[30] Although France was overall in favor of the concept, Aillot-Marie made it clear that "the force should not operate outside Europe, be used in a preemptive manner, or operate without a UN mandate." Peter Struck, German defense minister at the time, echoed his French colleague, remarking that it "would be wrong to assume that the United States could simply use the Response Force in any corner of the world."[31] Since then both France and Germany have become more sympathetic to a globally engaged

NATO—at least on a rhetorical level. Hitherto, the acceptance of a less-constrained role for the alliance in terms of geography has not, however, translated into deeds. And there is still little prospect of the NRF being deployed to Afghanistan.

Common Funding

The development of the NRF has in all likelihood been hampered by NATO's "costs-lie-where-they-fall" principle. According to this analysis, allies have been reluctant to make CJSOR commitments because of the potential high costs of an unanticipated deployment. This hindrance to adequate fill rates was already identified by then Secretary General de Hoop Scheffer at the Munich Security Conference in February 2006 (shortly after the NRF deployment to Pakistan), where he warned that under the existing funding arrangements, "participating in the NRF is something like a reverse lottery": "If your numbers come up you actually lose money. If the NRF deploys while you happen to be in the rotation, you pay the full costs of deployment of your forces. This can be a disincentive to countries to commit to participation in the NRF. And that is something the Alliance can't afford."[32] About a month later his concerns were repeated by then SACEUR, General James Jones, when he told the U.S. Senate Armed Services Committee that the NRF's future viability would "depend on member nations' willingness to resource the necessary forces and commit to a structure of common alliance funding."[33]

Partly as a result of these and other warnings, the allies decided to make the strategic lift portions of unanticipated NRF deployments eligible for NATO common funding for a two-year "trial" period at the Riga Summit (the "experiment" was later extended for another year). If successful—that is, removing disincentives to NRF pledges without undermining the nations' willingness to invest in modern, efficient equipment—it was expected that the time-limited common funding scheme would be widened to cover other costs associated with participation in the NRF. However, in October 2009 the NATO Senior Resource Board reported that the effects of the experiment had been somewhat inconclusive. There were no clear signs that making strategic lift portions of unanticipated NRF deployment eligible for common funding influenced the allies' willingness to contribute to the force.[34] Nonetheless, common funding for unanticipated NRF deployments was extended to 2013. The sharp disagreements between advocates of increased NRF common funding and supporters of the "costs-lie-where-they-fall" principle have therefore not been settled.[35]

On the one hand, a number of member-states, headed by the United States, have been strongly in favor of increasing the use of common funding. Seen from Washington, collective action problems and related free-riding strategies create considerable obstacles to the international deployment of NATO troops and the development of an effective and usable NRF. Given the staunch U.S. support of NATO's taking on an active operational role beyond the Euro-Atlantic area, it is therefore hardly surprising that successive American governments have argued consistently that extending the criteria for NATO common funding would alleviate the NRF's growing pains. Besides the United States, particularly smaller nations—fearing the unpredictable but potentially significant financial burdens of an unexpected NRF deployment—are said to belong to this category of allies. Others, such as the Netherlands, have called for enhanced employment of common funding for the NRF on the grounds that the alliance's operational activities should be given first priority. At a time of high operational tempo, increasing common costs in Afghanistan, and the most serious economic crisis in decades, this also entails cutting expenses related to the alliance's static infrastructure.[36] In addition to this group of member-states, NATO's strategic commanders—SACEUR and SACT—have been solidly behind plans to increase the use of common funding. SHAPE is even reported to "have some sympathy for a more UN-like funding-arrangement."[37]

On the other hand, France has led the opposition to a more comprehensive NRF common funding scheme. Seen from Paris—and to some extent from Berlin, London, and Madrid—expanding the common funding mechanisms to other portions of agreed NRF deployments and exercises would mean that countries (like France) that are already shouldering a fair share of the common burden would pay twice. As noted by the British government in 2008: "[H]aving paid for their own capabilities nations should not then have to subsidize those that contribute less than their expected share."[38]

Although the opponents of further common funding are usually arguing against the funding system due to its unfairness in terms of financial burden sharing, there is some evidence that, for example, France's stance has been partly informed by political motives. In the words of a senior NATO diplomat: "France's standpoint on common funding must also be understood in the light of Paris's appetite for security cooperation in an EU-environment."[39] This view is corroborated by the French government's apparent willingness to use common funding for the EU Battle Groups. Thus, during the French EU presidency, Paris "specifically called for the 'costs lie where they fall' concept to be abandoned in the name of so-called financial solidarity."[40] To the French—so it seems—common funding is not objectionable in principle.

Conclusion

When the NRF initiative was launched in late 2002, it was projected to provide the transatlantic alliance with a vehicle for modernization as well as an agile war-fighting capability with real teeth: transformation, operational capacity, interoperability, and burden sharing were thus at the heart of the scheme. Hitherto, however, the force has been unsuccessful in meeting these ambitious objectives. While the NRF has had a transformational impact, its inability to meet the requirements of the CJSORs and failure to agree on a clear operational role for the force have turned it into a net liability.

Most importantly, the ongoing operations in Afghanistan and elsewhere have stretched the available pool of deployable NATO troops to the extent that nations have been reluctant to make sufficient NRF commitments. Although these basic conditions are unlikely to change in the near future, there are reasons to believe that the latest revisions of the construct will improve the image of the NRF considerably. Rightly so, the alliance has moved beyond the self-inflicted and unproductive fiasco reporting linked to the first two incarnations of the NRF. Also, the latest signals from Allied Command Operations indicate that allied capability offers are indeed increasing.

A major question, of course, is whether the NRF will be more than "just" a transformational tool in the years to come. Or put differently: Are the political and strategic disagreements that have so obviously afflicted the NRF likely to be overcome, allowing the force to be used in real-world operations? Will the NRF also become an operational tool? The answer to these questions depends closely on the future balance within the debate on the geographical remits of allied activities.

As discussed above, the in-area versus out-of-area debate is thus the key political theme framing the issue. As long as a number of European powers remain instinctively opposed to engaging NATO in extra-European operations, the cutting edge and—if necessary—hard-hitting military instrument that was introduced at the Prague Summit and declared FOC in Riga four years later is destined to "stay in the drawer." Surely the NRF will be exercised on alliance territory—which in turn will make NATO more visible—and hence satisfy those member-states concerned about the intentions of a self-assertive Russia. But an exclusive in-area focus will keep the force linked to its transformational purpose, as there is little prospect of contingencies requiring a military response within the NATO treaty area.

Yet given American preferences for European participation and burden sharing in future military operations, I predict that the NRF—sooner or later—will be employed in missions outside the Euro-Atlantic theater. This is good news for the NRF, as its basic health is predicated on the fulfillment of *both* its transformational and its operational purposes. In the post–Cold War period, Washington has persistently sought to move the alliance to adopt a more global outlook and—as clearly indicated by, for instance, the three Strategic Concepts embraced since 1991—not without effect. NATO has indisputably become less Eurocentric since the fall of the Berlin Wall. While the appetite for major out-of-area operations will surely be very modest in the years following the projected withdrawal from Afghanistan, the globalist camp (including the United States) will keep calling for a NATO role in more limited extra-European engagements (i.e., not another operation like those in Iraq and Afghanistan). Therefore, the alliance is likely to continue on the trajectory toward a less territorially constrained grand strategy. Of course some nations will object to this long-term course of events. But as Washington's commitment to NATO is likely to depend on the acceptance of a less pronounced in-area focus, the alliance will be moved. Embedded in this overall political and geostrategic context, the NRF is designated to become an instrument of both military modernization and real-world military operations.

At the same time, the rocky development of the NRF reflects the difficulties and limits of transatlantic ambitions in relation to smart defense and the pooling and sharing of allied defense capabilities. Undoubtedly the multiple initiatives taken by NATO in this regard are rational and could potentially strengthen the alliance. However, as demonstrated by the rather discouraging history of the NRF, they are also destined to come up against a political reality characterized by sovereign nation-states with different strategic visions for NATO. This will not change fundamentally as long as the alliance is perceived to be different things by different members.

NOTES

All Web sites last accessed in November 2013 unless otherwise noted.

This chapter was previously published in another version as "NATO's Response Force: Finally Getting It Right," *European Security* 18, no. 3 (2009): 287–304.

1. Richard Kugler, *The NATO Response Force 2002–2006: Innovation by the Atlantic Alliance* (Washington, DC: Center for Technology and National Security Policy, National Defense University, 2007), 4.

2. Hans Binnendijk and Richard Kugler, "Transforming European Forces," *Survival* 44, no. 3 (2002): 117–32.

3. Nicholas Stringer, *Refining the NATO Response Force: Improved Utility from a Revised Construct* (Montgomery, AL: Maxwell Air Force Base, April 2008), 5–8; Nicholas Fiorenza, "Ready for Action," *Jane's Defence Weekly*, September 27, 2006.

4. Senior NATO official, interview with author, NATO Headquarters, October 2009.

5. Senior officer, SHAPE, interview with author, October 2009.

6. Senior official, Danish Ministry of Defense, interview with author, August 2009; interview, senior NATO official, October 2009; "Eingreiftruppe am Ende," *Der Spiegel*, September 17, 2007, http://www.spiegel.de/spiegel/print/d-52985261 .html; Judy Dempsey, "NATO Retreats from Establishment of Rapid-reaction Force," *New York Times*, September 20, 2007, http://www.nytimes.com/2007/09/20 /world/europe/20iht-force.4.7587514.html; John Mark, "NATO to Scale Back Reaction Force," *Irish Times*, October 26, 2007.

7. Allied Command Transformation, *NATO Response Force: Transformational Benefits* (Norfolk, VA: Allied Command Transformation, 2009); interview, NATO Headquarters, October 2009; interview, Danish Ministry of Defense, August 2009; senior NATO official, Allied Command Transformation correspondence with author, December 2009. At the Riga Summit in 2006, NATO claimed that all of the 460 or so commitments made by the allies at Prague would be fulfilled in 2009.

8. See, for example, House of Commons, Defense Committee, "The Future of NATO and European Defense" (Ninth Report of Session 2007–2008, House of Commons, 2008), 50.

9. Mats Berdal and David Ucko, "NATO at 60," *Survival* 51, no. 2 (2009): 55–76, 65.

10. Joris Janssen Lok, "NATO Response Force Falling Short of Target," *Jane's Defence Weekly*, May 17, 2006, 5. See also Robert Bell, 'Sisyphus and the NRF,' *NATO Review* (Autumn 2006), http://www.nato.int/docu/review/2006/issue3/english /art4.html; John R. Schmidt, "Last Alliance Standing? NATO after 9/11," *Washington Quarterly* 30, no. 1 (Winter 2006–2007): 93–106.

11. The American decision to contribute the missing capabilities was made during the night between the first and second day of the two-day Riga Summit. Interview, NATO Headquarters, October 2009.

12. Interview, SHAPE, October 2009.

13. North Atlantic Treaty Organization, "Questions and Answers: The NATO Response Force," September 21, 2007, http://www.nato.int/cps/en/SID-42E2C9C3 -8722613F/natolive/opinions_8494.htm?selectedLocale=en.

14. Interviews, NATO Headquarters and SHAPE, October 2009; "Schrumpf-kur: NATO verkleinert schnelle Eingreiftruppe," *Der Spiegel*, October 25, 2007, http://www.spiegel.de/politik/ausland/schrumpfkur-nato-verkleinert-schnelle -eingreiftruppe-a-513688.html; Tom Kington, "NATO May Relaunch Response Force in June," *Defense News*, May 11, 2009, http://www.defensenews.com/story .php?i=4083046; "Transformation Reversed: NATO Rapid Reaction Force to Be Eliminated," *Der Spiegel*, September 20, 2007, http://www.spiegel.de/international /world/transformation-reversed-nato-rapid-reaction-force-to-be-eliminated-a -506905.html.

15. The usability goals were agreed to at the Istanbul Summit in June 2004 and embraced in the "Comprehensive Political Guidance" (approved at the Riga

Summit in November 2006). In June 2009 NATO ministers of defense agreed to enhance the goals from 40-8 to 50-10. For an assessment of most NATO members' numbers of deployable and sustainable forces, see European Defence Agency, *Defence Data of EDA Participating Members in 2007* (Brussels: European Defence Agency, 2007).

16. Interviews, NATO Headquarters and SHAPE, October 2009; Lok, "NATO Response Force"; Fiorenza, "Ready for Action."

17. Allied Command Operations, *The NATO Response Force—The Way Forward* (blog), August 4, 2009, http://acositrep.com/2009/08/04/the-nato-response-force-the-way-forward/; interview, Danish Ministry of Defense, August 2009; NATO official at International Military Staff, correspondence with author, NATO Headquarters, October 2009; senior NATO official, correspondence with author, ACO, Mons, March 2011.

18. Guillaume Lasconjarias, *The NRF: From Key Driver of Transformation to a Laboratory of the Connected Forces Initiative*, NATO Defense College Research Paper No. 88 (Rome: NATO Defense College, 2013).

19. Jeffrey P. Bialos and Stuart L. Koehl, *The NATO Response Force: Facilitating Coalition Warfare through Technology Transfer and Information Sharing* (Washington, DC: Center for Technology and National Security Policy, National Defense University, 2005), 2.

20. See, for example, Jens Ringsmose and Sten Rynning, *Come Home, NATO? The Atlantic Alliance's New Strategic Concept*, DIIS Report (2009:4) (Copenhagen: Danish Institute for International Studies, 2009).

21. House of Commons, "Future of NATO and European Defense," 57.

22. Vladimir Socor, "NATO's Response Force, Other Planned Capabilities Stillborn," *Eurasia Daily Monitor* 6, no. 38, February 26, 2009, http://www.jamestown.org/single/?tx_ttnews%5Bswords%5D=8fd5893941d69d0be3f378576261ae3e&tx_ttnews%5Bexact_search%5D=NATO%20response%20force&tx_ttnews%5Bcategories_1%5D=6&tx_ttnews%5Btt_news%5D=34556&tx_ttnews%5BbackPid%5D=7.

23. NATO official, correspondence with author, September 2009.

24. North Atlantic Treaty Organization, "Active Engagement, Modern Defense: Strategic Concept for the Defense and Security of the Members of the North Atlantic Treaty Organization" (adopted by Heads of State and Government in Lisbon, November 19, 2010), www.nato.int/cps/en/natolive/official_texts_68580.htm.

25. Mark Joyce, "NATO Must Decide How to Use Its Response Force," *Financial Times*, April 21, 2005; Lok, "NATO Response Force."

26. This group of countries also includes a number of the East European member-states. These nations, however, have hidden quietly behind Germany and France. NATO official interview, August 2009.

27. Fiorenza, "Ready for Action."

28. Interview, NATO Headquarters, October 2009.

29. Interviews, NATO Headquarters and Danish Ministry of Defense, August and October 2009.

30. Ronja Kempin, "The New NATO Response Force: Challenges and Reactions from Europe," COPRI Working Paper (Copenhagen: Copenhagen Peace Research Institute, 2002), 10.

31. Michael Mihalka, "NATO Response Force: Rapid? Responsive? A Force?," *Connections: The Quarterly Journal* 4, no. 2 (2005): 67–79.

32. Jaap de Hoop Scheffer, "Speech given at the 42nd 'Munich Conference on Security Policy,'" 2006, http://www.nato.int/docu/speech/2006/s060204a.htm (accessed January 28, 2010).

33. Senate Armed Services Committee, March 7, 2006 (statement of General James Jones, Commander, United States European Command), http://www.global security.org/military/library/congress/2006_hr/060307-jones.pdf, 43 (accessed January 28, 2010). SACT, General Lance Smith, made a similar statement in May 2006: "You can put your forces in a NRF rotation and if nothing happens during those six months you're fine, but if there is an earthquake in Pakistan, as happened last year, those forces would have to deploy and it could become very expensive . . . costs that are not planned for in the national defence budget"; Lok, "NATO Response Force."

34. NATO officials, interviews and correspondence with author, October and November 2009.

35. Senior NATO official, correspondence with author, August 2013.

36. Predictably, Turkey, a net recipient of NATO budget funds and a warm supporter of common funding in general, has been a firm opponent of a more operationally focused common funding system.

37. NATO officials, interviews and correspondence, October and November 2009; See also Bell, "Sisyphus and the NRF"; Herman Shaper, "Informal Suggestions on Innovative Funding of NATO Operations," *Europe's World*, February 27, 2009.

38. House of Commons, "Future of NATO and European Defense," 12.

39. Senior NATO official, interview with author, NATO Headquarters, November 2009.

40. Liam Fox, "The Case for Financial Reform of Both NATO and ESDP," *Europe's World*, Spring 2009, http://europesworld.org/2009/02/01/the-case-for -financial-reform-of-both-nato-and-the-esdp/#.Uo-CxMTmPCs.

Conclusion

Building on ISAF, Looking to the Future

Andrew A. Michta

This volume has been conceived around the central argument that NATO remains essential for the protection and preservation of Western security and the open liberal international order. The argument stipulates at the same time that today the overall global security environment is in flux, with a greater potential for conflict than at any time since the end of the Cold War. Since the onset of the Great Recession of 2008 in particular, those risks have grown greater each year, with wealth, power, and technological changes accelerating faster than previously predicted. The attendant global power shift to Asia, driven by the rapid rise of China as an emerging peer-competitor to the United States, and the resurgence of Russia's power along NATO's northeastern flank have been accompanied by several deepening regional crises, especially the unraveling of the MENA region.

NATO tasks that used to be largely theoretical some decades ago, such as counterterrorism, energy security, cyber defense, counter piracy, and missile defense, are today very much at the center of security debates. Given the combination of regional crises and global threats, state and nonstate, NATO has been thrust ever more strongly into a global security role, whether it acts on its own or in partnerships with non-NATO states. In fact, through close cooperation, shared threat assessments, and interests, NATO has seen its relationships expand into a global network, rendering the "why" increasingly a moot question, but leaving the "how" just as relevant as during the first phases of NATO's post–Cold War adaptation.

NATO's global outlook and global relationships today are not just about defense and security, but increasingly a political web of networks, relationships, institutions, and values.

The year 2014 marks a cognitive shift in how the NATO alliance will define its tasks and its mission, and whether it can reach an enduring consensus as to its area of responsibility. The spring 2014 election in Afghanistan was the de facto prelude to the closure of NATO's most global mission to date. The ISAF in Afghanistan has been the longest, most sustained, and most costly military campaign in its history: a decade-long commitment. If the United States finalizes its Bilateral Security Agreement with the Afghan government, and NATO its SOFA negotiations, the alliance will then move to its planned training and support Operation Resolute Support, marking the end of direct combat involvement in that country. The year 2014 will also see the next NATO summit, scheduled for September 4–5 with the United Kingdom as its host.[1] The process of absorbing the lessons from the mission has been underway and will accelerate as the transition nears.

But what lies ahead goes beyond assimilating the ISAF experience. NATO needs to engage in a serious conversation about how it will respond to the changing regional power balances, both along its periphery and farther afield. Another urgent topic is its devolving relationship with Russia, as Moscow reasserts its influence in the post-Soviet sphere along NATO's northeastern periphery. The future of NATO enlargement is directly linked to this problem. Next come two overarching questions: about the political will of governments to spend on defense and the overall tenor of U.S.-European relations. For Europe, more than ever before, it is imperative to properly resource defense, as this will determine its ability to maintain core capabilities needed to work with the United States and to invest in key programs including missile defense. The United States needs to reinvest in the transatlantic relationship, not as a counter azimuth to America's "pivot to Asia," but as its necessary foundation, precisely because working through NATO and drawing on shared resources will be essential going forward. These are interlocking tasks and are treated as such in this conclusion.

Afghanistan and Shifting Regional Balances

The road NATO traveled in Afghanistan has been marked overall by a successful adaptation to the different phases of the conflict, evidence that the alliance is capable of operating at a distance and under difficult conditions.

During the greatest paradigm shift of the "surge" in the operation, especially in 2009 as it moved from operations led by coalition forces to increasingly partnering with the Afghan National Security Forces (ANSF), ISAF doubled from 69,000 to 132,000 personnel in the country. As NATO prepares to leave Afghanistan and shift to Resolute Support, it can look at the military side of the ledger in 2013 with a justifiable sense of accomplishment. Despite the casualties suffered by the Afghan National Army (ANA), reaching as high as one hundred per week during the peak of the fighting season, the ANA has continued to hold its ground and perform. Today the ANA has twenty-four infantry brigades partly or fully capable of autonomous operations, with an improving command environment and improving skill levels, despite the fact that training opportunities have been impacted by operational tempo. None of those gains have been consolidated, and they may be undone as soon as there is rapid disengagement, but NATO's military record in Afghanistan remains solid.

The conclusion of the ISAF mission is an inflection point for NATO, for it lifts the immediate military and political imperatives imposed by an ongoing operation, creating the space for reevaluation and future planning. The easing of the current operational burden associated with ISAF will free the alliance to ask fundamental questions about its future. Regardless of how Afghanistan evolves politically after the 2014 deadline—and there are worrisome signs that rocky times lie ahead for both the central government and continued NATO presence in the country—the ending of the ISAF mission closes a decade of allied planning, organization, force structure, and procurement decisions that have in effect reshaped the alliance to meet the mission requirements. ISAF has seen NATO's mission redefined several times, and on balance it has been the largest and longest resource commitment to date by NATO to a sustained combat operation. Although it would be a mistake to speak of Afghanistan as a test of NATO, it was without question a major task for the alliance.

Today there is already an accelerating debate among NATO members about important and continually valid lessons for the future of the alliance to be drawn from the last decade. This is not an easy task, as Afghanistan has always been seen in a different light by the United States than it has by the Europeans, although there are also differences of opinion on this issue in Europe. Most directly, the U.S./European divergence on the significance of Afghanistan reflects the different original rationales for the campaign. For the United States, Afghanistan was always part of the original "Global War on Terror," driven home by the searing memories of 9/11. For Europe, where the shock of the 2001 terrorist attacks on the United

States was also profound, the war in Afghanistan registered in a different way—as an act of solidarity with a key ally—and was less immediately felt than in America. Regardless of the motivation, however, ISAF has shown that NATO retains a necessary reservoir of allied solidarity. This is the most important legacy going forward.

It has become commonplace to assert that a conventional attack on a NATO member is highly unlikely today. And yet for the remainder of this decade change in the most traditional areas of national security, including territorial defense, is likely to occur faster than many experts have predicted. In 2014, as the MENA region continued to sink deeper into sectarian strife; Ukraine was rocked by a popular rebellion seeking alignment with the West vs. Russia, with Russia then seizing Crimea undermining Ukraine's territorial integrity and threatening its sovereignty; Turkey moved further away from the Ataturk paradigm; and China began to contest the power distribution in Asia, challenging the closest U.S. allies and America itself. For NATO post-Afghanistan it is time to set aside the mantra of traditional territorial security versus global expeditionary missions. As territorial security shifts and interlocks with global threats, reflecting the changing power distribution along NATO's periphery in Europe and Asia, the alliance is fast becoming ever more enmeshed as a global security provider, not because that is a role it chooses but because if it is to remain relevant the nature of the security environment has made this choice for it.

There may be a lot of continued political resistance in a number of European capitals to this view, but the reality of a global NATO is here in more ways than many thought possible a decade ago, even a few years back as NATO argued over its new Strategic Concept. Moreover, if properly thought out and linked, there should be no contradiction between the traditional and global perspectives. This transformation is also dictated from the ground up through operational experience, from Afghanistan to Libya and beyond, and demands more readiness along the rapidly congealing NATO frontiers in the northeast and the south of Europe's periphery, and across the wide spaces of the Pacific. Simply put, NATO is at a decision point about whether it will play a dominant global structuring role in twenty-first-century security or become hollowed out and ultimately irrelevant.

The "Fifth Phase" and Russia

As one analyst/practitioner noted a year ago, in its history NATO has gone through four phases, beginning with the original founding experience of the Cold War; shifting to the initial post–Cold War downsizing and reassessment, with enlargement into postcommunist states as its principal driver; shifting to the south and southeast of Europe, from the Balkan wars to the Mediterranean; and finally entering the 9/11 phase after the terrorist attacks against the United States,[2] with the Afghanistan operation included in this phase as well as NATO's marginal involvement in Iraq with the training mission. The post-9/11 phase added new tasks, including cyber defense, energy security, and counter-piracy missions. To build on this analytical framework, the conclusion of the ISAF mission has now ushered in the next phase in NATO's storied history. Today NATO is on the cusp of the fifth phase, unequivocally global in terms of the nature of the security environment, marked by the resurgence of traditional geostrategic concerns in Europe, Eurasia, and the Pacific, bringing state-on-state competition ever faster back into focus.

The United States and its NATO allies are facing a series of accelerating threats, some functional, some transnational, and some territorial in nature. Although the effort to reign in Iran's nuclear weapons program will continue despite serious doubts about its long-term prospects, the threat of nuclear proliferation, in combination with the spread of long-range ballistic missile technology, is fast redefining the global security environment that NATO needs to face. In regional terms, the Middle East and North Africa are in an accelerating downward spiral, with pro-Western regime alignments fracturing and new alignments emerging with breathtaking speed. This changing global picture is stitched from regional power balances, including the increasingly contentious relationship with Russia. Following the Syria crisis, MENA is witnessing the return of outside great power competition on a scale unseen since the collapse of the Soviet Union. Moscow brilliantly exploited an opening presented by the Obama administration's bungled threat of force over the Syrian regime's chemical weapons use, and it has shown every determination to return to the region.

Since the end of the Cold War, Russia has remained an important subject of concern for NATO, which has repeatedly tried to engage Russia in a partnership that would go beyond transactionalism. Initial hopes for NATO's productive relations with Russia had been high, especially during the heady years of enlargement and the Boris Yeltsin presidency, leading senior U.S. officials to seriously entertain the idea of bringing Russia into a structured relationship with the alliance, with some even suggesting that Russia's membership in NATO was not out of the question.[3] That enthusiasm has progressively waned, especially after Vladimir Putin's 2007 speech in Munich heralded Russia's determination to chart an independent course. The 2008 Bucharest NATO Summit that failed to generate consensus on Ukraine and Georgia's Membership Action Plan further underscored that the NATO-Russia relationship was rapidly devolving, followed by the shock of the Russia-Georgia war the same year. By the time of the Chicago Summit in 2012 it was clear that, absent a major policy change in Moscow, only the starriest eyed among NATO members would still entertain expectations that a meaningful partnership with Russia was actually possible. No other event has contributed more to the change in NATO's perception of Russia than the 2008 Russia-Georgia war, even though a number of European leaders put the blame for escalation squarely at the doorsteps of Georgian president Mikheil Saakashvili. Even more importantly, Moscow's staunch opposition to U.S. missile defense plans put paid to NATO's early hopes for cooperation with the Kremlin.

In 2014 NATO is entering a qualitatively new relationship with Russia. Decline in NATO-Russia relations has been tied to Moscow's larger goal of rebuilding its dominant position in the post-Soviet "near-abroad," especially in Eastern Europe and Central Asia. The progressive reintegration of Belarus into Russia's security system underscored the seriousness of Vladimir Putin's plans for the Eurasian Union and served as a prelude to bringing Ukraine into the Russian orbit. The crisis in Ukraine in the winter of 2013, following President Viktor Yanukovych's decision not to sign an association agreement with the European Union, set the stage for the closing of NATO's eastern frontier. The deepening confrontation between Russia and the West over Vladimir Putin's drive to restore Moscow's sphere of influence in Eastern Europe created the most dangerous East-West crisis since the end of the Cold War. The escalation of the crisis in Crimea, then in the Donetsk region and Odessa raised the possibility that the Ukrainian state could break up. For NATO, Russia's take over of Crimea, and the risk that eastern Ukraine might be next, called for action to reassure allies in Central Europe and the Baltic States. As the confrontation with Russia deepened, in addition to public condemnation, the U.S. administration sent F-15s to strengthen air policing in the Baltics, as well as F-16s to Poland for joint training, followed by additional forces. Even before the crisis in Ukraine, the joint Belarusian/Russian Zapad/Ladoga maneuvers in 2009 and 2013 added a military dimension to the Kremlin's project. Moscow seems now determined to deflect even the prospects of countries from the former Soviet Union ever associating with the European Union—something that not long ago was touted as an acceptable alternative to NATO membership. Likewise, Russia has seen NATO's involvement in the Middle East—especially in Libya—as another example of NATO's disregarding Moscow's interests and wishes. Combined with continued criticism by the allies of Russia's human rights record, including the undeclared de facto boycott of the winter Olympics in Sochi by key Western leaders, Moscow sees itself in an increasingly adversarial position vis-à-vis the alliance. Depending on the final outcome of Russia's confrontation with the West over Ukraine, NATO may face a period of renewed tension along its eastern periphery, requiring an adjustment of allied strategy. Hence, NATO urgently needs to shore up its northeastern flank, including military deployments in Poland and the Baltic states.

For NATO's relations with Russia the largest question is whether they have reached the point at which there is no reason to maintain the pretense of working together to build a relationship resting on common foundations, notwithstanding counterterrorist intelligence sharing. An added variable is the changing security perceptions among allies in Northern and Central Europe, which already manifested themselves in 2010 in the run-up to the new Strategic Concept. With the cooling of relations with Russia and the hardening of Moscow's position on key issues such as missile defense, it is difficult to imagine that NATO could continue business as usual with Moscow. The alliance may be approaching a moment of truth about its relations with Russia since the end of the Cold War: that the idea of a shared interest platform was largely the result of Moscow's weakness in the Yeltsin era. With Ukraine subject to direct Russians economic, political, and military pressure and intermittent reports that Moscow plans to or has already stationed Iskander missiles in the Kaliningrad District, to say nothing of the Zapad/Ladoga exercises targeting the Baltic States and Poland, NATO needs to respond to the deteriorating security environment along its eastern frontier.

The shift in Russia's relations with NATO, coupled with the announced Russian military modernization set at $700 billion in the coming decade amid collapsing defense budgets across Europe and serious sequestration cuts in the United States, has exposed the balance along NATO's northeastern flank. In 2013 Russia's defense budget rose by 26 percent,[4] with a series of new platform contracts for aircraft and ships, not just for Russian industry but also including purchases from the West, as has been the case with the Mistral landing ship purchase from France.[5] But even assuming its military modernization does not fully materialize in the coming decade, Russia is reemerging as a longer-term threat for NATO.

Political Will to Resource Defense

The challenge remains how to keep the organization energized and able to commit resources now that the ISAF mission has ended. Finding a formula for the interim period that would link the expectations of various regional players and generate sufficient resource commitment will be the key challenge. Regardless of whether one sides with the argument that NATO needs to revert back to its traditional Article 5 defense objectives, as favored by its Central European members, or that it should continue to take on global tasks, as is preferable from Washington's perspective, all can agree that as security challenges multiply the alliance is fast entering an era in which resource constraints reduce its strategic reach. Here the conclusion of the mission in Afghanistan will play a defining role. The end of the mission will redefine the debate about defense budgets among the member countries and in the internal political context. Prior to 2014, even though many countries in Europe underwent a considerable reduction in defense spending, the commitment to the mission served as a means to galvanize the political will, however tenuous at this point, to salvage core defense programs, especially those relevant to the ongoing Afghanistan mission. The transition to Resolute Support post-2014—or the "zero option" and withdrawal should it come to that—will mean the reopening of an essential debate on how the alliance is to be resourced going forward, this time without the imperative of having to fund troops already on the ground.

The end of the Afghanistan mission will also challenge an essential element that had pushed the European security optics closer to the U.S. view of an alliance with a global mission to deliver security where needed. In that sense, Europe's security risks becoming "unmoored" from the U.S. view. Amid the ongoing economic crisis, Europe will find it ever more difficult to hew to the U.S. perspective. Here there is the added complication of the shifting regional security optics within Europe itself, with different countries focusing on the southern or eastern azimuth. The shifting regional balance along the northeastern periphery of the alliance has already forced a rethinking of some of the dogmas from the 2000s. The resurgence of Russian state power and its geostrategic assertiveness along NATO's periphery has alarmed Central Europe and the Baltics. Likewise, France has eyed with growing concern the deteriorating conditions in North Africa and the Mediterranean, while Norway looks to a shifting balance in the High North.

As the U.S. military footprint in Europe continues to shrink, with current projections of no more than thirty thousand U.S. troops deployed by 2017, exercises will become the critical glue holding NATO together. The successful 2013 Steadfast Jazz in northeastern Poland and the Baltics needs to be followed up by similar—and preferably larger—exercises that can become routine going forward. Steadfast Jazz notwithstanding, the real question will be the extent of U.S. direct participation in those events. The United States announced it would send 250 troops[6] to the exercise in

Poland in 2013—politically significant but militarily limited. In the end, even fewer participated.

And so the defining question for the alliance will continue to be the issue of resource allocation for defense. Amid dramatically declining defense budgets, whereby the European NATO members are now contributing only about 30 percent of the organization's military capabilities—while eight years ago they provided half—it is clear that NATO will be doing smaller operations going forward. The training mission in Afghanistan if/when it takes shape will be small, and while NATO will continue to plan for similar operations in the future, there is no doubt that the size and duration of such operations will have to decrease. While ISAF has for the most part been a successful military mission, given the current resource constraints, no one in the alliance is interested in doing "another Afghanistan." This raises the question of how to meet global requirements with the requisite resources.

Enlargement and Missile Defense

The year 2014 is also a time when NATO's drive to enlarge has clearly been put on the back burner. NATO has effectively reached the limit of how far east it will go in bringing new allies into the fold. The "Europe whole and free and at peace" mantra of the Clinton years—symbolic of the drive to enlarge the alliance—seems to have been replaced with a new paradigm: Europe perhaps not quite whole, with some parts unfree, but preferring to remain at rest. Most of the enlargement fatigue dates back to the 2008 Bucharest Summit and the Russia-Georgia war that followed. Although NATO officials continue to deny it, there was a degree of finality in the decision not to offer Ukraine and Georgia the Membership Action Plan. The simple reality is that there is no consensus to be found in NATO, not just about which countries to bring into the alliance but about the very rationale for continued enlargement. While there is some willingness to complete enlargement into the Balkans, in the current political climate in Brussels and Washington the key question of membership for Georgia is clearly a bridge too far.

In 2014 NATO members are likely to have a discussion—in Brussels, at national capitals, and at the UK summit—about the future of enlargement. Not as a political exercise, as was the case in the Clinton era and in part in the early 2000s, but in terms of the actual hard security commitments for the alliance. Even if enlargement is to continue, most likely into the Balkans to complete the project of stabilizing southeastern Europe post-1990, the criteria will be different, with tough questions raised about not just the contributions of prospective entrants but also the price of commitments that NATO would be asked to make. It remains to be seen how the crisis in Ukraine will affect this debate.

No issue is likely to reopen the question of equitable burden sharing more than the missile defense (MD) issue, repeatedly raised at earlier summits.[7] On this issue U.S. views have evolved with the changeover from the Bush to the Obama administrations. Currently the United States remains committed to the European Phased Adaptive Approach (EPAA), but that idea may dissipate and eventually die as the cost issue moves front and center in the internal NATO conversation. It is also unlikely that Europe will pick up a large part of the cost, as MD has always been a divisive issue there. Here MD has a dimension that touches on the larger NATO solidarity issue, as the Obama administration's decision to eliminate Phase IV of the EPAA has raised serious questions about long-term U.S. commitment to the project. Few among border allies now seriously believe that the U.S. Congress will fully fund the program without Phase IV in place.

Likewise, with the Iran 5+1 negotiations on the nuclear program under way, Russia will make the case that the MD issue ought to be subject to its consideration. The NATO MD issue has been political from the get-go, and with the first three phases focused on protecting the territory of Europe, it will fast become a test case for allied solidarity, as well as for NATO's ability to reaffirm the transatlantic link. At a time when sequestration and budget cuts wreak havoc with U.S. military recapitalization goals post-Afghanistan—and while Europe is dismantling its own defense budgets—it will be a tough sell to argue that the U.S. taxpayer should be paying for a system with no direct applicability to the country's national territorial defense. How the final decision on the funding will be resolved remains an open question; still, there is a growing groundswell in Congress to demand more from the allies in terms of financial contributions.[8] Again, the crisis in Ukraine will be a new factor here as well.

U.S.-European Relations Amid Power Transition

The greatest challenge facing the NATO alliance in the post-Afghanistan era, however, is not a lack of money or even the deteriorating security environment along its eastern and southern periphery. The central question, tied closely to the experience of ISAF and Afghanistan, is the long-term relationship of the United States and Europe going forward, especially as the imperatives of "getting along" due to the common operational requirements in Afghanistan begin to fade. The last decade has not been the most auspicious for transatlantic relations, first scarred by the intra-alliance rift over policy responses in the post-9/11 world during the George W. Bush administration, then over the past five years, with President Obama's series of initiatives to "engage" with difficult states, pivot to Asia, "reset" with Russia, and, most important, "lead from behind" as America did in the Libyan campaign.

In just one brief decade, the U.S. relationship with Europe has traveled the full gamut from America the overbearing to America the increasingly absent, with different shades in between marking the progressive widening of the distance between the United States and its allies. In retrospect, perhaps the original sin lay not in the post-9/11 response but in the burning experience of the Balkan wars—the conflict that saw Europe at its worst, the United States still in a strong and balanced leadership position, and NATO in its finest hour bringing about the end of war on Europe's own turf. And yet the Balkans exposed the incipient unraveling of what had been the foundation of the NATO bargain from the start: that despite the uneven distribution of power within the alliance between the United States and the Europeans, the two could plan and work together effectively. Before there was IFOR and KFOR, nobody seriously questioned that the allies had the foundations of doctrine, technology, and training to fight hand in hand. No one, that is, until the Balkan wars; for this showed that in a new type of limited war the Americans and the Europeans, though singing from the same prayer book, came from different churches. In that war, while the United States paid the political transaction costs of going to war in an alliance, it saw little relief in terms of military transaction costs by pooling its resources with those of Europe. The Balkans exposed the scope of the military capabilities gap between the United States and Europe in ways that no one truly suspected. And so with the Soviet threat receding, the shared capabilities argument was exposed as hollow, posing a simple question for U.S. military planners: What is this alliance ultimately capable of if/when it actually has to fight?

Hence the Balkans put the ISAF experience in Afghanistan into sharp relief. To a large number of observers ISAF is going to be seen—for many it has been so from the start—as the ultimate test of the NATO alliance, following so to say the prelude of the Serbian campaign. This would be only partly a problem if the test were limited to the military component, for as I have argued, NATO has done well overall in the military arena. But the political component in Afghanistan is likely to become messy; worse yet, it is likely to turn into a multi-billion-dollar fiasco. If Afghanistan comes to be seen as a test of the alliance by these criteria, than NATO is genuinely in trouble.

It complicates the transatlantic relationship further that the United States now sees challenges looming large for America mainly in Asia. The Obama administration's "pivot to Asia" has been notable for two factors: first that America's resources continue to lag behind its rhetoric, and second that Europe remains absent from that theater in any meaningful way. Few in Europe would believe that today the United States looks at Europe as the primary area where threats are likely to generate America's response. And so the Obama administration's policy means clearly that Europe should rely on its own resources to an unprecedented degree since the creation of NATO. We shall see if and how the current confrontation with Russia changes that.

So the alliance has already been changed by the fact that the United States has openly redefined its strategic focus. Despite all the rhetoric and discussions about a "global NATO," Europe has not come to terms with how profoundly America's security environment has changed in the past decade, especially since the 2008 onset of the global economic crisis. Two factors are going to be very powerful limiters for America's continued willingness to accept "business as usual" in its relations with Europe when it comes to defense. First, at no time since 1945 has the United States operated under such severe resource constraints as it faces today. The U.S. public debt, projected by some estimates to reach $20 trillion at the end of the Obama presidency;[9] its structural deficits; and its deep political divisions mean that the United States is now operating on a de facto power deficit. This is a qualitatively new experience for the United States, one that makes the implications of a possible implosion of the Afghan project very different from previous failed U.S. interventions. While in 1973, after the collapse of South Vietnam, the United States retained vast margins of power and could rapidly rebuild and recapitalize its military, today it lacks the resources to do so on a comparable scale.

The second dramatic departure from the past is even more jarring for American security and also remains not fully appreciated by Europe. For the first time since the early nineteenth century the United States is in a situation where it faces in China a potential peer competitor which, if current growth projections hold, will command a greater economic power than America. This is precisely the trajectory in Asia that the United States is likely to face in its competition in the Pacific against an increasingly geostrategically assertive and nationalistic Chinese state, whose economic weight is slated to outstrip that of the United States in the next decade or so. Of course current trends need not become outcomes, and a lot may change based on both the structural constraints that China is facing and the continued reservoir of human and institutional capital in the United

States. Still, even if the probability is 50/50 that the U.S. economy will slide into second place, this is a new security environment for the United States to adapt to, and one in which NATO will be viewed in Washington as an asset or liability, depending on the added value it brings to America.

In the next decade a NATO that is unwilling or unable to contribute in the area where it matters most to the United States—Asia—will quickly find itself reduced to a political talking shop. If NATO does not reach the consensus that it needs to be in Asia with the United States, Europeans may discover that they are unable to count on America's staying in force with Europe as need arises. This potential tension is not about transactionalism, but rather about a shared view of security and about allied solidarity. The signs are already there, with the continued reduction of American troop deployment in Europe, the closing down of bases, and some voices in the U.S. analytical community demanding that the EUCOM be physically moved out of Europe to the United States.[10] A Europe that continues to disinvest in its defense and remain absent in Asia will find that there are fewer and fewer people on the other side of the Atlantic willing to accept the argument that the collective West constitutes a larger value in and of itself.

Building Consensus and Support

And so as NATO enters its fifth phase in the post-ISAF era, it needs to ask the most fundamental question of whether and how the threat perceptions and the particular interest and priorities of the members align. In a sense, in the fifth phase NATO does not need to justify its existence so much as accept that going forward it will face a mixture of territorial and global threats and understand and embrace its new global role.

One last outstanding challenge is to bring the very idea of the NATO alliance back into focus with public opinion. In that sense the 2012 Chicago Summit played an important public relations role by creating awareness in America's heartland about the existence of this venerable alliance. In this new security environment in Asia, MENA, and along Europe's southern and eastern flanks, for NATO to thrive it needs to rely more on public diplomacy to cut across the policy elites and into the parliamentary and public spheres. The global mission post-Afghanistan requires building a consensus, the most difficult consensus NATO has yet to reach: that it is still, as I believe, central to the future of transatlantic security.

The experience of ISAF is NATO's capital, which can and should be the foundation of the new consensus, for in Afghanistan NATO has already acquired a global role, notwithstanding current debates about whether the organization's primary function is to preserve the integrity and security of the territory of the principal members, or if operations such as ISAF fall into that category. These lessons need to be absorbed into the NATO DNA so as not to waste the experience of an integrated operation unprecedented in NATO's history. Because of the ISAF mission the alliance has the potential to become a hub for global security networking, including working closely in partnership with other countries in a number of contingencies. This role should grow in the coming years. And the United States should lead this effort. Some of the operations, such as Libya, have demonstrated how important NATO remains to addressing urgent crises and also how important partnerships have become to NATO's functioning. Libya also showed how ultimately counterproductive for NATO the Obama administration's mantra of "leading from behind" was.

There is, finally, the larger issue of NATO's importance as a check against state-on-state threats against members of the transatlantic community, especially now as the threat of war on Europe's eastern periphery has grown and tensions in Asia are only beginning to rise. Today, with Russia increasingly operating from a competitive position vis-à-vis the West and asserting its strategic prerogative in Eastern Europe, the overall tenor of European security has already changed. Developments in MENA and in Asia are increasingly interconnected with the overall rebalancing taking place in the global security landscape. In that sense NATO is a hedge against future contingencies of the shifting balance of power, whether along Europe's periphery, in Asia, or in the Middle East. It is in the U.S. interest, therefore, and in the interest of the Europeans, to support NATO going forward. This means that while Europe develops its own defense framework within the Common Security and Defense Policy, it must ensure that such developments do not undermine NATO's ability to work as a collective defense framework. Getting the balance right after ISAF means ensuring that the U.S. commitment to Europe and to the traditional Article 5 security function is not questioned, and in turn, that Europe is prepared to remain relevant in the changing global security environment, understanding that threats to U.S. security require NATO's collective response.

The drawdown of U.S. deployments in Europe may still be—a reality that Europe must come to accept. But it is essential for the future of the alliance that this drawdown does not serve as a chip in the political argument about the overall future of the transatlantic relationship. NATO fulfilled its task in Afghanistan, meeting the military requirements and paying the price in blood and treasure. This is capital for the next decade that should make it possible for the allies to reach consensus on how to meet both its territorial defense tasks and global obligations.

Today there are some who have declared NATO defunct, its mission accomplished, and who argue that the time has come to dismantle it. It is often repeated that although NATO has been the most successful military and security organization in history, its time has long passed and its recent record is questionable. But all the issues facing NATO notwithstanding, it remains without a doubt the most comprehensive and multifaceted security organization with real capabilities to act in a crisis, locally and globally, and to serve as the ultimate security guarantor for its members. This value of the alliance cannot be overstated, and Afghanistan proved that militarily there is no substitute for what NATO can do. Although the members continue to struggle with insufficient funding and conflicting political priorities at home, the West is better off with NATO than without it, for it provides not only hard military power but also the means for continued transatlantic connectivity.

The value of NATO going forward still rests on these very fundamentals: collective defense and the larger political framework with which to bind the two sides of the Atlantic.

NOTES

All Web sites last accessed in January 2014.

1. North Atlantic Treaty Organization, "NATO Secretary General Announces Dates for 2014 Summit," http://www.nato.int/cps/en/natolive/news_104982.htm.

2. W. Bruce Weinrod, "The Future of NATO," *Mediterranean Quarterly* 23, no. 2 (Spring 2012): 1–13.

3. Senior members of Clinton administration, conversation with author, late 1990s.

4. "NATO's Future: Back to Basics," *The Economist*, November 16, 2013, http://www.economist.com/news/international/21589900-atlantic-alliance-wants-new-role-after-afghanistan-time-being-it-looking.

5. "Russia Orders French Mistral Amphibious Assault Ships," *Defense Industry Daily*, October 9, 2013, http://www.defenseindustrydaily.com/russia-to-order-french-mistral-lhds-05749/.

6. "USAREUR to Participate in Steadfast Jazz 2013," *U.S. Army*, October 25, 2013, http://www.army.mil/article/113882/USAREUR_to_participate_in_Steadfast_Jazz_2013/. Some sources put U.S. participation at closer to two hundred troops or even fewer.

7. Karl-Heinz Kamp, *NATO's 2014 Summit Agenda*, NATO Defense College Research Paper no. 97 (Rome: NATO Defense College, September 2013).

8. Kamp, *NATO's 2014 Summit Agenda*.

9. Paul Roderick Gregory, "President Obama's Legacy: $20 Trillion in Debt for 2016 Victor," *Forbes*, December 25, 2012, http://www.forbes.com/sites/paulroderickgregory/2012/12/25/president-obamas-legacy-20-trillion-in-deficits-for-2016-victor/.

10. Sean Kay, "Time to Pull Our Troops from Europe," *Foreign Policy* (June 18, 2013), http://www.foreignpolicy.com/articles/2013/06/18/time_to_pull_our_troops_from_europe.

About the Editors and Contributors

DEREK AVERRE is senior lecturer in Russian Foreign and Security Policy at the Centre for Russian and East European Studies (CREES), University of Birmingham. His main research interests center on Russian foreign and security policy, Russia-Europe relations, and arms control/nonproliferation issues, and he has written numerous journal articles and book chapters and presented widely in the United States and Europe on these topics.

HELGE DANIELSEN is associate professor at the Norwegian Institute for Defense Studies, Norwegian Defense University College. He holds a PhD in history from the University of Oslo (2004). His fields of interest include modern and contemporary Norwegian history, U.S. foreign policy, transatlantic political and cultural relations, and NATO during the second cold war. Before joining the IFS in 2008, Danielsen was a postdoctoral fellow at the Forum for Contemporary History at the University of Oslo.

HELGA HAFTENDORN is professor emeritus at the Free University of Berlin, where she was director of the Center on Transatlantic Foreign and Security Policy Studies (1986–2000). She received her DPhil in 1960 from the University of Frankfurt and her Habilitation (venia legendi) in 1972 from the University of Hamburg. She has taught at the University of Hamburg and German Military University and has been a visiting professor at Georgetown University, Stanford University, the European University Institute in Florence, Harvard University, and the Woodrow Wilson International Center of Scholars. Her special interests are transatlantic relations and NATO. Dr. Haftendorn has received many prizes and honors and has published widely on foreign policy, international security issues, and theory.

PAAL SIGURD HILDE is associate professor at the Norwegian Institute for Defense Studies, Norwegian Defense University College. He received his DPhil in politics at the University of Oxford in 2003. His main research interests include Norwegian security and defense policy and NATO. Before joining the IFS in 2008, Hilde was a senior adviser in the Department for Security Policy, Norwegian Ministry of Defense (2004–2008), where he also served as a secretary for the Norwegian Defense Policy Commission (2006–2007).

JANNE HAALAND MATLARY is professor of international politics, Department of Political Science, University of Oslo, and adjunct professor at the Norwegian Defense University College. Her main academic fields of interest are European foreign and defense policy and international security policy. Matlary was state secretary for foreign affairs between 1997 and 2000. She has been a member of several governmental and parliamentary commissions in Norway and is a member of the board of The Swedish Defense College's research group on strategy. Matlary is a columnist on foreign affairs in several papers, has worked as a foreign policy adviser, and has published widely on European and international security issues.

SVEIN MELBY is senior fellow at the Norwegian Institute for Defense Studies, Norwegian Defense University College. Melby received his Cand-Polit degree from the University of Oslo in 1979. He held scholarships at the Norwegian Institute of International Affairs (NUPI) between 1979 and 1983. Melby was an executive officer at the Department of Security Policy, Ministry of Defense in 1983–1984. He worked as a researcher on security policy and U.S. foreign policy at NUPI between 1985 and 2005 and was a visiting researcher on Fulbright scholarship at the Centre for International and Security Studies at Maryland (CISSM) at the University of Maryland in 1995–1996.

ANDREW A. MICHTA is the M. W. Buckman Distinguished Professor of International Studies at Rhodes College and a senior fellow at the Center for European Policy Analysis in Washington. Professor Michta holds a PhD in international relations from The Johns Hopkins University. He has published books, book chapters, and articles on U.S. and European security, NATO, transatlantic relations, civil-military relations, and democratization. He has special expertise in Central European politics and security and U.S. security policy. He is a frequent media contributor and government consultant.

JENS RINGSMOSE is associate professor at the Center for War Studies, University of Southern Denmark, where he also earned his PhD in international relations. His main research areas are NATO, strategic studies, counterinsurgency, and new wars. From 2006 to 2008 he worked as a research fellow at the Danish Institute for Military Studies in Copenhagen. He has published widely, including articles in *International Politics*, *Contemporary Security Policy*, *European Security*, and *Cooperation and Conflict*, on counterinsurgency, transatlantic cooperation, and Danish security and defense policy.

STEN RYNNING is professor of international relations at the Department of Political Science and head of the Center for War Studies, University of Southern Denmark. His main research interests are the Atlantic alliance, Afghanistan, strategy, and geopolitics. He is the author of *NATO in Afghanistan: The Liberal Disconnect* (Stanford University Press, 2012), *NATO Renewed: The Power and Purpose of Transatlantic Cooperation* (Palgrave 2005), and other books and numerous articles on European and Atlantic security.

HELENE F. WIDERBERG contributed to this book as a research fellow at the Norwegian Institute for Defense Studies, Norwegian Defense University College. Widerberg received her MA in political science at the University of Oslo in 2005. She works as a project coordinator in the Department for Security Policy and North America at the Norwegian Ministry of Foreign Affairs (2013–).

Index

Abkhazia, 55
academies, military, 145
ACE. *See* Allied Command Europe
    (ACE)
ACO. *See* Allied Command Operations
    (ACO)
ACT. *See* Allied Command Transfor-
    mation (ACT)
"Afghan Compact," 113
Afghanistan, 177–79
    Bilateral Security Agreement with,
      177
    Comprehensive Approach and,
      113–14, 117–20, 130–32
    counterinsurgency in, 42
    Germany and, 168
    NATO in, 2, 27, 28, 39, 40–41, 55,
      60, 63, 76, 82–86, 83, 84, 85, 86,
      122–23, 159, 177, 188–89
    NATO Response Force and, 161,
      162, 167–68
    Norway in, 85–86
    Obama and, 38–39
    provincial reconstruction teams in,
      117–20, 121
    Resolute Support of, 183
    Russia and, 63–64
    September 11 attacks and, 178–79
    Soviet Union and, 21, 22, 23
    terrorism and, 97
    as test, 27–28

United States in, 5, 26–27, 36,
    38–39, 185–86
Afghan National Army (ANA), 178
Afghan National Security Forces
    (ANSF), 178
Aillot-Marie, Michele, 168
al-Assad, Bashar, 98, 127
Albright, Madeleine, 14, 59, 116
alliance dependence, 84–86
"alliance dilemma," 81–82
Allied Command Europe (ACE), 137
Allied Command Europe Mobile
    Force-Land (AMF-L), 166
Allied Command Operations (ACO),
    138, 157
Allied Command Transformation
    (ACT), 138
Allied Solidarity Force (ASF), 166–67
Al Qaeda, 38, 40, 97, 127. *See also* Sep-
    tember 11 attacks
AMF-L. *See* Allied Command Europe
    Mobile Force-Land (AMF-L)
ANA. *See* Afghan National Army (ANA)
ANSF. *See* Afghan National Security
    Forces (ANSF)
Arab Spring, 68, 97
arms reduction, 94, 101
Article 4, 18, 19, 20, 28, 29–30, 30–31
Article 5, 14, 15, 18, 19, 23, 25, 26,
    28–29, 30–31, 47, 56, 77, 80, 86,
    91, 98, 115, 138, 165–67

TNW. *See* tactical nuclear weapons
(TNW)
Tow, William, 17–18, 20
"traditionalists," 78, 79–80
transatlantic community, 49–51
Turkey, 103, 115, 127, 140, 141, 162

Ucko, David, 27
Ukraine, 4, 68, 96, 98, 99, 105, 139,
179, 180–81, 182
UK Stabilization Unit, 125
United Kingdom
in Afghanistan, 26–27, 39
Allied Solidarity Force and, 166
Suez crisis and, 20
United States and, 83
United Nations Protection Force
(UNPROFOR), 25
United States, 2–3. *See also* September
11 attacks
in Afghanistan, 5, 26–27, 36, 38–39,
177, 185–86
arms reduction with, and Soviet
Union, 94
Asia and, 187
burden sharing and, 77
China and, 37, 42, 48, 187–88
counterinsurgency and, 42
European relations with, 185–88
in European security, 45–48
European Union and, 45–46, 47
Hurricane Katrina in, 158
Iraq War and, 5, 27, 42
Korean War and, 16–17, 137
Libya and, 4, 27, 36
missile defense and, 44–45, 56, 59,
61–63, 99, 102–3
NATO and direct threats to, 37–43

NATO Response Force and, 170, 172
nuclear weapons and, 101–2
in original purpose of NATO, 155
as power deficit, 187
Riga Summit and, 123
Russia and, 44
September 11 attacks and, 4–5
shift away from European focus
of, 15
Soviet Union and, 43
Steadfast Jazz and, 183–84
Suez crisis and, 20
in transatlantic community, 50–51
value of NATO to, 42–43
UN Security Council (UNSC), 25, 113

Vallance, Andrew, 138

Wallander, Celeste A., 146–47, 148
Walt, Stephen, 23
"War on Terror," 116, 178–79
Warsaw Pact, 18
Washington Summit, 114
weapons of mass destruction. *See*
nuclear weapons; terrorism
Weapons of Mass Destruction Control
and Disarmament Committee,
103
Western European Union (WEU),
140, 147
Western Union, 79
Westerwelle, Guido, 101
World America Made, The (Kagan), 49

Yemen, 127
Yugoslav Civil War, 24, 60

Zapad/Ladoga exercises, 181, 182

Printed and bound by CPI Group (UK) Ltd, Croydon, CR0 4YY

09/06/2025

14685669-0001